LIVES OF THE DEAD POETS

Sara Guyer and Brian McGrath, series editors

Lit Z embraces models of criticism uncontained by
conventional notions of history, periodicity, and culture,
and committed to the work of reading. Books in the series
may seem untimely, anachronistic, or out of touch with
contemporary trends because they have arrived too early or too
late. Lit Z creates a space for books that exceed and challenge
the tendencies of our field and in doing so reflect on the
concerns of literary studies here and abroad.

At least since Friedrich Schlegel, thinking that affirms
literature's own untimeliness has been named romanticism.
Recalling this history, Lit Z exemplifies the survival of
romanticism as a mode of contemporary criticism, as well
as forms of contemporary criticism that demonstrate the
unfulfilled possibilities of romanticism. Whether or not they
focus on the romantic period, books in this series epitomize
romanticism as a way of thinking that compels another relation
to the present. Lit Z is the first book series to take seriously this
capacious sense of romanticism.

In 1977, Paul de Man and Geoffrey Hartman, two scholars
of romanticism, team-taught a course called Literature Z
that aimed to make an intervention into the fundamentals of
literary study. Hartman and de Man invited students to read
a series of increasingly difficult texts and through attention
to language and rhetoric compelled them to encounter
"the bewildering variety of ways such texts could be read."
The series' conceptual resonances with that class register
the importance of recollection, reinvention, and reading to
contemporary criticism. Its books explore the creative potential
of reading's untimeliness and history's enigmatic force.

LIVES OF THE DEAD POETS

Keats, Shelley, Coleridge

———+———

Karen Swann

Fordham University Press

New York   2019

Fordham University Press gratefully acknowledges financial assistance and support provided for the publication of this book by Williams College.

Fordham University Press has no responsibility for the persistence or accuracy of URLs for external or third-party Internet websites referred to in this publication and does not guarantee that any content on such websites is, or will remain, accurate or appropriate.

Fordham University Press also publishes its books in a variety of electronic formats. Some content that appears in print may not be available in electronic books.

Visit us online at www.fordhampress.com.

Library of Congress Cataloging-in-Publication Data available online at https://catalog .loc.gov.

Printed in the United States of America

21 20 19   5 4 3 2 1

First edition

for Anna and Doug

Contents

Introduction

This book explores the insistence of biography in the reception histories of Keats, Shelley, and Coleridge, three British romantic poets who could be said to have shared a condition of premature arrest. My title, *Lives of the Dead Poets,* aims to conjure the hagiographic, cultic dimension of this biographical interest as well as its resiliently undead character. Even today it would be difficult to engage the work of Keats, Shelley, or Coleridge without confronting the role biography has played in the canonization of each: hard not to come across the widely circulated stories of careers and lives cut off by a bad review or wasted in indolence; the anecdotes related by friends and other contemporaries that describe their subjects as not quite suited for life in this world; and the archival materials—letters, death masks, bits of bone, a heart, a text meant for a tombstone—preserved by circles and then, by proxy at least, circulating more widely, often in tandem with literary remains. Even for today's readers, the pervasiveness of this biographical material can have the effect of catalyzing untoward reading-effects, when a poetic line, phrase, or figure sparks the memory of biographical information, generating a feeling of pathos, a sense of prolepsis, a recollection of a death to come. Especially when it centers on the early deaths of Keats and Shelley, biographical interest is often deplored as a largely Victorian and sentimental phenomenon that we should by now have gotten over. That these materials and effects continue to inflect our experiences speaks of fascination, the involuntary *clinging* of attention to its object beyond reason. When it endures, biographical fascination is "posthumous" in Keats's evocative sense of the term, its life equivocally sustained beyond its allotted period.[1]

This period—British romanticism, its Victorian reverberations, the modernity to which it responds and that extends into our present—is itself difficult to circumscribe. Like many others who work in the field, I am interested here in the undead character of romanticism itself. The poetic and biographical materials that figure most prominently in this study, however, were primarily generated during the years we associate with second-generation British romanticism—roughly the period of the British Regency, sometimes held to account for the deaths of Keats and Shelley and into which Coleridge survived as a kind of remainder or ghost-effect of an earlier, more promising moment in the formation of this aesthetic movement. In this interval all three writers struggled with limited sales, skeptical and increasingly reluctant publishers, scandalously hostile reviewers, and lack of money. They also lapsed out of this struggle, Coleridge in a life widely agreed to have been marked by his failure to produce the great work and his expenditure of himself in fugitive writing, prodigious talk, and opium-taking; Shelley, often richly productive during the same period, could not find publishers to touch his work, much of which was not published until long after his death; and Keats, before illness circumvented all plans, was expressing an intention to sign on as a ship's doctor in the event of bad sales of his 1820 volume. The glamor that colors the afterlives of all three poets is bound to the stories they and others tell of promise wasted or prematurely cut off, either to be forever unfulfilled or, at best, to be belatedly redeemed by a future they shaped but did not live to see. Creative life is unsustainable under the conditions of modernity, these stories suggest. Thus each of these lives also seems to speak to another sort of failed promise, now on the part of a culture that has abrogated its end of a deal in which something might be owed to art. The biographies of these three figures have for these reasons informed constructions of romanticism itself: in Marc Redfield's words, which ventriloquize without endorsing the sentiment, romanticism "is, after all, a movement destined to die young or end badly, bequeathing only its promise to us as our own utopian possibility."[2]

The three romantic figures of premature arrest that I focus on here precipitate out of a broader period context, characterized by culture- and nation-building projects that centered around the deaths of poets. Samantha Matthews, in *Poetical Remains: Poets' Graves, Bodies, and Books in the Nineteenth Century,* Andrew Bennett, in *Romantic Poets and the Culture of Posterity,* and Deidre Lynch, in *Loving Literature,* have all anatomized and explored these projects, examining the centrality of the author's (and, especially, the poet's) death to the afterlife of literature during this period. Matthews's study, a rich cultural history of the nineteenth-century fascination with the deaths of poets, traces the period's identification of the poet's bodily and textual "remains," which ensured both death and biography a place in the textual afterlife of the corpus.[3] Bennett and Lynch focus more specifically on the way the (actual or anticipated) death of the author works to secure the prestige of British literature and a canonical romanticism. For Bennett, the cultivation of a discourse about posthumous fame solidified the stature of elite poetry in a period that saw its threatened marginalization in a market-driven book economy. With romanticism, he argues, the biographical figure of the author comes to be cast as an "originating subjectivity," anchoring a structure by which a poetry seen to be ahead of its time and thus uncontaminated by market concerns could proleptically claim recognition in the "future perfect."[4] Bennett's work suggests how the strategic foregrounding of the lives—and, more pointedly for both Bennett's and my project, the deaths—of poets falls in with a more general aim of aesthetic discourse, which is to consolidate a heterogeneous citizenry around a culture the values of which are recognized to be human and universal, but where that recognition is imagined to emerge belatedly, beyond the vicissitudes of the market. If Bennett's account centers on an emergent sense of futurity that allows the imagining of the future retrospective validation of the present, Lynch's work focuses on the way a prestigious national literature during this period becomes aligned with an illustrious past and the absent dead. Taking seriously the extent to which reading was shaped as a private and affectively rich experience during the romantic period, Lynch traces the ways in which a new construction of reading—as binding the reader in a form of human relation to the book, imagined as a ghostly incarnation of a biographical person—fashioned a Burkean body politic, attached through its affiliations with the dead to the canonical forms and institutions of British literature. For Lynch, oft-repeated claims about the anticipated "death" of poetry serve to shore up a readership's hopeless love for what is gone. Canonization, argues Lynch, is a "mortuary process"; the modern love of literature is thus at its core elegiac.[5]

The cultural projects Bennett and Lynch anatomize were from the first contested and internally riven, especially in the cases of the famously dead Keats and Shelley. Even during the early decades of the nineteenth century, efforts to use biography to promote the work of both writers were accused of being crassly manipulative and opportunistically complicit with the commodification of literature and the beginnings of celebrity culture (even as the stories of artists unsuited to survive in this world attempted to register a protest about these terms, and thus also served to sell "aesthetic" values). Versions of these charges were articulated very early on from within the Keats and Shelley circles, suggesting something of the complexity of this history: Friends and family at once hoped to deploy biography as a way of creating interest in the literary remains, but also accused such projects of falsifying or betraying their subjects. (This sometimes played out as a contest or fissure within a circle—say, between Edward Trelawny's more worldly Percy Shelley and Mary Shelley's idealized one—but also as equivocations within a biographical project, for example, within Richard Monckton Milnes's biography of Keats, which at once relied on the pathos of its subject's death and claimed to rescue Keats from the particular forms of pathos that had already attached to him.[6]) By the later nineteenth century, with the ascendency of supposed "idealizations" of these biographical subjects (a Keats "consumed" by a passion for art, Shelley as "ineffectual angel"), the work of biography could appear a deliberate strategy to contain potential scandal—political, religious, personal, the potential scandal of the writing itself—in the interest of promoting a sanitized corpus, refashioned to conform to the biographical image.[7] Versions of this last complaint have animated academic criticism ever since: Under modernism, sentimental interest in Keats was seen perversely to dog and belie the cool impersonality of a poetry of "negative capability," for example, and more recently Thomas Pfau has characterized romantic studies as "enthralled" by the death of Keats, at the cost of adequate readings of Keats's work.[8]

For Pfau, an adequate reading of Keats's work would attend to the way it engages *critically* with aesthetic ideology—that is, with the very cultural narratives that Bennett and Lynch describe as taking shape during the period. Both Bennett and Lynch persuasively examine how authorial biography— and the author's death—function to shore up and produce forms of allegiance to emergent aesthetic projects and discourses that aimed to secure the prestige of a national literature and culture: the story of the poet who, out of step with the times, aligns himself with the illustrious dead and gestures toward the art that is to come served and continues to serve to prop up romantic constructions of the writer as autonomous and prescient genius, and, by extension, to glorify a national literature that can act to "bind" a community of readers into a body politic. Pfau and many other contemporary critics might argue that this use of authorial biography overwrites dimensions of romantic literature that could be said to challenge these narratives and projects—for instance, its forms of *refusal* of the conventions of authentic subjective expression, or its resistances to being put to use or to work by cultural narratives that would see the past, present, and future bound in relations of filiation or into a developmental or progressive trajectory.[9] Here, we might think of Marc Redfield's account of the quixotic nature of the strategy that would use romantic literature to secure the ends of aesthetic ideology. Drawing on de Man's work on both aesthetics and romanticism (which, Redfield persuasively argues, amount to the same thing), Redfield unpacks the way romantic texts, through a consistent flagging of and attention to rhetorical effect, "resist" the romantic aesthetic that they also fashion.[10]

Compelling recent scholarship on British romanticism explores romantic poetic practices that could be said to function recalcitrantly with respect to the period's grand and aggrandizing narratives and projects.[11] Some although not all of this criticism focuses in particular on Britain's second generation and its responses to the Regency period, arguing that the innovative poetics of Keats and Shelley, especially, engage with their moment not so much in the way of overt challenge (although neither is this excluded), but in terms of sustained, unsettled, and unsettling engagements with literary form and convention. Examples of work that especially touches on the concerns of this project include Jacques Khalip's exploration of anonymity and negativity as political and ethical modes and postures that counter what is often declared to be the centrality of the subject—its modes of expressivity, its agentive force—to romantic aesthetics; Thomas Pfau's investigation of the "mood" of melancholy that underpins the formal inventiveness of Keats's verse— especially the poet's deployment of the poetic conventions of authenticity in a manner that exposes them as exhausted; Sara Guyer's tracking of modes of poetic figuration that survive romanticism in ways that refuse recuperation; and Emily Rohrbach's attention to the "out of time" character of romantic temporality, which unsettles both narratives of progressive development and the conditions for attachment to the past.[12]

There is broad agreement that the romantic aesthetic emerges both in tandem with perceived threats to poetry's prestige (and perhaps to its very survival) by an increasingly market-driven print world, and—as William Wordsworth and Walter Benjamin might argue—as a result of challenges to poetry's old allegiances to long practice and authentic experience presented by shifts in the very character of social experience under commodity capitalism.[13] If the romantic aesthetic's narratives and projects are ideological and recuperative, contemporary theorists of romanticism point out that they are also internally riven, incapable of fully containing the literariness of the romantic literature they presume to conscript. In terms of these accounts, biographical discourse and effects are almost always assumed to function in ways that shore up ideological designs, while effects that appear to fall into the category of "the sentimental"—effects that cling to Keats and Shelley in particular—tend especially to be aligned with benighted ideological complicity. A modest goal of this project is to complicate this view. Charges of sentimentality tend to be leveled at literary techniques and readerly responses that in one way or another expose a factitious dimension to effects of subjectivity—that is, that potentially fall on the side of romanticism's resistance to itself. That the lives of the dead poets I consider here have in common a certain failure to thrive, moreover, suggests that they bear a critique of the culture that would enlist art and artists into its designs.

—+—

Each of the chapters in this volume explores biographical fascination as it is catalyzed by the chiming of biographical materials (themselves primarily textual) with moments in poetic or other more properly literary texts. The biographical remains that especially interest me share a certain family resemblance in that they tend to conjure their subjects as at once thinned out and untimely—as virtual, denatured, iconic, and existing in the mode of character. (Writing to Keats's publisher John Taylor, Richard Woodhouse refers to Keats as Taylor's "personage." I hope "character" here has the same whiff of the celebrity and poetic commodity, but that it also evokes some of Keats's own uses of the word, for example his description of the "poetical character" as possessed of "no character," as well as the term's allusion to the depthless, apparitional sign.[14]) Some of the most smiting instances of the sort of thing I have in mind appear among the many extant anecdotes of Coleridge in his later life, when he is described by contemporaries as inhabiting London as an otherworldly figure, "dropt from the moon," making his way through the city "*as if* he had been earthy, of the earth."[15] Not of *this* place or time, he seems to occupy his modern, urban, quotidian world as a visitant from elsewhere. To William Hazlitt and others, Coleridge endures into the present as an anachronism: Hazlitt's Coleridge, having outlived both his own promise and the heady beginnings of British romanticism, haunts contemporary London as a ghost or revenant, "his lips ever moving, his heart ever still."[16] Others cast him as the precipitate of a still more ancient world: his talk, his listeners claimed, transports them back to the time of the peripatetic philosophers of ancient Greece, when Isocrates, Milton's "old man eloquent," walked the streets of Athens. Spellbinding like his own ancient mariner or the chaunting poet of "Kubla Khan," Coleridge bears his listeners to another place at once momentarily accessible and radically distinct from their ordinary modes of existence. When they return, they purport to bring nothing back from their travels, "no recollection," often, of a word he said.[17]

Coleridge himself seems to share this general sense of his difference from ordinary mortals. He writes in a notebook entry of this period:

> And yet I think, I must have some *analogon* of Genius; because, among other things, when I am in company with Mr. Sharp, Sir J. Macintosh, R. and Sidney Smith, Mr Scarlet, & c & c, I feel like a Child—nay, rather like an inhabitant of another planet—their very faces all act upon me, sometimes as if they were Ghosts, but more often as if I were a Ghost, among them—at all times, as if we were not *consubstantial*.[18]

Gregarious and captivating to the extent that he is perfectly abstracted, an *analogon* of Genius, he seems to occupy the world as a different order of being from Mr. Sharp, Sir J. Macintosh, R. and Sidney Smith, Mr. Scarlet, & c & c; at the same time, his coming into their presence potentially sets in motion reversals of this effect, in which the company itself becomes ghosted, eerily exposed as the mere simulacrum of a living social, collective body.[19]

In the accounts of those who knew him, Shelley likewise appears as a wonderful alien animated by hectic, unnatural life. Thinking back to his second encounter with the poet, Thomas Hogg describes visiting the former's Oxford room and quite literally becoming caught up in his magnetism. Shelley, Hogg finds out, has been experimenting with electricity. His disordered room is pocked with acid burns in floor and furniture, and in the midst of all is a small generator worked by a hand crank: "And presently," Hogg attests, "standing upon the stool with glass feet, he begged me to work the machine until he was filled with the fluid, so that his long wild locks bristled and stood on end." Hogg had begun that day having entirely forgotten the seven or eight hours he had spent with this "preternatural" "character" the night before, a fact he is "unable to account for . . . in a satisfactory manner." After longer acquaintance, however, he is in a position to generalize about the poet's convulsive swings between "periods of occultation" and hectic animation, rhythms that produce similar effects in Hogg himself:

> at six he would suddenly compose himself, even in the midst of a most animated narrative or of earnest discussions, and would lie buried in entire forgetfulness, in a sweet and mighty oblivion, until ten, when he would suddenly start up, and rubbing his eyes with great violence, and passing his fingers swiftly through his long hair, would enter at once into a vehement argument . . . with a rapidity and energy that were often quite painful.[20]

This virtual or unnatural life possessed by the poet is perhaps most famously evoked by Keats's accounts of the poetical character that, after flying out of himself, does not "go home to" himself, or, more plangently, by his late letters and Severn's accounts of his last days in Rome, which describe the period of the "posthumous existence," that indefinite interval that survives "real life" but precedes actual death. For both Shelley and Keats, however, I draw from a more capacious reliquarium that includes contemporary accounts of Shelley as a Narcissus perilously lost in a book and on the verge of going under; of a heart and bones that continue to circulate after life has stopped; and for Keats, of a face suddenly blanched, become countenance, and finally, death mask—the perfectly withdrawn, perfectly apathetic remainder of the lost singular biographical subject whose passing it carries as trace.

In plainer terms: The essays in this volume tug at biographical material that presents these romantic subjects as "not of [our] order," as Byron's Manfred might put it.[21] Manfred is making a little joke here: He is "not of the order" of the men he addresses and who are obsessed with him precisely to the extent that he is a poetic convention, a Byronic hero, and by the time of his appearance, a sensationally recognizable and very nearly depleted one. He is letting us know he belongs to the order of literary convention, and throughout *Manfred* his protestations of weariness and ennui point to the exhaustion of the particular kind of figure he is. (Those to whom he addresses his complaints are also fictions, of course, but first-order ones, and thus unconscious of their status as resurrected and last-gasp conventions inhabiting a closet drama.) I am interested here in biographical moments that are reflexive in this way: in anecdotes and descriptions that flag the figurality of the biographical figure, its character as personified analogon of the abstracted categories of Poet and Genius.

That these biographical figures are *figures* (and figures of the Poet or Genius) is of course not news. Lynch, for instance, observes that from the time of Samuel Johnson on, living authors often appear "abstracted" and anachronistic in contemporary anecdote because of the way literature is becoming identified with the illustrious dead of the British canon,[22] while the sources in which these particular examples appear are frequently accused of idealizing and sentimentally overdrawing their poetical characters, which nonetheless and scandalously seem capable of commanding belief, mobilizing attachments, and even producing bizarre forms of mass hallucination. I will come back to these claims and accusations. For now, though, I want to explore further the *kind* of figures these are. They are "allegorical," I propose, in the sense that they are second-order, like Manfred: They speak to their own predicament, and, I will argue, to the conditions of their coming-into-being.[23] More precisely, they speak to the ways in which romantic constructions of the Poet and of Genius are melancholic rather than full, and to the mode of survival of a function, role, or character that, having outlived its day, lives on in the manner of any exhausted convention transiently restorable to hectic life.[24] This, I propose, is the logic of the biographical figure's appearance as an untimely survivor of some other moment ("my real life having passed") lasting into indefinitely suspended posthumous time. The biographical figures of Keats, Shelley, and Coleridge inhabit their and our modernity as simulacra, a fate Hazlitt extends to all men of letters, whose living deaths in turn suggest the poverty of the landscape in which they move as strangers: "The life of a mere man of letters and sentiment appears to be at best but a living death; a dim twilight existence: a sort of wandering about in an Elysian fields of our own making; a refined, spiritual, disembodied state, like that of the ghosts of Homer's heroes."[25] Pointing to the diminishment of the age, men of letters, Hazlitt suggests, at the same time serve to inject their disenchanted world with a minor frisson of wonder; by the same token, the more radically abstracted figures of Keats, Shelley, and Coleridge infuse with an equivocal charm the quotidian landscape in which professional men of letters (Mr. Sharp, Sir J. Macintosh, R. and Sidney Smith, Mr. Scarlet, & c & c) go about their business.

Representing the poet as at once prematurely arrested and posthumously surviving, these lives of allegory anticipate still other figurations that will appear on the horizon of romanticism, including the character of Charles Baudelaire as Walter Benjamin describes him. "The image of [Baudelaire's] life," Benjamin claims, is a function of his moment, in which a "social contract" between poet and bourgeois audience is about to be annulled:

> No study of Baudelaire can fully explore the vitality of its subject without dealing with the image of his life. This image was actually determined by the fact that he was the first to realize, and in the most productive way, that the bourgeoisie was about to annul its contract with the poet. Which social contract would replace it? That question could not be addressed to any class; only the market and its crises could provide an answer.[26]

Elaborating on this insight elsewhere in "Central Park" and again in "On Some Motifs in Baudelaire," Benjamin suggests that Baudelaire appears— as biographical character, as body of poetry—at a juncture when the lyric, especially in its romantic introspective or expressive form, is losing relevance for a modernity in which the "structure of experience" has changed. Baudelaire, Benjamin speculates, "apes the 'poet' before an audience and a society which no longer need a real poet, and which grant him only the latitude of mimicry."[27] Dilettantish (because in want of other more substantial "parts"), combative, and often comically exaggerated, the figure of Baudelaire analogizes both a distinctive poetic practice and, simultaneously, the predicament to which this practice responds, a predicament of poetry itself.[28] Benjamin's perception that Baudelaire's image at once limns and creates the conditions of poetry's survival into the future, precisely *as* an exhausted virtual category, resonates with Rei Terada's more recent claim that "working through lyric includes accepting that the perception of lyricism may continue even as belief in the significance of that perception may not."[29] The lyric, like the poet, may live on, posthumously, beyond all reason; and it may do so in part because of the particular way the fates of poet and poetry are intertwined under modernity.

The juncture Benjamin describes, and even his diagnosis of it, predates Baudelaire, of course. In his 1800 "Preface" to *Lyrical Ballads,* Wordsworth is already articulating similar claims about the challenges that commodity capitalism poses to the aspiring poet. These challenges are at once economic and practical—is it possible for a distinctive writer to break into and survive in a market-driven print economy?—and aesthetic—how can poetry engage the new forms of subjectivity and social relation that are emerging in relation to phenomena that include urbanization, the rise of a mass media, and the resulting intensification of the shocks of daily life? In the next section and throughout the book, I connect the biographical figurations of Keats, Shelley, and Coleridge that emerged during this period to the very particular ways in which their poetic strategies reflected upon and renegotiated the "contract" between poet and audience. Here, though, I simply want to make the broader claim that in the manner of Baudelaire as Benjamin describes him, the "images of the lives" of Keats, Shelley, and Coleridge speak to the perceived equivocal status of the poet and poetry (and, in Coleridge's case, of intellectual life more broadly) at a moment when one sort of social contract was eroding, new ones were in the making, and, at this juncture, making themselves around figures of poetic originality and genius. Their appearance can thus be understood in terms of a protracted beginning of the end that, Lynch argues, dates at least from the period of Samuel Johnson and, if Terada's speculations are correct, stretches into our own times.

Lynch suggests that readerly attention to the biographical figure of the author, always to some degree a form of affection for the dead, serves to foster a "love of literature" as a kind of Burkean filial "human relation."[30] While I agree with the broad strokes of this argument, I would argue that pressing on the figurality of these figures—and here I am especially interested in the figures of Keats, Shelley, and Coleridge—serves to expose the deep strangeness of the interspecies romance that blossoms between readers and textual materials, a strangeness that has to do with the nonhuman logic of figuration. Attending to this logic, I would argue, helps to account for the volatility of the reception histories of all three of these romantic writers and the undead character of the fascination that continues to clings to them. It helps to explain as well the motives and predicaments shared by a long march of magisterial biographies, each intending to put to rest, once and for all, sentimental accounts of the poets' lives. Pace Paul de Man, biography can only always be a fleshing out, a belated and reactive attempt to root out or at least naturalize what is constitutively and adamantly virtual in the figure.[31] Biography produces reality-effects that mask the fictiveness of their subjects and mute the particular modes of life available to them—the hectic animation that depends on affective transference; the pathos-inspiring apathia of countenance, emblem, mask; the shocks that open to the deadness at the core of the "living" subject. We might think here of Paul Monette's verdict on Walter Jackson Bate's biography of Keats, to which he turned following pilgrimages to Keats's rooms and grave that were propelled by a fascination generated by one "whose name was writ in water": "weighty as a tombstone," the sum of its monumentalizing ambitions. In this context, I would argue, a sentimental reading alive to biographical fascination—to responses and effects that disturb the very monumentalizing programs of aesthetics that provoke them—can perhaps tell us more about romantic poetry's modes of survival into the future.[32]

---+---

The lives of Keats, Shelley, and Coleridge were prematurely arrested: by early death in the cases of Keats and Shelley; in Coleridge's case by a widely acknowledged collapse that, while not as precisely datable, can for convenience's sake be held to have occurred around the time of his trip to Malta in 1804.[33] Biographical accident thus mobilizes effects of untimeliness and pathos that cluster around each of these poetical characters and is crucial to their allegorical functioning and to the sentiments that adhere to them: The life prematurely cut off speaks to the spirit of an age that, Hazlitt suggests, refuses the means of thriving to its arts and artists, at best consigning them to a kind of living death. The premise of this study, however, is that biographical fascination, both its forms of attachment and its failures to let go, does not depend on biographical accident alone. Rather, the valence of biographical accident, and, especially, that its effects so tenaciously cling to these particular writers, can equally be understood as a working of the writing itself. If Wordsworth's response to the modernity he diagnosed in the 1800 "Preface" to *Lyrical Ballads* was the form of the innovative, introspective lyric that has come to signify romanticism for almost everyone but professional romanticists, the Regency-period writing of Keats, Shelley, and Coleridge tends to flaunt conventions of authentic expression, foregrounding instead the "literariness" of its rhetorical materials. (In this respect, the second generation is more closely aligned with Baudelaire as Benjamin describes him.) These particular strategies of figuration, I propose, are deeply implicated in the centrality of biography to the reception histories of these writers.

Biographical fascination arises out of the concatenation of biographical figures with poetic and rhetorical ones. Obvious examples of such concatenations are when a biographical anecdote overtly draws on a poetic figure or character ("like his own ancient mariner"). More interesting to my mind are the less predictable conjurations of biographical materials and narratives by poetic figuration. Sometimes these effects are broadly acknowledged: Think of the final stanza of Shelley's *Adonais,* or of Keats's "This Living Hand." One gets a sense of how idiosyncratic such couplings can seem, however, when an editor is struck by one and puts it in a footnote: here, we might think of Miriam Allott's gloss of "full-throated ease," which refers us to the sore throats Keats had been suffering at the time he composed "Ode to a Nightingale."[34] Even when widely acknowledged, effects like these depend on the way they befall the reader singularly and intimately, in the privacy of reading. A line of verse madeleine-like opens to the landscape of biography, to a previously dormant provenance. Although these effects depend on a familiarity with biographical materials that circulate in print culture, they are at odds with projects of historical contextualization. Rather, they ambush, captivate, and even call us, in ways that can provoke an unsettling recognition of a gap between an imperfectly recoverable context and the poetic text.

A moment in a poem of Keats stages this sort of biographical fascination, anatomizes its working, and potentially solicits this fascination in its turn.[35] The passage concludes "Lines on Seeing a Lock of Milton's Hair":

> For many years my offerings must be hush'd.
>   When I do speak, I'll think upon this hour,
> Because I feel my forehead hot and flush'd—
>   Even at the simplest vassal of thy power;
>   A lock of thy bright hair—
>   Sudden it came,
>   And I was startled, when I caught thy name
>   Coupled so unaware;
> Yet at the moment, temperate was my blood—
> Methought I had beheld it from the Flood.[36]

The lines dramatize the poet coming into a sense of calling, precipitated by the "sudden" appearance of the lock of Milton's hair. The passage is often praised as a harbinger of Keats's mature poetic accomplishments by virtue of its economic telescoping of the complex, riven moment it describes. Finding himself "coupled unawares" with Milton, the young poet, even as he declares his intention to delay his poetic effusions "for many years," seems precociously to break this promise, getting ahead of himself in the space of a shock of an antediluvian recognition. His response splits him temporally, but also affectively, into shame—the flushed forehead, the sense of having anticipated himself—and confident expectancy, an anticipatory leap toward his place among the English poets.

This drama of recognition lends itself to a story of triumphal developmental breakthrough, made plangent by the reader's knowledge of Keats's early death, and in this respect the poem is readily absorbed into cultural narratives about poetic genius and posthumous fame. But such a reading fails to read the pivot on which these effects depend, the "bright" lock of hair—at once intimately connected to the lost singular subject and surviving that subject as an impersonal and inanimate thing. A bit of the body that stupidly endures and circulates after life is gone, it can only be "coupled unawares" with the famous name, the referent it cannot know it bears and that attaches to it in a manner at once despotic and contingent. The poet's intimation of immortality is thus shadowed by a prematurely experienced fatality of a particular sort. "Coupled unawares" with this odd couple, which comes "sudden," before he can guard against the shock of its mildly traumatic appearance, the poet is arrested and riven.[37] The odd couple—name attached to material remain—figures the personification that structures biographical figure, and calls the poet—his starts and flushes already suggesting his capture in the reversive energies of trope—into an anticipatory identification of himself with the order of the cobbled-together thing that he apostrophizes as "Milton."

Keats's poem may solicit the sort of fascination it explores if the line "for many years my offerings must be hush'd," or the poem's last line, which seems eerily to address us from the place of the illustrious dead, happens to conjure the prematurely arrested life of the singular subject John Keats. At such moments the poetic line contracts into something obdurate to hermeneutic labor, taking on the character of a relic, a dumb material remainder of that which has passed on. The line-as-relic is extraneous and unassimilable to an understanding of the sense of the poem.[38] Attached to the proper name, it produces effects of reference to a biographical subject, but in a context that suggests the irrecuperable nature of this subject except as the dumb, enigmatic remainder or trace. The poem thus at once solicits and rebuffs an illusion of reference.[39] If historically, effects like these have produced attachments to "Keats" and to literature in ways that have been turned to cultural account, the poem suggests that modes of securing the meaningfulness of literature through biography may defend against the shock of more untoward attachments resistant to the work of humanism and what Lynch might characterize as a filiating sense of "human relation": here, the improbable and hopeless coupling of affect with poetry in its materially resistant dimension. The whiff of fatality that attends the artist's coming into his calling, that is— an attachment to the obdurately nonhuman thing—may drift over toward what we sometimes call the love of literature.

Against this passage I want to place lines taken from one of Coleridge's notebook entries, part of the poem eventually published as "Limbo." (I discuss the entire notebook entry at greater length in Chapter 5.) These lines initially appear to take us far from Keats's poem. Although the passage does include a muted biographical reference, it does not seem to explore or to stage biographical fascination. It does, however, dramatize and explore a moment of ambush by effect in a way that resonates with and glosses the workings of biographical figure in Keats's poem. Coleridge's poem germinates out of this notebook entry's struggle to describe a "state": limbo—a "den" visited only by shadows and cordoned off from hope or *any* sort of imagined temporal trajectory, *any* sense of space and time as meaningful. The poem can only approximate this landscape through sequentially offered poetic figures, each of which in turn comes to bear an excess of meaning and must therefore be canceled, to be succeeded by another. The turning of tropes halts, however, with the arresting appearance of a negative image of the conditions that make meaning possible. The poet has just compared the "unmeaning" space and time of limbo to "Moonlight on the Dial of Day." But he takes that back:

> But that is lovely—looks like Human Time,
> An old Man with a steady Look sublime
> That stops his earthly Task to watch the Skies—
> But he is blind—a statue hath such Eyes—
> Yet having moon-ward turn'd his face by chance—
> Gazes the orb with moon-like Countenance
> With scant white hairs, with fore-top bald & high
> He gazes still, his eyeless Face all Eye—
> As twere an Organ full of silent Sight
> His whole Face seemeth to rejoice in Light/
> Lip touching Lip, all moveless, Bust and Limb,
> He seems to gaze on that which seems to gaze on Him! [40]

For a moment, the figure of the blind man held by the moon fixes the non-progressive movement of the poem, although not by offering an alternative to limbo. Halting a sequence of canceled possibilities, the specular image figures, in a negative mode, the tendency of metaphors and similes to take on meaning through relations of semblance: "Moonlight on the dial of day," evoked to convey time and space as "unmeaning," is too "lovely" an image for the state it is invoked to convey, resembling human time in the way a blind man turned toward the moon resembles a sighted person scanning the skies. The last in a recursive series of figures of nonmeaning, the blind man that "seems" to gaze on the moon that "seems" to gaze on him does not salvage or redeem anything: Like the figures that precede its appearance, it is not "like" the experience of limbo, and it conjures only by negation the fullness of "human time."

And yet the "sweet" image arrives to move the poem out of limbo den for a brief while until it is in turn retracted: "No such sweet Sights doth Limbo

Den immure." The ecstatic feeling conveyed here—by the dwelling on the image, the incantatory doublings and echoes of the verse, the exclamatory final line—is on one level puzzling, since the image itself is one of radical nonrelation and thus functions as a sort of prosopopoetic limit-figure to the state of deprivation that is limbo. The face caught in an apparent exchange of gazes, a mask bathed in nonseeing light, can only convey a *seeming* reciprocity, the mere mimicry of a structure of mutual care, mutual holding: "A statue hath such Eyes." Yet from a distance—the distance to which the poet and we are transported by these sequenced tropes—this image nevertheless appears "lovely," transfixing, perhaps, in part *because* of the way it refuses the lures of meaning and relation.

The passage quietly alludes to biographical figure, the famous marble busts of the blind Homer and the blind Milton, and by way of these conjured stony memorializations of poetic genius we enter the tropic field that interests me in this study. But the strangely moving blind man of this strangely moving lyric, which takes negative measure of a den that does not properly belong to any singular consciousness, although any consciousness could perchance find itself there, may also call up the character of "late Coleridge"—the large-eyed, balding, and touched sage of Highgate, an immured figure who, by virtue of possessing some analogon of genius, glows with a transfixing and socially refracted light.[41] This effect of reference does not secure the poem (the poem can almost strike us as a primer on the lures of prosopopoeia, which, it turns out, may be maximally alluring in this fully negative modality). At most it produces one more turn of a tropic structure that exposes the specular figures of autobiography or self-reflection as incapable of securing reference, because gestures of meaning are always bound in the rhythms of unmeaning (and, in this case, especially, vice versa). But the likeness, if it befalls us, is arresting: The figure of the blind man conjures a "Coleridge" who inhabits the world as an unfathomable simulacrum, at once gripped and charismatic. Like the image of the Brocken specter[42] that concludes "Constancy to an Ideal Object" and that Coleridge elsewhere identifies as illuminating "Genius," "Coleridge" could be said to exist as a projected shadow or image "with a glory round its head," a charged absence surrounded by aura.

In Keats's *Fall of Hyperion* the poet comes into the unseeing gaze of the goddess Moneta and is captivated by a look about which he has no illusions but which nonetheless "comforts" and "holds" him in its "benignant light." In the manner of the passages we've just looked at, this scene also equates coming into a calling (however that may be defined) with entering "unawares" into a specular effect. The moment he steps into the unseeing "benignant light" of Moneta's eyes, the poet finds himself to be already posthumous ("Thou hast felt / What 'tis to die and live again / Before thy fated hour," declares the goddess [141–43]), already "pulled" into an archaic landscape that he comes to inhabit as one of its exhausted denizens ("and every day by day methought I grew / More gaunt and ghostly" [395–96]). Both the image from "Limbo" and this scene replay, in the mode of disenchantment, the many instances in the poetry of Keats and Shelley in which an aspirant to poetic fame happens to catch the eye of one or another immortal; and all of these scenes, whatever their valances, obey the logic of ambush that structures Keats's "Lines on Seeing a Lock of Milton's Hair." If Wordsworth's answer to the question "What is a Poet?" is "a man speaking to men,"[43] the poetry of Keats, Shelley, and late Coleridge would seem to answer, "one singled out by the [dead] gods." These renderings of modern poetic vocation (or of what, following Benjamin, we might describe as the contract between poet and the social world that emerges as an older one is being annulled) suggest that being singled out entails stepping into a place that already awaits one's appearance—that is, into culturally salient structures of expectancy. Thus the one singled out in this way, recognized for the distinctive originality of his gifts, is also and always one in a series. Arriving in this place, one may find oneself "among the English poets," and indeed, it is only by virtue of appearing in this fated spot that the very type of the Cockney poetaster can enter into the series of recalibrations by which he becomes the guarantor of a prestigious literary culture. But these scenes remind us that charisma, the gift of the gods, tends to be fatal: It demands the subjection of singular life to the logic of poetic figure—to effects of premature arrest, untimeliness, abstractedness, untoward reference, and posthumous life.

These scenes dramatize poetic calling as the capture of a subject in an effect that arrests and abstracts. The universalizing gestures of the aesthetic, we are reminded, entail the sublation of particular life. What I am calling biographical fascination involves the redounding of that knowledge in the reader, when a biographical figure concatenates with a poetic figure in a way that catches one unawares, bringing home to the pulses a sense of the lost and unrecoverable singularity of that which has passed on or gone under. In a sense this frisson and the effects that occasion it comprise just one subset of a more general class of effects that can befall a reading, of the sort de Man describes in his analysis of Wordsworth's *Essay on Epitaphs*, in which he is struck by the odd animosity the poet displays to epitaphs that speak in the voice of the dead: Wordsworth's discomfort, de Man speculates, must arise from the way this kind of address causes the bystander to feel "not only the prefiguration of one's own mortality, but our actual entry into the frozen world of the dead."[44] His words could as easily describe the ambushing effect of

"Milton's Hair": Conjuring the premature arrest of Keats, the poem freezes, becoming a relic, a remainder attached to a name, and it simultaneously pulls us into its landscape and a recognition of the illusionistic character of poetic voice. The effects I pursue here are thus on one level merely special cases of the way poetic figure and poetic language work, and more particularly, of the working of autobiographical figuration as de Man describes it. I would argue, however, that the vagaries of these particular figurations open in salient and unsettling ways to the modes of poetry's survival in this (protracted) period of the renegotiation of the contract of poet and public. They speak to and personalize a dimension of loss that cannot be recuperated within the monumentalizing and aestheticizing projects of modernity but that poetry can bear as recalcitrant trace. This loss is connected both to the operations of those projects and to the ascendency and expansion of commodity capitalism to which they respond, a regime that demands, in Jennifer Bajorek's suggestive formulation, that the commodity "cut itself off from those parts of itself that were human in the past."[45] Biographical fascination, which ambushes us into a recognition that these romantic figures "are not of [our] kind," may thus also open us to the way in which *we* may be "of *their* kind," a recognition that takes on a particular valence (and violence) at this (long) juncture when "the human" increasingly seem to inhabit the world as simulacrum of something that has passed on. At the same time, it binds readers to what is recalcitrant to these regimes, to the posthumously surviving figure and the loss it bears as a trace.

—+—

The "image of the life" cast up by Benjamin's Baudelaire of course differs in significant respects from the lives of allegory lived by Keats, Shelley, and Coleridge. For Benjamin, Baudelaire's posing—his aggressive and theatrical fencing with the world—is at once heroic and suggestive of a certain clarity about the new poetry's need to register and parry the shocks of modern life. In contrast, these earlier images of the poet's lives, as thinned out and turned away, are frequently characterized as sentimental fictions eliciting sentimental response: If they speak to the perilous status of poetry in modernity, they are said to do so in blindly ideological as opposed to critical modes, falling in with what Bennett describes as the calculated narratives of posthumous fame and genius. To explore biographical effects like the ones I am trying to understand, then, may entail being alive to sentimental effect.

Impressions of sentimentality involve ideas about decorum. A response may seem emotionally extravagant, and/or it may appear to attach itself to a narrative or poetic effect that may itself seem "overwrought" (in the sense of factitious and calculated). In either case, the extravagantly factitious combines with the excessively emotional to at once promote and mask ideological interests. Pointing out sentimentality thus tends to involve judgments about authenticity, intention, and knowledge: A subject may be suspected of passing off histrionic expressions of emotion for genuine feelings so as to manipulate others; or the intensity of her passions, which she experiences as authentic, may strike another observer as out of proportion to a trumped-up object; or a narrative may flag its designs on us, too baldly sporting its ideological interests. In each of these examples, a presumption about the authenticity of emotional response is disturbed by the obtrusion of an apparently overly worked, overtly interested demand. Writing on romantic-era emotion, Adela Pinch describes "the concept of sentimentality" as "defined precisely as a confrontation between the personal and the conventional": The decorum at stake in charges of sentimentality concerns a lack of "fit" between a supposed "real" passion and a literary or cultural convention. With reference to Adam Smith's writings on sentiment and sympathy, Pinch proposes that effects and charges of sentimentality can thus be read as symptomatic of cultural anxieties about the indeterminacy of the grounds of feeling: "'Sentimentality' reveals the *arbitrariness* of the distinctions with which we . . . discriminate inauthentic from 'appropriate' emotional expressions. Sentimentality is the affective dimension of an epistemological conflict over the origin of feelings."[46] An impression or accusation of sentimentality thus reacts to the scandalous possibility of the intrinsic fictiveness and conventionality of feelings (a scandal that, for our purposes here, directly challenges the prestige of the romantic lyric, dependent as it is presumed to be upon the expressive hypothesis); and it tends to displace that possibility onto classes of texts and readers (female, Victorian, middle-brow, queer) imagined not to know the degree to which they are caught in ideological effect.

Diagnosing the impression of the sentimental as arising out of anxiety about the (possibly fictive and conventional) genesis of feelings, Pinch's claims resonate with the distinctive poetic practices of Keats, Shelley, and Coleridge that I have been describing. As I noted earlier, much recent contemporary scholarship on second-generation or Regency poetics has seized on ways it could be said to resist, expose, or refuse the naturalizing strategies and assumptions about lyric expressivity and subjectivity that shore up poetry's prestige during the period; in recent and influential work on Keats, especially, his poetic deployment of antique literary figures—poetic convention—has been centrally important to these arguments.[47] A beautifully schematic example from Keats's *Isabella* quite precisely demonstrates the disconcerting relays of passion and poetic figure characteristic of his verse. Describing the genesis of the protagonists' love affair, the poem's narrator casts their fluxes of passion as a hydraulic exchange: Isabella's waning (her "untouch'd cheek / Fell sick within the rose's just domain") prompts a "ruddy tide" in Lorenzo; when he in turn "[waxes] very pale and dead," she flushes (33–54). Both are antique but lately revived figures, coming as they do from Boccaccio: in a manner that might remind us of Manfred's allegorical joke, the poem dramatizes love as a matter of transferential crossings between feelings and tired but revivifiable conventions that are indeed reanimated by these attachments they inspire. Keats's lines might call to mind Hogg's account of Shelley's circuits of occultation and hectic life, or the stops and starts of Coleridge's ancient mariner, or Keats's blanching and flushing on the sudden appearance of Milton's hair, or the "living hand" that, if cold, could revive at the cost of our own "heart's blood," or, possibly, the infatuations readers often profess with "Shelley" or "Keats."[48]

I have twice referred to Manfred's statement as a joke, but this is of course a judgment. His words *may* be a send-up of the self-serious Byronic hero, but they could also be one more instance of a glamorized Byronic ennui that we are encouraged to take seriously. I know what *I* think, but the figure of Manfred has been read both ways. Similarly, in the history of Keats criticism, moments like this one in *Isabella* (a set that includes much of Keats's early verse) have sometimes provoked embarrassment on the poet's behalf and charges of sentimentality or mawkishness directed at the poem (including, in this and other cases, charges coming from Keats himself).[49] Pinch's analysis helps us see why. The oscillating possibilities here—is *Isabella* a sentimental poem ("bad," in Marjorie Levinson's formulation, ideologically complicit in a way productive of sentimental response?) or does it knowingly and wittingly expose to critique the very cultural assumptions and norms that sentimentality is said to enforce?[50]—are typical of those informing the reception and critical histories of all three figures in this study, although most strikingly of Keats and Shelley. Especially but not exclusively when biographical fascination comes overtly into play, these histories take shape around perceived instances and effects of sentimentality on the one hand, and correctives to the sentimental on the other. The latter camp accommodates a host of examples, including claims for the poetry's cool modernity, or for the poet's or the poetry's virile engagement with the world (the obsessive theme of Keats biography and criticism of the 1960s and '70s), or for the seriousness of the poetry's political engagement, or of its critical anti-aesthetics. That is, it includes any reading that makes claims to critical rigor and seriousness.

This history obeys a familiar logic. If sentimentality exposes, by an obtrusive inauthenticity, what it is understood as trying to mask, the function of criticism, and of a critical poetry, is to point out what sentimentality doesn't know it is revealing. A poetry, a strain of which flags the conventionality of the lyric subject and resists the allure of the expressive "I"—that aspires by times to anonymity or subjectlessness—is likely to produce these oscillating judgments in a particularly volatile way, since some version of the expressive hypothesis, some imputation of what is or is not intended, tends to be invoked to settle questions of sentimentality. All of which suggests that so-called sentimental effects do not unfairly befall these writers but are generated, risked, *intended* in some sense, by the most distinctive features of their work.

Sentimentality may thus be less the symptom of critical naiveté than an effect generated from out of an anxious dynamic that hinges on the possibility of discriminating between blind captivation by effect and critical purchase on it. In an essay on William Butler Yeats's "Among School Children," Anita Sokolsky describes the resistance to sentimentality on the part of literary critics as, potentially, a resistance to *sentimentality*'s power to unsettle criticism's claims to "expose entrenched presuppositions": "The resistance to sentimentality may stem from a suspicion that it masks its ideological investments with an apparent access of emotive illogic. But even to attribute to sentimentality such tactical shrewdness may underestimate its power to unsettle the very activity of exposing entrenched presuppositions—a power which critiques of sentimentality may serve only provisionally to ward off." She goes on, "It is precisely the attempt to exorcise sentimentality that dictates the fetishistic moment."[51] Sokolsky's argument suggests that the dynamic I have been describing is caught up in the logic of what Marc Redfield describes as a "spiral of ideology and critique" informing the broader reception history of romanticism. Because romantic texts at once fall in with and resist "romanticism," Redfield claims, "the mutual implication of aesthetics and theory accounts for the endless back and forth of criticism, whereby literary or other aesthetic works are by turns judged ideologically complicit and subversive."[52] Her reading goes further to suggest that effects associated with "the sentimental" have the capacity to undo the distinctions which this "spiral" fetishizes and upon which it feeds. "Sentimental" effects may be efflorescences of romanticism's resistances to the terms of its contextualization and valuation; charges of sentimentality may at once respond to and attempt to settle an anxiety about not knowing how to read the intention of a particular effect, but also, of a romantic poetics more generally.[53]

—|—

The effects isolated and explored in these essays perhaps more properly fall under the sign of pathos. In his *Romantic Moods,* Thomas Pfau describes the period of the British Regency as melancholic, lacking in both revolutionary hope and revolutionary outrage. The melancholia of this time bleakly acknowledges a world in which possibilities appear foreclosed in advance, in which social and economic systems are seen inevitably to coopt human energies, abstracting them and putting them to use.[54] The mood of "lucid despair" he describes could well describe that of William Hazlitt's *Spirit of the Age*: What most of Hazlitt's subjects share is less their political apostasy or quietism (although many are so charged), but a kind of willingness to settle and accommodate, to channel talent, industry, and even genius into narrow disciplinary bounds. Coleridge is an exception, but his exceptionality has consigned him to the punctum of the *nunc stans*, a place that is "no abiding place nor city of refuge."[55] The subjects I focus on here speak to this mood. Prematurely arrested, they survive posthumously to inspirit but also to chastise the thinned-out world that has failed to sustain not just its arts and artists, but life. At their most extreme they can suggest at once the limit-case of a complete opting-out of the business of getting and spending and the limit-case of a complete opting-in: the person given over to a complete, impenetrable, and deadly privacy, fully absorbed in "the life of the mind"; and the person fully abstracted into the petrific and virtual sign, into the form of the commodity.

Pathos is the emotion appropriate to these figures. As Rei Terada argues in *Feeling in Theory,* her investigation of "emotion after the death of the subject," "pathos" is the name we give to the second-order passion that registers the conventional and figurative status of emotion when it attaches to literary figures and modes. In Terada's words, "*pathos* conveys the explicitly representational, vicarious, and supplementary dimensions of emotion."[56] Connected to representation and "techniques of perpetuation," pathos is the feeling that posthumously "lives on" in the wake of an imagined authenticity of response. Pathos can thus be described as "the phoenix emotion": "Pathos assumes the death of other passions and fixes the conditions for their revival." Acknowledging the figural status of the poet, we nonetheless mourn, and our mourning has in part to do with our acknowledgment of the figure's subsumption into itself of biographical life, now revealed as unrecoverable. An example Terada gives that is especially pertinent for this study is the figure of apathia—that is, of the complete withdrawal from human relation and response: We might think here of Keats's death mask, the Witch of Atlas's hermaphrodite, Coleridge's marmoreal blind man or the "nonconsubstantial" Coleridge himself, Moneta's unseeing face. The apathetic image, attesting to the absence of relation, nonetheless generates pathos, an emotion connected to the aura or glamor attending such remote objects.[57]

Because it registers its own second-order status, pathos is thus linked to allegory (and could be said to be the austere twin of sentimentality, which it tends to risk: If for Pinch, a sense of "the sentimental" registers epistemological anxiety about the grounds of feeling, for Terada, "pathos" is the emotional response that registers the indeterminacy of the grounds of meaning). In a reading of de Man's theory of emotion, Terada explores this affinity of pathos and allegory. According to de Man, she argues, emotions "display the allegorical patterns of figures," for like and in tandem with rhetorical and poetic figures, they produce reality- and reference-effects, betray these effects as effects, and allegorize their own processes. These local oscillations and reversals are especially volatile where explicitly *biographical* figures are concerned, I would argue, and this local volatility affects the larger-scale oscillations of the reception history and the undead quality of biographical fascination, when poetic effects chime and concatenate with biographical figure in ways that produce crises of reference, effects of pathos, and romanticism's particular modes of survival into the future.

Commenting on the baroque drama, Benjamin links its allegorical form to a structure of mourning in which feeling "revives the empty world in the form of a mask." In the baroque drama this "mask" is masque-like, a formal, impersonal, choreographic arrangement of archaic and conventional materials. As Benjamin states, the melancholy it instantiates is "a feeling which is released from any empirical subject."[58] I have been suggesting that Benjamin's understanding of allegory helps us to understand the character of the romantic poet as a resuscitated convention equivocally surviving into modernity in a manner that points to its depletion. Overwrought yet undermotivated, too full yet eviscerated, by turns this character can seem to possess the cultural gravity of the exemplar, or to partake of the bright hollowness of the commodity. But *biographical* figures of the poet are also special cases within this larger set: They are personifications that bear effects of reference to a singular if resolutely occulted empirical subject, a subject that has irrevocably passed on, leaving only its mute imprint or trace on the underside of the mask. Concatenating with poetic materials that themselves resist the expressive hypothesis, the biographical figure carries these burdens and residues of reference in a way that unsettles both poetry and biography. Called up by the poetic line, memory interrupts our reading by opening the text to biographical reference, but in a manner that exposes the figurality of the subject it conjures. The yoking of poetic figure and biographical figure thus produces crises of reading, provoked by this unsettling of the relation of author to text, of context to work, the disturbances of which have historically troubled the reception history of these three poets. The dead poets cannot be put to rest because of their capture in structures of figuration.

Pathos is the companion of the undead, revenant character of biographical fascination. Some of the pathetic effects that attach to the figure of the poet in this period can strike us as oddly autonomous, unmoored in any particular consciousness. Here we might recollect the striking unanimity of contemporaries about qualities of charm or grace that can seem to bathe a biographical figure in effulgent light, the source of which, we could speculate, is the oscillation of reality-effects and their undoing projected back onto the figure. But others, more wayward and idiosyncratic, are felt on the pulses by readers in the privacy of reading. These personalize a sense of the precariousness of poetry and the poet-function in modernity, binding poetry to an irrecuperable empirical subject, and the reader to both. All these attachments have historically functioned to stabilize, fix, and memorialize romantic poetry and romantic genius. As Lynch points out, enlisting this glamour and pathos of the poets in the cultivation of a "love of literature" is an essential strategy of aesthetic education. But I would suggest, with Terada, that these stabilizing moments continually fissure and prove unstable. Love and loss strike one, and attachments to the romantic poets, and especially, to these particular arrested figures, come in the form of apprehensions of the strange posthumous life of poetry, its survival due to the capacity of its undead materials to spark and bind emotional response. Our attachments to what is impervious to our regard ensure that mourning will always become melancholia where literature is concerned. The artist whose fame and work live on into posterity is also the dumb material thing attached to the proper name, the odd couple that bears the trace and the loss of an occulted singularity: unassimilable to the "work" demanded by the projects of aesthetics and of mourning alike, it ensures that the world that would outlive romanticism cannot completely move on from its haunting figures.[59] The intractability of romantic figures to processes of working through ensures, in Sara Guyer's words, that "romanticism remains what can only be unfulfilled."[60] The arrested characters of Keats, Shelley, and Coleridge, speaking in allegorical fashion to the poet's survival into modernity as that which cannot thrive—speaking, that is, to the possibility of the end of poetry—do so in a way that posthumously sustains poetry's unsettling life, its capacity to bear "those [lost] parts . . . that were human in the past" into the future in the form of a trace.

—+—

The account of the concerns of this book that I have been offering here is retrospectively constructed, perhaps to a greater degree than are many such arguments. The chapters to come were originally written as essays, a form I have always loved for the way it accommodates errancies of attention and thought. Composed over a period of years and not in the order in which they appear here, each was first conceived as a self-standing foray into some dimension of biographical fascination under the sway of which I had fallen; biographical fascination thus simultaneously propelled and became the subject of each exploration. The chapters that follow speak to each other less as successive moments in an unfolding argument than as a series of paths through a common set of concerns that only belatedly emerged as the possible focus of this more extensive project.

Each chapter explores how biographical materials of the period, particularly those that foreground the belated, anachronistic, and virtual character of the poet, concatenate with strains of a poetics that are uniquely modern and critical, even in the context of second-generation British romanticism. These concatenations, I argue, serve to forge but also to trouble period conceptions of the poet and of poetry and the attachments readers form to both. Chapter 1, "Tracing Keats," examines Keats's "posthumous life," the name he gave the period that opened out between the knowledge of a death-to-come and actual death, in relation to the poetic strategies of *Endymion* and *Fall of Hyperion,* which, as other readers have pointed out, plunder the reserves of "literature" in ways that suggest the hollowness, opacity, and exhaustion of literary and broader cultural figural strategies, including figurations of the poet. The biographical materials generated out of Keats's "posthumous life," I argue, become a revivable but ultimately irrecuperable provenance that sharply personalizes the forms of cultural loss registered by the poetry. Chapter 2, "The Art of Losing," focuses on Shelley's choice to revive pastoral elegiac form in *Adonais,* his elegy on the death of Keats. Through this choice, Shelley engages Keats's melancholic, allegorical style in order to evoke the "passing on" of an unrealized and only imperfectly registered possibility. The poet's declared project of commemorating Keats and reshaping a literary movement around the writers of romanticism's second generation is thus shadowed by a sense of what cannot descend to the future. Chapter 3, "Shelley's Pod People," brings contemporary accounts of Shelley (and what we know about the deaths of the Shelley children) into conversation with Shelley's *Witch of Atlas,* which, I argue, figures the poet and poetry as radically withdrawn entities that are imagined to persist into the future as immured, dormant deposits—banked, perhaps, or planted, but in the absence of any promise of return or future growth, although neither are these possibilities ruled out. Written after the annus mirabilis that saw the creation of *Prometheus Unbound, The Cenci, The Mask of Anarchy,* and *A Philosophical View of Reform* and the publication of none of these works, Shelley's *Witch,* abjuring "human interest," suggests that poetry's and the poet's equivocal survival may depend on an obdurate refusal of human relation and social demand; paradoxically, the glamour that accrues to this flagged insularity may ensure the preservation of both, but in the form of occulted possibilities that may remain forever immured and undetonated.

Each of these chapters on Keats and Shelley shuttles between biographical and more properly poetic texts. The book's final chapters, on Coleridge, treat these two kinds of materials more separately: Chapter 4, "Late Coleridge," focuses primarily on Coleridge's later poetry and fugitive writing; Chapter 5, "Coleridge the Talker," focuses on contemporary anecdote and, treating Coleridge as a figure, not simply of the poet but of "the life of the mind," also broadens the argument of the book to some extent. Coleridge's late verse, I argue in Chapter 4, creates and falls into a category of "work without hope"—work reactive to "light," committed to an exploration of the negative spaces that open on this side of aim and end. It explores the "dens" of the mind without presuming a communicable interiority and an expressive subjectivity; rather, it traces movements of thought that push away from the world, that are "abstruse" in Coleridge's terms. In Chapter 5, I propose that Coleridge's late career as a prodigious talker—whose audience, enchanted by the experience of listening, comes away professing not to recall a word that was said—puts into circulation a mode of thinking that can perhaps only be inferred from the remains, and that cannot readily be marshaled into the service of the projects of modernity, including aesthetic projects and the disciplinary study of philosophy and literature. De Quincey describes Coleridge the talker as entering into a "silent contract" with his public, by which Coleridge performs "the life of the mind"—a life capacious, undisciplined, unproductive by social measures—for an increasingly regulated and professionalized class of writers. This contract, I would argue, speaks to the fascination that has historically clung to each of the writers of this study: a fascination with closed-off possibilities of thought, and even, of "life," losses that the lives of the dead poets cause us to feel on our pulses.

Readers may wonder about writers *not* included in this study. For instance, Byron—a second-generation poet who could be said to have suffered premature arrest, and whose biography was central to his place in a commodified literary culture. I hope it is clear to readers who have read thus far, however, that Byron's unprecedented commercial success and the remarkable fame and stature granted to him before his death distinguish him from the poets included in this study. The poets who interest me here are figures of *unfulfilled* promise or potential, of reserves held in reserve—sometimes, at least in retrospect, in a manner suggestive of a kind of fatal recalcitrance in relation to audience and market demands.

The omission of women poets of the period—who, as Tricia Lootens suggests, collectively have a particularly salient relation to fatality and death, and some of whose deaths (Mary Tighe's, Letitia Landon's) became central to their posthumous reputations—demands more explanation.[61] The explanation is in part circumstantial, having to do with the long history of this project. My very first attempts to write about these biographical materials, in the early 1990s, came out of an effort to understand the resiliency of the all-male romantic canon during a time (from the early 1980s on) when feminist scholarship was effecting the expansion and reassessment of many other period fields: In a series of talks and papers on the death of Keats, I argued that death positioned the male poet in a way that simultaneously capitalized upon the cachet of female poets, mobilized the energies of a "feminine" reading public, and at the same time preserved him, along with the set of illustrious canonized dead poets he comes to join, from "feminization." I dropped the idea of that project when other feminist scholars began to publish work that pursued this set of concerns, and then of course the romantic canon—or at least the set of objects of study pursued by professional romanticists—did eventually become more porous (a shift, one could argue, that could only occur in tandem with our *profession's* shift from aesthetic to historicist methodologies, which allowed the recasting of "romanticism" as "British literature of 1790–1830"). Now, as I write this, there exists excellent scholarly work on the way death inflected the posthumous reputations of Tighe and Landon, on the particularly close relation female poets of this period were seen to have with death and disappointment, and on the way this relationship marked a path to "canonization" that ultimately served to consign them to minority status.[62] When I finally returned to the materials that had interested me earlier, my own questions continued to center on the complex relation these particular male figures of arrested development had and have with the construction of a prestigious and entrenched British romanticism, considered as both canon and aesthetic. I can see that a different sort of project—one, perhaps, focused exclusively on the cases of Keats and Landon—could have opened to these questions as effectively and in ways that would have kept gender more squarely in focus. But that is not the book I ended up writing.

Finally, a word about the critical and theoretical terrain on which these essays are located. My primary engagements are with contemporaries who work in British (and in some cases European) romantic studies and who remain caught up, however tendentiously, with the legacy of deconstruction, especially the work of Paul de Man. My choice of theorists is in other respects somewhat opportunistic. Thinking about Keats, whose reception history is so preoccupied with the early imbrication of his work and reputation in contemporary print and commodity culture, drew me to Walter Benjamin's writing on Charles Baudelaire, while Benjamin's important accounts of allegory in *Origins of the German Tragic Drama* served to open and deepen my understanding of Shelley's choice of Greek elegiac form in *Adonais*. Other chapters—especially the readings of Shelley's *The Witch of Atlas* and of Coleridge's late poetry—draw upon on psychoanalytic theory (especially the work of Maria Torok and Karl Abraham, D. W. Winnicott, and André Green) that grapples with questions that interest me more broadly in this study: What sort of contract comes to exist, what volatile relations come about, between persons or objects that can appear withdrawn, that can even flag an extreme of privacy, noncommunicativeness, or nonrelationality, and those readers or auditors they nonetheless transfix and enchant? Finally, my chapter on Coleridge's talk is indebted to Hannah Arendt's *The Life of the Mind*, in its own way a late-romantic reflection on the prospective end—the already-posthumous-status—of modes and traditions of thought it remains compelled by.

A love of poetry is quixotic, even hopeless, involving as it does an attachment to linguistic figures that avert themselves from us, eluding our grasp and failing to accommodate themselves to human plans. As is the case with most nonnormative attachments, this love is relatively unsupported and unsupportable when support is gauged by the obvious measures. Those of us working, or attempting to work, in the humanities at this particular historical moment need not be reminded of this.[63] Yet it is poetry's capacity to inspire attachment beyond all reason that at the same time has sustained its life, from the romantic period to our own, which is to say, its "posthumous life" in the Keatsian sense—the life that occurs in the interval stretching out between a death sentence and a death, a death that in poetry's case has been indefinitely deferred. The poetry that engages me in the essays to come reminds us that modernity's exhausted landscapes and dry bones can be exceptionally generative, in proportion, perhaps, to the extremity of the conditions in which we find ourselves, over the course of this protracted romantic period.

1. Tracing Keats

When one knows that something will soon be removed from
one's gaze, that thing becomes an image.
                                    —Walter Benjamin, "The Paris of the
                                        Second Empire in Baudelaire"

In the age of the media, people and things *come to pass* . . .
                                    —Samuel Weber, *Mass Mediauras*

The Masks of Keats

On the cover of Andrew Bennett's *Keats, Narrative and Audience* is an image of
the life mask Benjamin Haydon took of Keats in 1816.[1] The mask fascinates
in part for its promise, before the advent of photography, to show Keats as he
was: to catch the singular beauty of countenance attested to by his contemporaries, and, even, perhaps, that look of being lost to some other scene—
the worlds of billiard balls or sea-shouldering whales, or the landscape of
the posthumous existence—that charges this form taken from life with the
pathos of a death to come. In his reflections on the death of Keats, Stanley
Plumly includes Keats's life and death masks among the few images of the
poet that to him seem to capture the Keats of biographical record, and which
he prefers to the several posthumously executed oil portraits of the poet: for
Plumly, the more formal portraits, which often show Keats amidst his books
or in the posture of the thinker, chin in hand, are guilty of generalizing the
singular person into the type of the Poet.[2] But the masks of course affect a
comparable conversion. If the portraits depict Keats as the social character of
the nineteenth-century literary man, the masks show the face become image,
loosed from context; if the former resuscitate their subject to ensure that the
British canon gets its full set, the latter evoke a loss that feels constitutive
to another sense of literary history, for which this particular truncated life
metonymically evokes romanticism itself as cut short, an unfulfilled promise.
If by a kind of inept taxidermy the portraits revivify and display Keats as a
member of a presumed still-living species, the masks suggest that the figure
of the poet may be an afterimage, surviving anachronistically into the present
as an untimely and allegorical figure. The portraits invite us to participate in

public commemoration of the worthy dead; the masks provoke attachments that feel private, intimate, even prurient, and that bear a charge of loss.

The masks of Keats have the status of relics, with plaster copies enshrined in private collections, in Hampstead House, and the Keats–Shelley museum in Rome, but they are also iterable and commodifiable, now in ways Haydon could not have anticipated: Both Bennett's and Plumly's books reproduce versions of Haydon's life mask on their covers, while a quick internet search of "Keats's masks" brings up numerous links to images appearing on Keats fan sites, discussion and Pinterest boards, references to collections, the occasional auction, and so on.[3] The proliferation of these images suggests that Keats descends to our own moment by way of nineteenth-century strategies of representation in which his biography played a central role, and which academics, however gratified they may be to discover these signs of Keats's afterlife, tend to find sentimental or kitschy. One could argue, however, that Keats's mask figures forth what to his best readers constitutes the distinctive, and distinctively modern, power of his work, its consistent exposure of the movement through which the aesthetic appears as such.[4] Peeled off from a singular body and its historical moment, but bearing the imprint of that body and moment as a trace of what has passed on, the bright image takes on an allegorical character as Walter Benjamin describes it, appearing in our present as the denatured remainder of a lost context, evoked *as* inaccessible and unsalvageable. Thus, even and especially in its aspect as a collectively available cultural form that circulates as commodity, exists as museum display, participates in projects of nation-building and shores up institutions of culture, it finds its analogue in Keats's urn, the relic of a disappeared world that, borne away from context to appear in its new setting as remote "attic shape," provokes untoward attachments that can only ever be incommensurable to it.[5]

Keats's masks open to the volatility and ironies of the history of Keats's reception and criticism, to the often-lamented way that biographical fascination, especially with the poet's death at age twenty-six, paradoxically clings to the poet of "negative capability" and "no character." At least since modernism, Keats's distinctiveness has been seen to lodge in his resistance to lyric conventions of interiority and expressivity—for instance, in his explorations of what Jacques Khalip describes as modes of "impersonality" or "anonymity," the ways of being of the alienated, fractured subject of modernity.[6] The fascination with Keats's death thus appears, for many critics of different stripes, to dog his reception as a sentimentalism that unfairly befalls the corpus. As Thomas Pfau exasperatedly comments in the context of his sustained examination of the allegorical style and melancholic mood of Keats's work, the popular imagination and romantic studies remain "forever enthralled by Keats's death at age twenty-six in Rome."[7] That enthrallment is not easily broken, I argue here, because it is deeply responsive to the impersonal, allegorical dimensions of Keats's poetry that both Khalip and Pfau persuasively demonstrate are central to its timeliness.

Keats's mask is like and not like "the empty world in the form of a mask" to which Benjamin refers when he describes the melancholic pleasure of dwelling on petrified surfaces in the German *Trauerspiel*.[8] Benjamin's allegorical dramas register mood as impersonal, formal structure. In contrast, the mask, like the abstracted image of the Poet as it emerges under romanticism, bears the trace of a singular untimely death. This capacity of the factitious, formal sign to elicit a sharp, specific acknowledgement of loss opens Keats's reception to charges of sentimentality. I would suggest, however, that the so-called sentimental response is in tune with Keats's distinctive aesthetic practices, which habitually explore the capacity of the theatrically withdrawn image, the charismatic appearance of which depends on the sense it conveys of something having passed on, to elicit untoward attachments.[9]

It is in the nature of a truism to link the character and fate of romanticism—its prematurity, its belatedness, its untimely survival into our present as anachronism and as arrested, unfulfilled promise—to the fate of its singular personages and the attachments its readers form to them.[10] This chapter explores this truism, taking as its subject the figure and work of Keats. The biographical fascination that has historically marked the reception of Keats's work is, I contend, deeply responsive to the peculiarly Keatsian character of the materials of the posthumous life. These materials are themselves allegorical, melancholic, and poetic. Insistently refusing narratives of progress or even of working through, they instead convey a sense of a world suspended and withdrawn, its figures become abstracted, phantasmagorical. Circulating in print culture, the remains of the posthumous life chime with and charge with pathos the figures and landscapes of Keats's poetry, which speaks to experience under modern commodity capitalism through its resuscitation of evacuated poetic conventions, including the figure of the poet. The reception history of Keats registers art at a particular juncture, one that may extend into our own moment, and thus his modern verse descends to us burdened by these traces of lost and irrecuperable singularity, of that which must pass on as the condition of its emergence.

"it comes like Ice"

As any lover of Keats knows, his death was preceded by what he called his posthumous life, the interval that opened between the death sentence he avidly constructed as absolute and the moment of his actual demise. The beginning of that posthumous life is difficult to pinpoint, but this scene from Charles Brown's memoir of Keats has as good a claim as any for pride of place:

> I entered his chamber as he leapt into bed. On entering the cold sheets, before his head was on the pillow, he slightly coughed, and I heard him say,—"That is blood from my mouth." I went towards him; he was examining a single drop of blood upon the sheet. "Bring me the candle, Brown; and let me see this blood." After regarding it steadfastly, he looked up in my face, with a calmness of countenance that I can never forget, and said,—"I know the colour of that blood;—it is arterial blood;—I cannot be deceived in that colour;—that drop of blood is my death-warrant;—I must die." I ran for a surgeon; my friend was bled; and, at five in the morning, I left him after he had been, some time, in a quiet sleep.[11]

Charles Dilke called Brown's memoirs "a dream on the subject" of Brown's relation to Keats.[12] Yet the scene's highly signaled theatricality—its emphasis on the weight it doesn't quite manage to bear—captures the spirit of the posthumous life, which has the character of a repeated *tableau mourant*. Death irrupts into the quotidian world and at once the frame contracts, the candle picking out the deadly spot and the poet's steadfast look; pushed outside, the friend has nothing, really, upon which to intrude. Brown captures here nothing more than a vanishing: the poet bled of hope, his face become remote iconic "countenance."

The existence that dates from this moment ultimately takes over Keats's quotidian life, as posthumous time becomes increasingly untethered from London, the rhythms of ordinary days, even the constraints of the reality principle. Thus we aren't really surprised that Severn's account of Keats's final moments repeats Brown's story of the beginning of the end:

> Each day he would look up in the doctors face to discover how long he should live—he would say—"how long will this posthumous life of mine last"—that look was more than we could ever bear—the extreme brightness of his eyes— with his poor pallid face—were not earthly—
> . . . an immense sweat came over him so that my breath felt cold to him—"don't breathe on me—it comes like Ice"—he clasped my hand very fast as I held him in my arms—the mucus was boiling within him—it gurgled in his throat—this increased—but yet he seemed without pain—his eyes looked upon me with extreme sensibility but without pain—at 11 he died in my arms.[13]

Like Brown, Severn only registers what remains after a leave-taking—the distinctive, memorable utterances, the bright eyes and pallid countenance, the feeling of having been clasped fast, of having been interpellated, one could say, into his future role as "the friend of Keats."[14]

Reporting home from Rome, Severn sees in his friend's avid embrace of posthumous existence a symptom of the singularity or strangeness of a poetic mind: "Keats is desiring his death with dreadful earnestness. . . . The strangeness of his mind every day surprisses us—no one feeling or one notion like any other being" (*LJK* II:373). This mind, however, is now given over to a refusal of its own and others' hopes for the arc of a career. Imagined as a space of withdrawal from attachment, the posthumous life promises to relieve the poet of an exhausting obligation to show promise and to have prospects:

> He will not bear the idea of living much less strive to live . . . he will not hear that his future prospects are favorable—he says that the continued stretch of his imagination has killed him—and were he to recover he could not write another line—then his good friends in England—he only cherishes the idea of what they have done and this he turns to a load of care for the future—the high hopes of him—his certain success—his experience he shakes his head at it all and bids it farewell. (*KC* I:179)

Instead, Keats flies ahead to another shore, and from there lives out a virtual existence, a life of duration without trajectory: "I have an habitual feeling of my real life having past, and that I am leading a posthumous existence"; "every man who can row his boat and walk and talk seems a different being from myself—I do not feel in the world—" (*LJK* II:359, 349).

Severn's reports suggest that for Keats, posthumous life promises a respite from the shocks that inevitably befall one who possesses the negative "capacity to be in uncertainties, Mysteries, doubts," especially as these pertain to the vagaries that shape or befall love, poetic composition, and career: Embracing one's death sentence allows one to opt out of being buffeted by happenstance (*LJK* I:193). Poetry, Keats seems to think, has been lethal to him; posthumous life promises to afford relief from the burden of promiscuous responsivity and the uncertainty of the paths it opens. Yet, paradoxically, in his posthumous life he suffers from an intense, killing version of the plight of the poetical character, whose lack of proper identity makes him always vulnerable to annihilation. In his famous letter describing this character, Keats suggests that poetical speculation is a kind of defense against the pressures of sociality: Either he is filling and informing the bodies of "characters," or, in a strange but characteristic hydraulic calculus, the identities of those around him flood him: "When I am in a room with People if I ever am free from speculating on creations of my own brain, then not myself goes home to myself: but the identity of every one in the room begins to press upon me that, I am in a very little time annihilated" (*LJK* I:387).[15] In his posthumous life, having given up the "continued stretch of . . . imagination," Keats is morbidly and viscerally susceptible to the suffocating existences of others: "A person I am not quite used to entering the rooms half choaks me"; "a person I am not quite used to causes an oppression on my chest"; "Don't breathe on me—it comes like Ice" (*LJK* II:314, 321, 378). The references suggest a bodily hypersensitivity to the surprise advent of anything that threatens an avidly adopted insularity, an advent he at first connects to the chance appearances of strangers, but, as he becomes more ill, of all phenomenal traces of abjured social attachments. Thus he becomes preoccupied with controlling incursions into his world: He instructs people to limit their visits, and then, when visiting ceases, to limit their notes to bearable brevity, and finally, to the most minimal of indicators (+ or −) (*LJK* II:352). Eventually all communication ceases except what is "framed" to Keats's ear through Severn's mediation, for Keats, all attest, cannot bear the "hand" or any material reminders of persons ("to see her handwriting would break my heart"; "the silk lining she put in my travelling cap scalds my head"; "I cannot bear the sight of any handwriting of a friend I love as much as I do you"; "a letter to Keats now would almost kill him" [*LJK* II:370, 351, 360, 363]).

These strenuous efforts are doomed to fail, since the letter's power to traumatize only increases with the vigilance with which one puts up one's guards. In his efforts to cordon off the space of the posthumous life, Keats refuses, for himself and for others, the "working through" of loss, a coming to terms with death that might involve the opening of letters and the assimilation of the sentiments they bear. Leaving the letters unopened, he abjures small prophylactic doses of sociality that could make the prospect of letting go bearable, and instead keeps alive the possibility of the devastating chance appearance of the "hand," the material traces left by the persons now lost to him. No precautions, moreover, can preserve him from the scalding phantasms—sense information charged with the lost scene—that irrupt, willy-nilly, into consciousness: "Some of the phrases she was in the habit of using in my last nursing at Wentworth place ring in my ears"; "There is one thought enough to kill me—I have been well, healthy, alert &c, walking with her—and now—the knowledge of contrast, feeling for light and shade, all that information (primitive sense) necessary for a poem are great enemies to the recovery of the stomach" (*LJK* II:345–46, 360).[16]

If posthumous life promises an escape from the burdens that afflict the negatively capable poetical character, it ultimately and ironically delimits a terrain that is poetical in some of the ways we have come to associate with the landscapes of Keats's poetry. As Thomas Pfau has persuasively shown,

Walter Benjamin's account of the way allegorical intention works—"that which the allegorical intention has fixed upon is sundered from the customary contexts of life: it is at once shattered and preserved"—aptly describes Keats's distinctive poetic style, which obsessively plunders and restages the materials of antique literary worlds.[17] Benjamin's sentence, however, resonates equally with the stuff of Keats's posthumous existence. The litany of protests that runs through these late letters suggest the poet's keen sense, not of his coming death, but that he himself is a relic of a past time, improbably lasting into this brief afterlife—the lone survivor of a vanished and mourned world, the traces of which obtrude into memory as fragments ruptured from any trajectory of hope or desire. This world, in turn, possesses its own emptied, phantasmagorical existence as it endures without him ("I eternally see her figure eternally vanishing"). To the prematurely posthumous Keats every letter bears the trace of a lost "hand." Poet's poet, who always looked on fine phrases like a lover, loving, that is, the petrified "fine phrase" as it descends to him from an evacuated context, he is excruciatingly alive to the chance appearances of these estranged figures, responding to them with violent and unstable cathexes, suffering their promiscuous advents promiscuously, on the skin, in the stomach, the lungs and the heart.[18] Refusing the work of remembrance, he is attacked by figures of illimitable loss; giving up poetry, he sustains around him a charged, if vacated, poetic world.

These are the materials that have always circulated with Keats's poetic remains. Both the landscape they shadow forth and their mode of circulation are peculiarly modern, I want to argue now, drawing on Walter Benjamin's work on the poet Charles Baudelaire. In "On Some Motifs in Baudelaire," Benjamin argues for the centrality of the experience of "shock" to life lived under the regime of commodity capitalism, shocks that he, like Wordsworth, connects to the density of modern urban social life, with its multiplied possibilities of chance and transient encounters, including especially those with strangers; and to the rise of a mass media that continually delivers a surfeit of information to its consumers. (These affinities between Wordsworth and Benjamin, I would argue, allow us to think about British romanticism as an earlier moment in the modernity to which Baudelaire responds.[19]) Drawing from Freud, Benjamin speculates that in these conditions, consciousness takes on the role of defending modern subjects against the shocks of modern life by absorbing stimuli in a way that prevents the latter from flooding unconscious processes. The result is that under modernity, experience comes to take two mutually exclusive paths: The successfully absorbed stimulus, managed by consciousness, can make its way into public life and discourses; while stimuli that slip by this guard leave their traces in reservoirs of private and collective memory cordoned off from and unavailable to conscious remembrance, unless they happen to surface in the psychically disruptive *mémoire involontaire,* which can only be triggered willy-nilly, by accident—for example, in the famous example from Proust, eating a certain kind of cake dunked in a certain kind of tea.[20]

If Wordsworth sees the introspective lyric as having potentially salutary power vis à vis the shocks of modernity, for Benjamin, the waning of the lyric during the nineteenth century suggests that, in its traditional introspective (i.e., romantic or Wordsworthian) form, it no longer speaks to modern experience.[21] Baudelaire's work, which steadily gained readership during this period, would seem to be an exception. This, Benjamin suggests, has to do with the paradoxical way Baudelaire meets the shocks of modern life. His public persona is at once theatrically and constantly *on guard,* and everywhere failing: in this way, Benjamin claims, this connoisseur of shock "mimes the poet" for a culture no longer in need of such a figure. The essay suggests that Baudelaire's persona comes out of, and allegorically renders, a poet's feeling for the special predicament of his times: Baudelaire may parry so vigorously because only impressions that consciousness fails to capture can become the materials of modern experience and poetry.[22]

Benjamin is specifically concerned here with the work of memory, citing Theodor Reik in this context: "The function of memory (*Gedächtnis*) . . . is to protect our impressions; reminiscence (*Erinnerung*) aims at their dissolution. Memory is essentially conservative: reminiscence, destructive."[23] In an age of information, "reminiscence" (the transmission of information about the past in a way that makes it consciously and thus narratively and publically available) is of a piece with forgetting (the necessary, constant shedding of information as the next thing comes along). Given the divide between "consciousness" and "experience," for an event to become present to consciousness is "to isolate events from the realm in which they could affect the experience of the reader." What *can* affect the reader—affect the reader *in the form of memory unregistered by consciousness*—can only come in the form of a shock that slips past a guard, and the subsequent, accidental detonation of its trace in a way that ruptures the conscious, public narratives and contexts in which information becomes installed. In this way, Baudelaire's poetry at once necessarily blocks direct access to experience and effects its transmission beyond its encryption in a singular psyche. That is, as Jennifer Bajorek argues in a fine account of the shock effect in Baudelaire, it works in the manner of Proust's *madeleine.*[24]

Benjamin's essay on Baudelaire, in which Baudelaire's poetry becomes the way that true experience—that is, experience unabsorbed by consciousness—can move into collective memory, helps us think about both the dynamics of Keats's posthumous life and the "sentimental" effects that dog the reading of Keats. For we could argue that the materials of Keats's posthumous life model and create the conditions for the delayed openings of involuntary memory: The "strangeness of Keats's mind," legible in the protests about what he cannot bear to entertain—the letters that must remain closed and out of view; the "hands," material traces of singular persons, that accidently slip past the guard; the phrases and images that belatedly detonate in the defended mind; and the avidly refused telos of hope realized, promise fulfilled—suggests a mode of experience that is private and singular but not subjective, and that can be transmitted, through these nuggets of speech, embedded in Severn's letters, which are then circulated among the friends whose letters won't be opened and whose hands won't be borne, as an unassimilable burden of sociality. And we could extend our account of the movement of these materials into more broadly collective memory when we consider the sharp and unpredictable effects of pathos and loss that Keats's poetry has historically prompted in its readers, effects generated by shards of verse that can randomly and unpredictably revive the *mémoire involontaire* of the materials of the posthumous life.

One cannot hope to illustrate a random and idiosyncratic effect. But in the context of the materials recalled here, consider this description of an abstracted Endymion:

> Now indeed
> His senses had swoon'd off: he did not heed
> The sudden silence, or the whispers low,
> Or the old eyes dissolving at his woe,
> Or anxious calls, or close of trembling palms,
> Or maiden's sighs, that grief itself embalms:
> But in the self-same fixed trance he kept,
> Like one who on the earth had never stept—
> Aye, even as dead-still as a marble man
> Frozen in that old tale Arabian. (I:397–406)[25]

This passage, were we to meet it in the wilderness, would scream out "Keats." The hypertrophic and hyperallusive style (the arrested figure that demands not one but two similes, each of which introduces a new literary field); the rhymes, by turns jingling and forced; the affective responses that float free of any particularized subject; and, perhaps most salient, the passage's culmina-tion in this "frozen" antique "marble man," the fully evacuated figure that, the poem suggests, is perfectly captivating only as it approaches this limit: All are typical of a poetry that could be said to hold up to view the atrophied landscape of Regency literary culture by suggesting the exhaustion of its (still delightfully manipulable) conventions.[26] But the lines potentially spark more untoward attachments if they coax out of memory the particulars of Keats's posthumous life: the poet who claimed not to "feel in the world," the face become countenance and then mask, the body frozen, finally, under the breath that "comes like Ice," the rapt circle that formed around this withdrawn image. That is, for a lover of Keats, the scene might call to mind the passing of the particular and unique biographical subject into the already anachronistic but newly celebrity figure of the Poet; and it seems to intimate how the passions and agonies of the singular personage could begin to circulate into the social realm, initially through a circle bound in attachment to this at once prematurely arrested, belated, and modern figure.

Coming: Mr Keats

In his posthumous life, Keats was a negative collector of memorabilia—the "hands" he could not bear to look at, the letters he never opened. He was thus a rare negative instance of the archival activity that became central to the establishment of his reputation during the course of the nineteenth century. That the documents of Keats's life remain so familiar to this day—that these texts are in fact more familiar to most readers of Keats than the majority of his poems, especially those published prior to the 1820 volume—suggests how central his biography, and especially the circumstances of his death, were to the reputation he was to acquire.[27] The materials of the posthumous life had an immediate public career: Severn's letters, addressed primarily to William Haslam and John Taylor, circulated among Keats's friends, who from the first attempted to gain wider publicity for them. Both John Hamilton Reynolds and Bryan Waller Procter drew from Severn's letters in their obituaries, as did Leigh Hunt in his reminiscences and the biography he wrote for the pirated Galignani edition of Keats's work published in 1829.[28] When Richard Monckton Milnes began to gather information for the edition ultimately published in 1848, Keats's collected works accompanied by a biography, he borrowed extensively from these reports, along with other documents that members of the Keats circle, now long since having fallen out with each other, contributed to this "labour of love" that was also a work of mourning and remembrance.[29]

Writing of Walter Benjamin, Hannah Arendt points to the circle as a necessary precondition of posthumous fame, which she calls "the lot of the unclassifiable ones."[30] One cannot overstate the importance of Keats's circle in the making of his later reputation, or dispute the degree to which his supporters were bound to Keats and each other through a sense of the unclassifiable distinctiveness of his work and mind, a "mind like no other"; or, for that matter, dispute the degree to which this sort of impression of sin-gularity and originality is a necessary prerequisite for being counted "among the British poets" after one's death. But the ironies and paradoxes here are also striking, having to do with the fact that the *question* of Keats's class was so central, historically speaking, to the shaping of these dynamics. Keats's first appearance before the public was as a minor instance of a derogated class of persons and goods, the Cockney School of poetry. Marjorie Levinson's influential reading of the class-based vitriol of the *Quarterly*'s and *Blackwood*'s reviews of *Endymion* suggests the degree to which "Cockney" poetry, the poetry of the Hunt circle, in turn posed a threat to a certain class of literary gentlemen represented by the conservative Scottish reviewers. Levinson per-suasively connects the extremity of the attacks on Keats's class and youth that consigned him to "the shop" and perpetual minority status, the gleeful erotic opprobrium directed at the onanistic "young Cockney rhymester gazing at the moon," to an "allegorical" style that, by virtue of its pastiche recycling of "antique" figures, exposed poetry as just another commodity form, and challenged the assumptions about authenticity and expression that served to undergird its prestige (and that of its arbiters of taste) during the period.[31]

Levinson's account prompts us to ask: By what logic did *this* poet, who first appeared before the public as the very epitome of Cockney style and sensibility, come to take his place among the "unclassifiable ones"? To begin to answer this question we might turn back to *Endymion* and the passage cited at the end of the previous section. Swooning off, becoming abstracted, Endymion enters a chain of local equivalencies ("like one who on the earth had never stept," "as a marble man"), and simultaneously inaugurates another of the poem's figural series, the set of dreamy mortals who happen to catch the eyes of the immortals. (In addition to Endymion, this set includes Adonis, Hyacinthus, Glaucus.)[32] These eye-catching youths tend to wander about in the landscapes of *Endymion*, while the gods and goddesses who become smitten with them tend to be more or less anchored in one place: One almost gets the sense that the latter train their eyes on a particular spot and simply wait for some lovely youth to drift into it. This is one way of thinking about how Keats first appeared on the scene: He walked into *Blackwood*'s series on the Cockney poets, one of several more or less substitutable members of a class. (The number prior to his appearance announced: "Coming: Mr Keats.") We cannot know whether Keats arrived in the spot opened up by the *Blackwood*'s series by chance (any Cockney poetaster would have done as well) or because of some quality only he possessed. To be singled out in this way has the structure of fate. A particular subject appears in a spot that, at least retrospectively, seems to precede him and to await his arrival there, by a causality that feels at once arbitrary and overdetermined. He appears there, moreover, as at once arrested, morbidly thinned-out, and charismatic.[33] Thus a whiff of mordancy that we can think of as the off-gassing of a neutral and structural effect accompanies even Keats's first appearance before the public as a prematurely and permanently arrested "boy of pretty abilities"—"Master John," fatally afflicted by the "metromanie" and already the equivocal focus of a circle of gentlemen, which in this first case included John Wilson Croker, John Gibson Lockhart, Lord Byron, and anonymous. These intimations of fatality help to explain the Keats circle that promptly and defensively formed in response to the reviews: It was at this time that his friends began referring to him as "poor Keats," Richard Woodhouse began collecting "Keatsiana" at this moment, and protests about the reviews began linking him to Chatterton and Kirke White, poets cut off before their prime due to public neglect.[34]

Charisma, the gift or blessing of the gods, comes at a cost, the sacrifice entailed when the full, singular subject steps into the role of the singled-out, abstracted character.[35] In *Endymion* as in reviewing culture, this is fatality without gravity, and indeed, subjection to this structure may be the condition of a certain upward mobility. Thrust forward as a representative of a series, class, or movement, the unique historical individual transmutes into the "type" that stands in for the group or series by flagging a difference from it; while the equivocality and depthlessness of this virtual figure, appearing in the fated spot, makes it available to renewed figurations and projections by shifting constellations of circles.[36] Unmoored, the perfect avatar of the Cockney poet is now open to re-classification, readily integrated, for instance, into the class of youthful geniuses, ahead of the times and killed off by a hostile world. That in Keats's case this process was not dependent on the accident of death is suggested by these first comparisons of him to Chatterton and Kirke White, although the accident of death cemented Keats's place in this series, which Shelley's *Adonais* extended back to include Lucan and Sidney, and Barry Cornwall's obituary of Keats proleptically extended forward to include the as-yet-living Shelley and Byron, to the entire second generation ("he was the youngest, but the first to leave us").[37] By 1848, with the publication of Milnes's edition, Keats would become thoroughly absorbed into the set his own work had helped to establish, of youths fatally singled out by the gods: As Benjamin Bailey commented at this time, thinking back on the friend of his youth, "the favorite of the Gods dies young."[38]

Writing on Keats's biography, Jack Stillinger describes "two stories" that can be told about the poet. The "first story," the "sentimental" one, which begins with the negative reception of the Cockney poet and to which Keats's death is central, propelled him into public view; but once this happens, the "first story" falls away, or can and should *give* way to the "second story," the true story, which acknowledges the achievement and value of the poetry and a life actively and unpathetically engaged with literary history, contemporary literary culture, and the times.[39] The story Stillinger tells of Keats, of poetic accomplishment that ultimately breaks free from the contumely and vicissitudes of its early reception history, is a familiar one. Stillinger is of course not wrong: The initial attention to Keats's death was part of a vigorous and ultimately successful campaign to garner attention for the work; and the mere fact of his death cannot account for the endurance of the poetry. (Before Keats, Kirke White was being tried out for a similar sort of role as admonisher and reinvigorator of Regency letters but that project failed.) If we perform the exercise of imagining Wordsworth having died in 1802, however, it's hard to see him having the same sort of afterlife. Stillinger's account, that is, doesn't quite address Pfau's exasperated complaint that the "first story" is weirdly adhesive and persistent, never quite kicking away despite any number of magisterial biographies and critical assessments of the work intended to correct the record.[40] Keats's own poetry leads us to speculate that the first story, far from being an appendage that can fall away once the truth emerges, is the condition of, and remains imbricated in, all subsequent stories: It is only by virtue of Keats's appearance as an exemplum (with the neutral charge of fatality that this entails) that he could come to function as a nodal point around which new and renewed constructions of literary culture can form, ultimately serving as a guarantor of poetry's prestige under conditions that might seem to threaten its survival.

I have been arguing that Keats's poetry stages the coming-into-view of the depthless, arrested, charismatic figure, the "type"—the mode of existence of the commodity, the celebrity, the canonical work—that demands the passing on of singular existence in order to emerge as such; and that these scenes resonate with the emergence and after-life of "Keats." I want to stay with this claim a bit longer, turning now to a passage from a later moment in *Endymion* that, in an even more sustained way, dwells and reflects upon this movement. In pursuit of the goddess of his dreams, Endymion by chance comes upon Adonis, adored by Venus and kept by her in suspended animation until her periodic returns, and for an instant he sees as an immortal might see:

After a thousand mazes overgone,
At last, with sudden step, he came upon
A chamber, myrtle wall'd, embowered high
Full of light, incense, tender minstrelsy,

And more of beautiful and strange beside:
For on a silken couch of rosy pride,
In midst of all, there lay a sleeping youth
Of fondest beauty; fonder, in fair sooth,
Than sighs could fathom, or contentment reach:
And coverlids gold-tinted like the peach,
Or ripe October's faded marigolds,
Fell sleek about him in a thousand folds—
Not hiding up an Apollonian curve
Of neck and shoulder, nor the tenting swerve
Of knee from knee, nor ankles pointing light;
But rather, giving them to the filled sight
Officiously. Sideway his face repos'd
On one white arm, and tenderly unclos'd,
By tenderest pressure, a faint damask mouth
To slumbery pout; just as the morning south
Disparts a dew-lipp'd rose. (*Endymion* II:387–407)

Here again, this set-piece arguably displays the smart, melancholic modernity that Pfau admires in early Keats, whose "sly allegorical performance," he contends, "exposes literariness as a specious good—a commodity as-yet-unconscious of its commodity status."[41] The lines hold up to view what the gods really want—and what they want would seem to be the unconscious figure of a commodified literariness. The poem's officious display of the abstracted youth exposes his character as a specious good, one of the series of more or less interchangeable lapsed boys the poem singles out in this way.[42] It exposes as well the potential allure of the commodity "as-yet-unconscious" of its status: for some hand, knowing there's nothing so desirable as withhold-ingness, too officiously displays to view Adonis's retentive charms, too exactly offers him up to a powerful structural effect, whether that be installing him in the glance of Venus, or Endymion, or the reader. Keats's staging of Adonis exposes the paradoxes of playing hard to get, the determining bind of the commodity, the seductiveness of which could be said to lie precisely in its appearance of being "unconscious" of the economic and market structures on which its charm depends. What might make this staging seem particu-larly literary and modern to contemporary readers of Keats is its apparent acknowledgment that the belief in the commodity's reserves are face-saving but not necessary. The charm of the specious good is to charm anyway, to enthrall us despite our suspicion that we may be bound in a calculated effect, entranced by an abstracted, hollow figure.[43]

The relays of desire and identification in this scene—Endymion gazing on one who, like himself, has attracted the attention of the immortals—and the repetition of such scenes throughout Keats's work invites us to extend the series further, and to consider Adonis as a figure of the *poet* as specious good. But while we are tempted to insert Keats into this chain, we can't be sure in what spirit the fashioner of Adonis tips his hand; or rather, I would suggest, it's a commitment to a certain reading of Keats that tends to decide this matter. Could he be so enraptured by this wishful image of the head-turning youth that he is embarrassingly unaware of his vulnerability to our perspective? (*Is* he, perhaps, a young Cockney rhymester gazing at the moon, inviting and giving himself up to the sentimental narrative of fated and fatal (in)attention?) Or is he aggressively and self-consciously working here the only self-image one of his age and class could claim? Or, alternatively, is he involved in a send-up of an aggressively solicitous "Cockney" poetic style—the style of *Endymion* itself? or, perhaps, of an entire literary tradition whose prestige and effects of authenticity in fact derive from recycled and exhausted literary materials, including the glamorized figure of the poet?[44] Following Benjamin's argument about the German *Trauerspiel*, Pfau notes that in a Regency culture characterized by entrenched forms, "critique must formally mirror [the] very state of affairs" it holds to scrutiny. Given this, the passage suggests the difficulty of making a cut between an embarrassingly sentimental effect and a demystifying allegorical one, or between the structure of the commodity and the melancholic allegorical style that exposes the commodity structure of literary culture.[45] What equivocally "appears" theatrically flags the occlusion of a subjectivity, aim, or intention "behind" the appearance: It flags a now–unreclaimable context.

Like the earlier scene of Endymion swooning off, this one fascinates in part because of its anticipation of the structures by which Keats became singled out. Most obviously it inspired Shelley, whose *Adonais*, often charged with popularizing a sentimental story about Keats's death, can itself also be read as a deep, appreciative engagement with his fellow poet's prescient modernity, including his explorations of the posthumous modes of survival of the exhausted figures of poetry.[46] But the scene's resonances with Keats's biography are also odder and more slant. Onanistic, mortally wounded, plucked from the trajectory of narrative and suspended between life and death, Adonis, a boy of "no character," anticipates, even to his officious staging, the Cockney rhymester of the reviews, gazing at the moon; or posthumous Keats, the feverish, slumbering youth framed by his coverlids in Severn's wash drawings; or Keats "in life," loveable, according to the strikingly unanimous anecdotes collected by Milnes, for his beauty of person and his attention elsewhere. Keats's tableau of Adonis discomfits in the way the phenomenon of the biographical Keats sometimes does, when we seem to see the poet entrepreneurially presented as a youth unconscious of his effects, proffered to the glance that would single him out. "Keats"—the poet of "no character"—emerges and descends to us as the projected effect of a poetic practice deeply imbricated in the way of being of the equivocal good.

In both archaic and commodity forms of allegory, the denatured sign enters into relations of equivalence and substitutability with other such signs: whether we think of them as allegorical figures or poetic currency, Adonis is like Endymion is like Hyacinthus is like Glaucus (is like Lycius, is like the wight of "La Belle Dame," is like the poet of *The Fall of Hyperion*)—mortal youths all who come serially into the glance of the gods. "Keats" was also a fated wight. With Keats's death, however, structures of seriality and equivalency that characterize not only celebrity and commodity culture but also canonicity (the series of those who belong in no class) and that are predicated on the transmutation of the singular person into the type or image, become bound to biographical accident: The neutral fatality of the singular subject's interpellation into an iterative structure becomes burdened by the sacrificed unique life and corpus, radically incommensurable with any other.[47]

This concatenation of life and figure open Keats's work and its reception to charges of sentimentality, which register the effects produced when affect attaches, in a way that inevitably seems disproportionate, to the hollow or factitious image.[48] These effects are more properly pathetic. Rei Terada has called pathos "the revenant emotion of allegory," the emotion that persists in the wake of the death of the subject.[49] In the case of Keats, pathos describes the effects produced by the poetic corpus when its ostentatiously evacuated, self-consciously literary landscapes and figures nonetheless conjure the materials of a poignantly and famously truncated life, in a way that can feel unmotivated and scattershot, yet binding of a community of readers. Pathos also names the passions that attach to certain allegorical images of the poet, which, Benjamin suggests, have virtual life in a modernity no longer in need of the real thing. In the case of "Keats," this is a poetical character abstracted, prematurely arrested, not of the order of ordinary consciousness and quotidian life but yet bearing the trace of a singularity that has "passed on." Equivocally singled out to bear and fail to bear the shocks of a market-driven print culture and modern social arrangements, this posthumous figure finds its avatar, I will argue, in the poet that emerges in *The Fall of Hyperion*.

The Poet and the Goddess

If Wordsworth's answer to the question "What is a Poet?" is "a man speaking to men," Keats's would seem to be "one who strays by fate or chance into the glance of the gods." *The Fall of Hyperion* is a late and almost thoroughly disenchanted gloss on this theme. The goddess who presides over the world of Keats's late poem—the Titan Moneta, lone survivor of the lost world of Saturn—is beyond desire, beyond concern with all external things, and nearly impervious to the charm of the dreaming youthful aspirant; while within the dream-vision of the poem, the youth who comes before her gaze is fully awake and highly aware of the equivocality of his status. The question of *why* the poet has appeared in just this place, of whether his appearance here is deserved or arbitrary, comes between the aspirant and the goddess in an overt way. Significantly, the poet's questions turn on a problem of classification: *What* (and not *who*) am I to be thus singled out? What *kind* of thing, representative of which class or tribe?

> —"Holy Power,"
> Cried I, approaching near the horned shrine,
> "What am I that should so be sav'd from death?
> What am I that another death come not
> To choak my utterance sacrilegious here?" (*Fall of Hyperion* I:136–140)

In the extended exchange that follows, Moneta's hedging answers tend merely to reproduce the category confusion of the poem's introductory strophe, in which the poet discriminates among ways to classify the dream he is about to offer, only to challenge or erode the apparent distinctions among these categories.[50] Although she parries his direct appeals, however, Moneta does fairly consistently peg the poet, not as a member of a class organized around genre, style, or function, but as the *psychological* type of the melancholic, whose "happiness" it is to allow collective "woe" to leak into "all his days":

> Only the dreamer venoms all his days,
> Bearing more woe than all his sins deserve.
> Therefore, that happiness be somewhat shar'd,
> Such things as thou art are admitted oft
> Into like gardens thou didst pass erewhile,
> And suffer'd in these temples . . . (I:175–180)

Refusing the assurances his questions strive to solicit, Moneta's diagnosis suggests only that this poet's dream will bear the cast of a melancholic propensity—that is, he will dream in the allegorical mode.[51]

This part of their exchange helps to account for Moneta's very first response to the poet's "What am I," which sidesteps the question of authorial kind altogether to address the perhaps more basic ontological question of "what kind of *being* am I." For initially, she observes only that the speaker, having managed to climb this altar and approach her shrine, has entered a class of prematurely posthumans who have been reserved for an equivocal gift—one extra turn of the hourglass, a little bit of posthumous time, as it were: "Thou hast felt / What 'tis to die and live again before / Thy fated hour" (I:141–43). Or, insofar as he is *any* sort of poet or thinker, he is one who has outlived his own death sentence. As is the case with all of Keats's dreaming boys, of all his borrowed characters, the life he has remaining to him is that of an outworn but temporarily revivable figure, the figure, perhaps, of "the Poet," not immortal so much as suffered to endure somewhat beyond the moment of his cultural efficacy.[52]

The melancholic modernity of this poem is signaled by this belatedness of its protagonist and the antiquity of the setting his task it is to fathom—a temple so vast and ancient that, it is suggested, human senses may not even register it as such. The temple's roof "builded so high, it seem'd that filmed cloud / Might spread beneath, as o'er the stars of heaven" (I; 63–64); the "silent massy range / Of columns north and south, ending in mist / Of nothing" (I:83–85); the Image "huge of feature as a cloud" (I; 88): These descriptors suggest that what we call the phenomenological world could, and perhaps does, nestle within this capacious, desolated space, borrowing its features and obscuring from the uninitiated the framing architecture that comprehends the whole. The story of the Titans registers the defeat of an old order, and the poem to come, in the manner of much of Keats's poetry, will partially resuscitate that old tale in the knowledge of an end that has already occurred. The protagonists, already vanquished when we first encounter them, are decisively doomed by the full trajectory of Hesiod's story, which admits no comeback, affords no hope. And yet the world of Saturn lives on in the form of this vast indestructible temple, within which, we are invited to speculate, a claustrophobic and saturnine modernity may locate itself.[53]

What is the poet's role here? If the *Fall*'s epic structure and Dantean echoes encourage us to expect a project of historical and narrative retrieval, however skeptical and fissured, Keats's choice of Moneta as its presiding goddess warns us to temper these expectations. Moneta occupies the place of *Hyperion*'s Mnemosyne, occasionally even taking the earlier goddess's name. Simply in terms of the role she plays in the *Fall*, however, she descends from Mnemosyne/Memory in ways that trouble this equivalency and suggests that the conception of the new poem picks up at the point where the earlier one "flamed out," in Forest Pyle's suggestive formulation. One of Moneta's designations is "Shade of Memory"—shade or shadow of that earlier figure, and thus, more immediately evocative of what according to Benjamin becomes the fate of memory in modernity.[54] In response to the challenge posed by Moneta, the poet could be said to cultivate a strenuously disciplined openness to fugitive, encrypted materials, which entails an exhausting and self-sacrificial disabling of the shock defense. Aching to see the scenes "enwombed" in "the dark secret chambers of [Moneta's] skull" (I:277–78), ushered by her to the tableau of Saturn, Thea, and Clymene, he lets fail his guard and simply waits:

> Without stay or prop
> But my own weak mortality, I bore
> The load of this eternal quietude,
> The unchanging gloom, and the three fixed shapes
> Ponderous upon my senses a whole moon. (I:388–92)

This excruciated receptivity to the accident or chance that may or may not happen may or may not have an effect. Eventually these figures do begin stirring (as the animated fragments of the earlier avatar of this poem), but it's not clear what moves the *mémoire* out of its hiding place, which in any case happens only briefly and partially before the poem breaks off. *The Fall of Hyperion* orients itself toward a view of history as complex potentially unavailable to conscious experience. If the poet manages to bear the past, this might not, necessarily, result in his bearing it away, transporting it from out the crypt, the place of the Titans' live burial according to Hesiod.[55]

The youth who comes into the glance of the goddess thus enters into a peculiar kind of bond: an allegiance to that which may be decisively closed off to him, a loyalty that, the poem suggests, could kill him. This is already suggested in his encounter with Moneta's face:

> Then saw I a wan face,
> Not pin'd by human sorrows, but bright blanch'd
> By an immortal sickness which kills not;
> It works a constant change, which happy death
> Can put no end to; deathwards progressing
> To no death was that visage; it had pass'd
> The lily and the snow; and beyond these
> I must not think now, though I saw that face—
> But for her eyes I should have fled away.
> They held me back, with a benignant light,
> Soft mitigated by divinest lids
> Half closed, and visionless entire they seem'd
> Of all external things—they saw me not,

But in blank splendor beam'd like the mild moon,
Who comforts those she sees not, who knows not
What eyes are upward cast. (I:256–71)

Earlier versions of this sort of scene dramatize love at first sight, the goddess's infatuation with the mortal youth and/or he with her. While this poem abjures these forms of investment—the poet knows that the goddess sees him not—the passage describes enchantment nonetheless: the poet held and comforted by these eyes that do not see, that beam out of the face blanched to artifact. This, I would argue, is "the love of literature," the modern poetic calling rendered as a fatal attraction. Retaining the formal structure and affective residue of a relation of care, the mere structure of mutual looking holds and binds the posthuman poet to the inhuman countenance.[56] Relinquishing the project—if he ever entertained it—of bearing a retrieved story back into his human world, he instead gives himself over to an alien landscape that demands the sacrifice of his human "weak mortality" to the logic of the denatured trope or allegorical figure: and so he too becomes subject to depletion without limit, coming to resemble the statue-like forms of Saturn and Thea and the "blanch'd" face of the goddess herself: "Every day by day methought I grew / More gaunt and ghostly" (I:395–96).[57]

On different occasions in "On Some Motifs of Baudelaire," Benjamin describes glances resembling Moneta's—glances that, because they do not actually look back, serve to "pull" the human subject into the realm of the nonsubjective or inhuman. The most fully elaborated account of this sort of look comes up in a discussion of the aura, which, Benjamin has just proposed, can be defined as "the associations which, at home in the *mémoire involontaire*, seek to cluster around the object of a perception." This tendency of associations to cluster around an object can be linked, he suggests, to a presumed ability to *look back at us* that we grant to such an object:

> Experience of the aura thus arises from the fact that a response characteristic of human relationships is transposed to the relationship between humans and inanimate or natural objects. The person we look at, or who feels he is being looked at, looks at us in turn. To experience the aura of an object we look at means to invest it with the ability to look back at us. This ability corresponds to the data of *mémoire involontaire*. (These data, incidentally, are unique: they are lost to the memory that seeks to retain them. Thus, they lend support to the concept of the aura that involves the "unique apparition of a distance." This formulation has the advantage of clarifying the ritual character of the phenomenon. The essentially distant is the unapproachable: and unapproachability is a primary quality of the ritual image.)[58]

Data unretained in conscious memory but lodged in the *mémoire involontaire* produce a feeling of the object's ability to look back. The glance that appears to look back, however, does so only to communicate its reserve and remoteness: It is the expression of the inaccessibility of the data.[59] Benjamin's account suggests that the auratic object exists in a double relation to the *mémoire involontaire:* Its aura consists in the "associations"—traces of a provenance now lost to us—that attach to it, but in its ritual character—as an object that looks at us only to communicate its distance—it also functions as an apparitional or allegorical sign *for* the unique "data" lodged in memory that cannot be retrieved to consciousness. The feeling that this object "looks back" at the viewer expresses a sense of its lost intimacy with the human.

This passage provides a way of thinking about the challenge Moneta presents the poet in *The Fall of Hyperion,* a challenge dramatized in his encounter with her remote countenance. Descending from antiquity, "Moneta," in the manner of the auratic ritual image as Benjamin describes it, has a provenance. The associations that cluster around her were available to Keats primarily through classical dictionaries that, more than any single narrative, suggest both the character of collective memory as a repository of unconscious, palimpsestic, fragmentary experience, and the degree to which that experience is only problematically accessible to modern readers. Already the Greek Mnemosyne, mother of the Muses, has fractured and multiple roles. Born into the parental generation that would swallow up its children, at least according to some accounts she begets the new arts by consorting with the Olympian Jove. In *The Fall,* Moneta's name heightens the potential complexity of her allegiances, since one of its derivations is from Juno Moneta, a Roman Olympian figure who borrows from and at times covers or succeeds the more ancient Greek Titan goddess. "Moneta" identifies the promiscuous mother who has been through it all, who breeds, consorts with, and survives generations—the Titans, the Olympian gods, the muses, the poet himself.

Shade of memory, Moneta lingers beyond her apparent context and relevancy, her survival due, perhaps, to her capacity to mutate into ever-new forms of currency. As Benjamin declares and any lover of fine phrases knows, words, like ritual objects, possess auras, the accumulated traces of their provenance.[60] Coins, like words in so many ways, also have provenances. Early Roman coins were sometimes stamped with the figure or face of Dea or Juno Moneta, the goddess who presided over the first Roman mint, located near the first Roman bank, which was situated in what had been the temple of Saturn. "Moneta," her face "deathwards progressing toward no death," thus conjures the goddess whose face has been coined and circulated—and whose proper name, rubbed down with use, has became "moneta," the Roman and

Italian words for "money"; the English "money" and "monetary" thus bear the trace of the mother of the muses and goddess of the mint (although, by what the OED calls "popular etymology," these words are also transfer points to another cluster of associations connected to the Latin *monare*, "warn": admonishment, monitory). The first reference to "Moneta" in Lemprière's *Dictionary* is to her role as goddess of the mint: Keats would have known this fact about her provenance, and it's possible he would have seen the coin stamped with Moneta's face that is in the possession of the British Museum.[61] In Keats's dream vision, "Moneta" is thus a nodal point or *madeleine*, the point at which the singular auratic object is pinned to the inexhaustibly reproducible thing. Linking the ur-history of the Titans to the birth of empire and capital, to seriality, exchange, and technical reproducibility, Keats's choice of "Moneta" invites us to understand the setting of *The Fall of Hyperion*—the vast temple of Saturn, within which the landscape of modern capitalist society may nestle—as the first bank; and to entertain the possibility that the blank, auratic face of its presiding goddess can also be read as a coined face, and thus as an ancient avatar of the reproducible and socially circulating form that for Benjamin is linked to the decay of the aura in the modern era. Levinson's insight about Keats's work is that it understands and manipulates the way in which culturally prestigious forms, including "antique" ones, circulate as forms of cultural capital.[62] In this context, Moneta—the figure he dreams up to serve as the muse of his last poem—functions as a switchpoint between the unique, prestigious original and the serially produced iteration: between the ritual object, to which we impute the ability to look, and the face of the commodity form, which, according to Benjamin, in a way peculiar to modernity rebuffs our gaze.[63]

In *Endymion,* interspecies love—the poet's "love" of "fine phrases" (from Keats's phrase that, Levinson argues, betrays the aspirations of the youthful seeker of cultural capital[64])—is promiscuous and apparently without cost: In that poem, one fine phrase supplants another, one lovely youth supersedes another, as elements in an almost inexhaustible series. In *The Fall* the human attachment to the nonhuman signifier has a weightier charge. In a footnote to the passage quoted above, Benjamin characterizes the "wellspring of poetry" as the poet's capacity to endow the nonhuman object with the power to pull the observer into its distance.[65] *The Fall* dramatizes this "pull," felt on the pulses of the poetical character, whose gravitation toward Moneta and a distant world causes him to become like her, an exhausted, posthumous figure in a desolate landscape. This shift in gravity can perhaps be attributed to Keats's abandonment, in this late poem, of the enthusiasms of the youthful *arriviste*.[66] Yet his choice of "Moneta" suggests otherwise: Her ritual, auratic figure, coined and circulated, is the very image of the literary as cultural capital. Encountered in the shadow of the bank, these eyes that don't see, yet "hold" the poet and make him "ache," suggest a continuity between the melancholic fate of the ritual object that descends to us from a lost world and the pathos of the commodity, which, Jennifer Bajorek speculates, to appear as such "must cut itself off from those parts of itself that were human in the past."[67] Both, that is, can only appear as posthumous forms that testify to the loss of the singular existence and of a history of connectedness to the human. In Keats's Regency culture as in our own, these posthumous forms potentially include poetry (both because of its anachronistic attachment to "long practice" and "craft," and in its modern, commodity character), and the figure of the poet, which, Benjamin suggests, having outlived its cultural function and value, may only circulate as simulacrum.[68]

In this context, we might turn to Samuel Weber's reading of Benjamin's work. For Weber, Benjamin's efforts to discriminate between the unique work of art and the reproducible image, and to attribute the waning of the aura under modernity to the ascendency of the latter, inadequately reckon with the way in which the phenomenon of aura anticipates the "leave-taking" that is the very condition of modern experience. His argument centers on the distinction Benjamin attempts to make between the "look back" that we impute to the unseeing ritual object and the "glance that does not look back and yet sees"—the expression of the streetwalker or of the striking woman in mourning who briefly appears in the crowd in Baudelaire's "En Passant," the glance, registered as posthumous shock, of the one who has already passed on. Weber's remarks account for the persistence of aura under the regime of the commodity and its technological reproducibility:

> And with this glance that does not look back and yet sees, a very different kind of aura emerges: a singularity that is no longer unique, no longer the *other* of reproduction and repetition, but their most intimate *effect*. What Benjamin calls the "decline of aura" emerges here not as its simple elimination, but as its alteration, which, however, turns out to repeat what aura always has been: *the singular leave-taking of the singular*, whose singularity is no longer that of an original moment, but of its posthumous aftershock—"*Un éclair . . . puis la nuit!*"[69]

The Fall explores this singular leave-taking of the singular in its different modalities: The face of the ancient goddess transmuted into blanched or coined visage; the pilgrim, "pulled" into her distance, become the poet, whose "gaunt and ghostly" way of being at once marks his archaic status and the modern iterability of his figure, and whose reflexive "methought" ("methought I grew / More gaunt and ghostly" [I:395−96]) lightly registers

the "posthumous aftershock" of an insight that he has already been interpellated into a landscape that affords no "hope of change," no viable prospects.[70]

For Benjamin, the aura—the expression of an unknown provenance, the
affective residue of a forgotten relation to a singular thing—resembles the
"traces of a practiced hand" left by the potter on the pot.[71] Long practice,
he notes, is in decline, as the accelerated demand for goods and new modes
of producing them make obsolete the skill of the artisan. But poetry, a long
practice, endures anachronistically in this accelerated world. In the protracted
moment that has seen poetry's threatened loss of relevance to the character of
modern experience and the subsequent waning of the expressive hypothesis,
its craft can appear as "metromanie" but can also point to poetry's survival
beyond the death of the author. The *Fall of Hyperion* opens to this modern
landscape.[72] When the poet tells us that we will perhaps know what to make
of this "dream" when "this warm scribe my hand is in the grave" (I:18), the
line does not settle the question of how its story will end, of its ultimate value,
of its potential "immortality": It simply designates the poem's status as that
which will have survived if we are reading these lines. Like the masks that
quietly capture the imprint of a leave-taking, the lines simultaneously deliver
a subdued posthumous aftershock—kinder, less aggressive, more tuned to
what we can bear than "This living hand"—that detonates the provenance
of "Keats."[73] The modernity of Keats's poem involves this signaling and remembrance of lost particularity—a structural effect repeatedly felt on the
pulses as we read, binding us to that which must pass on in order for poetry
to have posthumous life.

2. The Art of Losing
Shelley's Adonais

Shortly into Percy Shelley's *Adonais*, the elegist urges us to "come away," to "haste" to the side of the dead Adonais. This call has precedents in the elegiac tradition: In pastoral elegies going back to Bion and Moschus, the mourner who comes into the presence of the as-yet-uncorrupted body is granted a space in which to entertain the vain belief that the dead one "is not dead" but merely sleeping, "still."[1] In Shelley's elegy for Keats, however, this fantasy is only half-heartedly offered. Adonais lies "*as if*" in sleep; "surely" he rests:

> Come away!
> Haste, while the vault of blue Italian day
> Is yet his fitting charnel roof! while still
> He lies, as if in dewy sleep he lay;
> Awake him not! surely he takes his fill
> Of deep and liquid rest, forgetful of all ill. (58–63)[2]

The following stanza, moreover, decisively retracts even this equivocally offered possibility:

> **8**
> He will awake no more, oh, never more!—
> Within the twilight chamber spreads apace,
> The shadow of white Death, and at the door
> Invisible Corruption waits to trace
> His extreme way to her dim dwelling-place;
> The eternal Hunger sits, but pity and awe
> Soothe her pale rage, nor dares she to deface
> So fair a prey, till darkness, and the law
> Of change, shall o'er his sleep the mortal curtain draw. (64–72)

Yet despite this refusal of the elegiac delusion, we are urged to attend the corpse while it is still arrestingly fair, suspended in this interval before the corruption that is inevitably to come.

Why the hurry? What motivates the urgency of this call, sounding as it does in the context of Shelley's skeptical, modern elegy? I propose that the elegist is here summoning us to another kind of liminal moment, the point at which the afterlife of "Keats"—an afterlife characterized by its posthumous effects—could be said to be generated out of his death. A bald example of the sort of effect I have in mind occurs just here, with the poem's staging of the youthful form that lies "as if" in dewy sleep. While this fair stilled body resonates with other avatars within Shelley's own oeuvre, here it most nearly recalls the "sleeping youth" Adonis, embowered in Keats's *Endymion*:

> In midst of all, there lay a sleeping youth
> Of fondest beauty; fonder, in fair sooth
> Than sighs could fathom, or contentment reach . . .

Conjuring this early scene, Shelley's image of the body lying "as if in dewy sleep" produces effects of untimeliness and pathos familiar to readers of both poets: With the retrospective look back, a recalled poetic figure comes to feel proleptic of a loss to come.[3]

The elegist invites us to linger here, to come into the field of these effects, the creation of which the poem attributes to a sort of dreamwork that concatenates biographical and poetic figures. Within the fiction of the poem it is not the elegist but "Dreams" that fall prey to the elegiac delusion that "our love, our hope, our sorrow is not dead":

9

> O, weep for Adonais!—The quick Dreams,
> The passion-winged Ministers of thought,
> Who were his flocks, whom near the living streams
> Of his young spirit he fed, and whom he taught
> The love which was its music, wander not,—
> Wander no more, from kindling brain to brain,
> But droop there, whence they sprung; and mourn their lot
> Round the cold heart, where, after their sweet pain,
> They ne'er will gather strength, or find a home again.

10

> And one with trembling hands clasps his cold head,
> And fans him with her moonlight wings, and cries;
> "Our love, our hope, our sorrow, is not dead;

See, on the silken fringe of his faint eyes,
Like dew upon a sleeping flower, there lies
A tear some Dream has loosened from his brain."
Lost Angel of a ruined Paradise!
She knew not 'twas her own; as with no stain
She faded, like a cloud which had outwept its rain. (73–90)

At one level, this scene acknowledges a newly weighted attachment, Shelley's heavy return to his contemporary in the knowledge of his death, suggested by the rhyme scheme's failure to progress in stanzas 9–10 and by the especially rich allusiveness of this passage to Keats's poetry: While some references are direct (to *Endymion*'s Adonis and other youths, to Isabella's tears that wash the dead Lorenzo's fringes), the cumulative effect is of a deep engagement with Keats's early mannerist, rococo style.[4] Within the fiction of the poem, though, it's not Shelley but the corpus that returns to the corpse. The Norton Critical Edition of *Shelley's Poetry and Prose* glosses the "dreams" thus: "Shelley personifies various aspects of Keats's mental life as his *flocks*, according to the tradition of the pastoral elegy."[5] As scholars note, Greek pastoral only comes into being with the loss of an "authentic" pastoral society.[6] Yet because its urban and cosmopolitan audience was still closely tied to oral performance, it is not hard to see how poems might be compared to "flocks"—attached to the person and voice of the shepherd, although capable of outlasting him in a forlorn and diminished way. Transported to modern print culture, the convention feels odder: odd to think of an unmaterialized "mental life" outlasting the "brain" or body; not odd at all to think of print materials having life radically independent of the author, but hard to think of them as really *caring* if the latter lives or dies.

What are we to make, then, of these dreams and splendors that return to the evacuated figure of the dead poet and set in motion the mutual, transient sensationalizing of both? The conceit suggests that these archaic figures of the Greek pastoral tradition, disobeying the dispersive logic of print culture, instead wander back to the evacuated figure of the poet, where they sparkle and fade, discharging their "life" in a way that momentarily stains that figure with the illusions of affect—tears, the flushing of blood. I propose that Shelley dramatizes here the dynamics of Keats's posthumous life, a dynamics that *Adonais* itself helps to create: of poetry that becomes flushed with the biographical situation, producing overwrought effects that are here carefully acknowledged to arise out of the relation between highly wrought poetic materials and the hollow, a-pathetic biographical figure.[7]

Shelley's depiction of this lurid exchange between corpse and corpus defines the form Keats's celebrity would take: the lines of verse that serve as constantly renewable evocations of the poet's experiences of suffering and dying; the death that perpetually reanimates the poems, perversely lending biographical fascination to writing that, perhaps more than any English romantic poet's, resists the lures of the expressive "I." Among scholars of romanticism there is a history of decrying these "sentimental" effects as unhappily befalling Keats because of the accident of his early death, and more tendentiously, as caused or at least amplified by Shelley's poem.[8] In the passage just cited, the poet suggests his own capture in the pathos and dynamics of posthumous reception. The figures of *Endymion*, of *Isabella*, of "Ode to a Nightingale," all poems that in letters Shelley has not singled out except for criticism or equivocal praise, insist themselves here, conjuring Keats's body of work in a context that reminds us of its end-stopped character. I would argue, however, that the move by which the poem opens itself to the energies of posthumous life is inextricable from its force. Calling the survivors around the stilled figure of the poet, *Adonais* seeks to crystallize a generational movement, and, ultimately, a romanticism, the sentimental effects of which are the lining of its complex modernity. At this liminal moment a future comes into view—a future ethically bound to that which cannot descend to it, to the evacuated figure of an unrealized promise.

Reviving the Empty World

In obvious, even, perhaps, surprisingly overt ways, given Shelley's claims elsewhere that poetry does not exist in a causal relation to events and effects, *Adonais*'s elegiac and anachronistic project is oriented toward the future in a practical or "gross" sense.[9] The poem seeks to transform the world that survives Keats into a world in which Keats's corpus, and in consequence Shelley's own work, could survive. It famously chastises modern print culture, especially the conservative review establishment of *Blackwood's* and *The Quarterly* (and even more especially, if misguidedly, Robert Southey) as sadistic and homicidal. This belated attack on the poet's enemies is accompanied by a concerted, strenuous reconfiguration of the cultural landscape.[10] As the poem unfolds, the elegist's grief ("I weep") is amplified into a collective, ritualized expression of mourning, as he commands, cajoles, and instructs a series of designated mourners to join into the general lament ("Oh weep," "wake and weep"). These choreographic efforts mobilize figures from pastoral tradition, a Greek pastoral world especially identified with Keats's oeuvre, to perform a belated recognition and legitimization of the poet's remains. At the same time, *Adonais* proleptically dramatizes a re-orientation of a contemporary world of letters around the figure of the neglected and prematurely arrested writer. Members of the Keats circle, the Cockney circle, the Hunt circle, and the Shelley circle convene at the grave and meld into a generation of Romantic Regency poets; their "tradition," a constellation including Lucan, Sidney, Chatterton and Keats, consists of writers who will never be fathers, but only ever *confrères*. These shifts in the literary-cultural center of gravity toward youth and the second generation are shored up by the attacks on the periodical press as losers in the long historical perspective that the elegist offers prospectively.[11]

By all sorts of markers these ambitions have succeeded: *Adonais* stands as one of Shelley's most successful and highly regarded works; historically, it has played a significant role in the shaping of both Keats's and Shelley's reputations after their deaths.[12] Yet the reception history of this "highly wrought" poem has proven almost as vexed as that of Keats's early work: the critical acclaim it has garnered has been marked by extremes of disagreement about its philosophical and argumentative assumptions and aims, while responses to it have always been shadowed by a queasiness attached to what have sometimes been seen as the poem's *over*wrought forms of special pleading—its perceived glamorization and sentimentalizing of the figure of Keats, and, for some readers, its willingness to capitalize on Keats's death in the service of a too-nakedly-revealed personal stake in the excoriation of the review establishment.[13] Shelley did not in fact invent the story that Keats was killed by a bad review, which was already anticipated by his circle's responses to the negative reviews of *Endymion*, responses that compared Keats to Chatterton and Kirke White.[14] But *Adonais* played a part in locking into place the narrative that grants cultural prestige to the pathos-laden figure of the artist seen as a victim or casualty of a world hostile or indifferent to genius. Susan Wolfson's implication of the poem in a history that summons "Keats" as the "evocative focus, even at the risk of parody, of a peculiarly melodramatic and sentimental romanticism" suggests something of the difficulty *Adonais* has posed for professional romanticists, when, intended or not, it seems to have participated in giving not just Keats but romanticism itself a bad reputation. (Wolfson suggests that the "cultural processing of Keats" is "one of the main routes by which the 'romance' of 'romanticism' emerged in the nineteenth century.")[15] At least at times, even for sympathetic readers of Shelley from Byron to Wolfson, Shelley's efforts to create a world oriented around the prematurely dead Keats appear overstrenuous, too overtly interested, too liable to fall into sentimentality, melodrama, and self-parody. The conversion of Keats into Adonais, the one who takes his place among the illustrious dead, perhaps too readily reveals the dependence of the aesthetic realm on the tastes it purports to educate and redeem.

In what follows, I will suggest that the volatility of the poem's reception is linked to the very formal and stylistic choices that announce its learnedness and aesthetic ambition—Shelley's turn to the archaic form and conventional materials of pastoral elegy. I argue that the poem's sentimental and scandalous effects derive from this untimeliness, which allows archaic poetic convention to collide with the conventions and structure of modern print culture, the sometimes overt topical focus of *Adonais,* and the terrain within which it circulates. I want to propose, further, that these scandalous reading effects attest to Shelley's grasp of and poetic allegiance to "Keats," the poetical character of "no character," to whom effects of reference befall. The result is a poetic project that orients the future around an open and unfinished project of memory and mourning while refusing strategies of biographical memorialization.

Peter Sacks points out that Shelley's choice to write a *pastoral* elegy on the death of Keats was by no means an obvious one. By the time of Milton's *Lycidas* the form would already have seemed outmoded, and by 1821 it had been decisively superseded by the expressively elegiac poems of Thomas Gray, William Collins, and, especially, Wordsworth. Sacks suggests, however, that we can make sense of Shelley's choice of pastoral elegy given the form's history of acknowledging premature death, especially that of a poet by a fellow-poet, and especially a poet seen in the context of a hostile world.[16] But just as pertinently, and as many critics have pointed out, the form allows Shelley to return to a Greek landscape closely linked to Keats's work, including both the 1820 volume, which we know Shelley was reading closely at the time of Keats's death, but also to *Endymion* and the volume of 1817.

We might ask what motivates this catholic a return to Keats's verse on Shelley's part, given the latter's equivocal reception of much of Keats's work during the former's lifetime, especially before the 1820 volume. The evidence of *Adonais* itself suggests that Shelley's interest in the earlier poetry was reinvigorated after Keats's death, while the biographical evidence, which testifies to his close, admiring reading of Keats's last poems, especially *Hyperion*, suggests that the last poems may have become a lens through which he revisited that earlier work.[17] Thus one could speculate that Shelley's reading of *Hyperion* may have moved him out of a camp of readers capacious enough to include both Byron and Marjorie Levinson, for whom the oversaturated, hypertrophic early poetry symptomatically betrayed the poet's arriviste aspirations (ambitions and effects which, Levinson argues, are muted or turned to account in the later work), and into the camp of a reader like Thomas Pfau, for whom Keats's early work is conceptually and aesthetically of a piece with *Hyperion* and already self-consciously working out an innovative, modern poetic practice that operates to expose the exhaustion of British Regency middle-brow culture and the projects it shored up. In Keats's reliance on archaism and pastiche, on figures that flag a denatured fictionality, Pfau recognizes a melancholic poetics of the kind elaborated by Walter Benjamin in his writings on the baroque drama and, later, on Baudelaire's modernism—a poetics that, in the case of Keats, exposes "romantic" values of expression and authenticity, most often (if unfairly) associated with Wordsworth's poetry, as poetic convention, and exposes as well the more general depletion of cultural life and the commodity that poetry has become. Pfau is in part concerned to dislodge entrenched, developmental accounts of Keats's life that would distinguish the early, "bad," "naïve," or refreshingly "embarrassing" Keats from the "late" Keats (accounts that often cast the early "immaturity" as predictive of a coming "maturity"); he himself reads Keats retrospectively, through *Hyperion*'s story of the melancholic survival of an archaic world that endures beyond its usefulness and significance in attenuated, faded form—a story that challenges any triumphalist narrative of progress or development, including the ones often told about Keats's own career.[18]

Pfau's construction of Keats's career helps to make sense of Shelley's engagement with both Keats's rococo style and the pastoral mode in *Adonais*. We can speculate that, looking back at the earlier volumes, especially *Endymion*, through the lens of an attentive, appreciative reading of the 1820 volume and in the light of his own struggles with publication and reception, Shelley recognizes, in the flashy mannerism of Keats's earlier poetry, a style aimed at the exposure of "the deeply alien norms of authentic sensibility and stylistic propriety" that govern a petrified landscape of modern Regency culture.[19] If this is the case, then *Adonais*, far from being guilty of the creation of a mystified, sentimental romanticism (charges that Wolfson describes and to some extent ascribes to), powerfully and decisively allies itself with a melancholic aesthetic that has come retrospectively to characterize the most radically modern, critical, and interventionist projects of second-generation romanticism.[20]

Indeed, and as many readers have noted, *Adonais* maintains a scrupulously self-conscious and critical relation towards its own mythmaking project, if we can even call it that.[21] Throughout the poem, the figure of Adonais is resolutely occulted, his body sometimes portrayed as grotesquely and disturbingly dead, and his aura, as in the "Dream" passage, exposed as a rhetorically refracted glamor. The world of *Adonais* is one from which the gods have receded, as here:

14

All he had loved, and moulded into thought,
From shape, and hue, and odour, and sweet sound,
Lamented Adonais. Morning sought
Her eastern watch-tower, and her hair unbound,
Wet with the tears which should adorn the ground,
Dimmed the aerial eyes that kindle day;
Afar the melancholy thunder moaned,
Pale Ocean in unquiet slumber lay,
And the wild winds flew round, sobbing in their dismay.

15

Lost Echo sits amid the voiceless mountains,
And feeds her grief with his remembered lay,
And will no more reply to winds or fountains,
Or amorous birds perched on the young green spray,
Or herdsman's horn, or bell at closing day;
Since she can mimic not his lips, more dear
Than those for whose disdain she pined away
Into a shadow of all sounds:—a drear
Murmur, between their songs, is all the woodmen hear.

16

Grief made the young Spring wild, and she threw down
Her kindling buds, as if she Autumn were,
Or they dead leaves; since her delight is flown
For whom should she have waked the sullen year?
To Phoebus was not Hyacinth so dear
Nor to himself Narcissus, as to both
Thou, Adonais: wan they stand and sere
Amid the faint companions of their youth,
With dew all turned to tears; odour, to sighing ruth. (118–44)

Once, Ovid tells us, gods and mortals metamorphosed into natural elements, lending enchantment to the world. *Adonais* tells this story in reverse, tracing the fading of pastoral figure. Here "aerial eyes" dim into recognizably modern, fanciful poetic diction, "Ocean" becomes the most minimal of personifications, "winds" lose their orthographic distinctiveness, and, with the figure of an Echo who has lost her interest in mimicry, animated pastoral convention fades into the muted, "drear" landscape of modernity.

Shelley's "highly wrought" poem thus revives archaic poetic figure, especially the figures and conventions of Greek pastoral poetry that so densely populate Keats's poems, to show them expiring once again. Through this stylistic practice he thus aligns himself with Keats, whose distinctiveness, according to our most powerful contemporary accounts of his poetry, inheres in his recycling of found poetic materials, the signs and detritus of a high literary tradition, in a way that suggests the factitious, exhausted, and commodity character of that tradition.[22] Keats's Echo, his Hyacinthus, his Narcissus, his Adonis reappear in *Adonais* as afterlives of afterlives. Wasted, "wan and sere" like the knight of "La Belle Dame sans Merci," they present themselves for a final curtain call that registers as such because of the finality of the death of the poet to whose distinctive practice they are attached, and then they evanesce into an unmoored sorrow: "dew all turned to tears; odour, to sighing ruth." "Ruth," whom Keats set sighing amid the alien corn, here vaporizes into a more generalized melancholic mood. As in the earlier scene of the dreams and splendors returning to the corpse, it is as though the figure dissipates and the traces of that dissipation register as an unmoored affect of mourning.

This reading, however, does not account for the reception history of the poem. If *Adonais* does not actively sentimentalize Keats's death, do the charges of sentimentality unfairly befall it, in a manner perhaps related to the way, critics claim, the broader reception histories of both Keats and Shelley have been unfairly colored by the accidents of their premature deaths?[23] In this context we might turn more directly to Benjamin's writing, especially, to his descriptions of the impersonal, formal character of the melancholic text. Here is a well-known passage from *The Origin of German Tragic Drama*:

> Mourning is the state of mind in which feeling revives the empty world in the form of a mask, and leaves an enigmatic satisfaction in contemplating it. . . . For feelings, however vague they may seem when perceived by the self, respond like a motorial reaction to a concretely structured world. If the laws which govern the *Trauerspiel* are to be found, partly explicit, partly implicit, at the heart of mourning, the representation of these laws does not concern itself with the emotional condition of the poet or his public, but with a feeling which is released from any empirical subject and is intimately bound to the fullness of an object.[24]

The mood of melancholy does not belong to a melancholic subject but is instantiated in the formal, mask/masque-like character of the text—in the formal, hyperbolic, archaic, declamatory style of the German baroque; or in the case of the modern allegory of Baudelaire, in practices that expose, in the "literary" figure, including figures of expressive voice, the empty form of the commodity.[25]

Writing his pastoral elegy, Shelley would seem to revive a form that is exemplarily allegorical in these terms: an archaic mode, the effects of which depend on ritualistically repeated, conventional elements, and the affective register of which is explicitly and thematically linked to mourning. Yet it is this latter dimension of elegy that also makes it potentially anomalous, or at least a special case, in terms of Benjamin's account of the melancholic allegorical text. In contrast to the diffuse and impersonal mood of baroque *Trauerspiel* or the verse of Baudelaire, elegy is directed toward the loss of a specific "empirical subject." It is thus the particular power of the belated English avatars of the pastoral elegy to connect the sense of an exhausted world, a world that has survived its own meaningfulness and "life," with the untimely death of a singular person. The fate of the one who dies prematurely comes to exist in a bound relation to that of the world that survives him as a system of evacuated signs.[26]

The English pastoral elegy shares with Benjamin's baroque drama, but also with Keats's own work, a deployment of flat and/or conventional figures uneasily yoked to the passions they purport to express and mobilize. All have in common a vexed reception history: on the one hand, a tendency to be pejoratively described as bombastic, sentimental, melodramatic, mawkish, and so on—the vocabulary reserved for perceived inauthenticity under the ascendency of naturalism or realism; on the other, an interest, especially since Benjamin, in the critical, "modern" power of this literature to register the constructed and hollow character of authenticity-effects produced by an array of cultural forms. The volatility of *Adonais*'s reception can thus be connected to a broader reception history of literary modes (melodrama, gothic, sentimental literature, and so on) that have in common this linking of passion to the ostentatiously factitious figure.[27] Among these forms, the English pastoral elegy is a special, and especially volatile case, since its figures—Lycidas, Adonais, the lorn poet/swain who weeps the dead one's fate—carry a burden of biographical reference that causes these inauthenticity-effects to redound to one or another empirical subject. Here we might recall Johnson's criticism of *Lycidas*: "Passion plucks no berries from the myrtle and ivy, nor calls upon Arethuse and Mincius, nor tells of rough 'satyrs and fauns with cloven heel.' Where there is leisure for fiction, there is little grief."[28]

But where Johnson accuses Milton of being unfeeling, Shelley is as apt to be charged with wearing his heart too much on his sleeve, even if there is a lack of consensus about *what* he is exposing (too near an identification with Keats? a willingness to sacrifice the latter for his own ambitions?).[29] The difference may hinge on the modern culture of personality that was taking shape during Johnson's time (and indeed, around Johnson himself) but by the Regency period could emphatically said to be the landscape within which Keats and Shelley wrote. Take, for instance, this scandalous passage from *Adonais*:

31

Midst others of less note, came one frail Form,
A phantom among men; companionless
As the last cloud of an expiring storm
Whose thunder is its knell; he, as I guess,
Had gazed on Nature's naked loveliness,
Actæon-like, and now he fled astray
With feeble steps o'er the world's wilderness,
And his own thoughts, along that rugged way,
Pursued, like raging hounds, their father and their prey.

32

A pardlike Spirit beautiful and swift—
Love in desolation masked;—a Power
Girt round with weakness;—it can scarce uplift
The weight of the superincumbent hour;
It is a dying lamp, a falling shower,
A breaking billow;—even whilst we speak
Is it not broken? On the withering flower
The killing sun smiles brightly: on a cheek
The life can burn in blood, even while the heart may break.

. . . .

34

All stood aloof, and at his partial moan
Smiled through their tears; well knew that gentle band
Who in another's fate now wept his own;
As in the accents of an unknown land,
He sung new sorrow; sad Urania scanned
The Stranger's mien, and murmured: "Who art thou?"
He answered not, but with a sudden hand
Made bare his branded and ensanguined brow,
Which was like Cain's or Christ's—Oh! that it should be so! (271–306)

On the one hand, this passage could hardly be more scrupulously aware of the fictive status of the "frail Form" that takes its place among the mourners. Appearing on the scene as a "phantom among men," that form moves with the mechanical and hectic life of poetry—of the turning, "breaking," and decay of trope following trope, the tremor of the thyrsis responding to the "beat" of the verse; marked in a way that only serves to flag a radical undecidability, the "Stranger" speaks "As in the accents of an unknown land," that is, in the denatured language of melancholy—formal and foreign, inflected by the Greek, the alexandrine, the archaic.[30] And yet this figure refers. When it weeps over the fate it shares in common with Adonais, we can speculate that this fate is that of the "poetical character," who, possessing no self, is nonetheless trailed and shadowed by the biographical referent, those accidents of class station, of education, of erotic entanglement, and of early death that informed the reception of both Keats's and Shelley's work, even though the practices of each resist and critique conventions of poetic self-identity and -expressivity.[31]

Registering a complaint about these ad hominem attacks, *Adonais* foregrounds the gap between poetical character—the bright, denatured image—and biographical person. Yet the result is not to clear up confusion but to invite, once again, a volatile, ad hominem response. When this particular fair form, decked out in its antique trappings, "weeps," it scandalizes in the manner of Keats's own work when the latter exposes the virtual and conventional structures of lyric authenticity. But compounding this, it also conjures, or provocatively risks, reference in a particularly volatile and unstable way, by flagging an aggressive but unfathomable intentionality.[32]

"Even whilst we speak," the "I" of the verse asks, "is it not broken?" The address, with its startling reference to "our" face-to-face, voice-to-ear relationship, is one of three such moments in this passage (along with "he, as I guess" and "Oh! that it should be so!"). Breaking the formality of the verse, these moments emphasize the fictive character of the "frail Form": "He, as I guess" pointedly establishes that "he" is not Shelley, "I" am not "he." Yet they do not especially lend authenticity to the lyric "I" that emerges in relation to the fictive "he." In the context of this highly wrought poem and this local play of figures, the "I" rather reminds us that the lyric "I" is also a figure, that "we" are "now" being addressed by one whose "natural" voice has been stilled long ago and never sounded here anyway. The aside instead sets up a relay among poetic postures that at once invites and resists biographical speculation.[33] Here "Shelley" becomes subject to volatile reception-effects that more consistently accompany the reception of Keats, in which questions of poetic value hinge on speculations about the poet's intention and degree of self-awareness (for example, in critical disagreements about whether a given moment performs the work of cultural critique or exposes an embarrassing, wishful effort at self-commodification).[34] We could almost say "he" sacrifices himself—and nowhere more flamboyantly than in this passage's notorious allusion to the mark of Cain or Christ. The posed alternative points to a *question* of intention that has historically engaged the poem's critical reception. Is it Shelley's genuine goal in *Adonais* to redeem Keats for posterity, or, wittingly or not, does he betray a brother-poet once again to public contumely by resurrecting old charges of Keats's "weakness," minority status, and inauthentic "Greek"? Or, willingly suffering contamination by Keats's Cockney baggage, does Shelley thus take on a kind of martyrdom?[35]

But the Cain or Christ question also, and even more unfathomably, seems to invite the virulent response it in fact received at the time, when critics answered the question "What possessed 'Shelley' to mark this self-image with just this scandalously illegible mark?" with reference to the poet's atheism, blasphemous impulses, and/or lack of impulse-control—that is, with biographical information circulating freely in print culture.[36] Even for critics relatively hostile to the intentional fallacy, this question (of what prompted the author to do just this?) may tend quietly to surface at moments when a sense of having worked something out produces a fantasy of having grasped something about the author's intentions. (So, for instance, the difference between Levinson's and Pfau's readings of Keats in part turns on a question of the extent to which Keats knew what he was doing, the extent to which the exposing qualities of his allegorical style either exposed *him* or were mastered by him; for me to suggest that Shelley is "reading like Pfau" rather than "reading like Levinson" is another turn of this casual critical reliance on that strategy.) *This* passage, I propose, exposes this fantasy for what it is. It produces the scandal of a flaunted, possibly perverse intention—an intention that asks to be read—but that cannot be attributed to a person.[37] The scandalous "fact" of Shelley's atheism, or, more recently, the charges that Shelley is exposing a mawkish or self-indulgent and unreflective self-pity or anger here, do not settle so much as mark the scandal of the text, which lodges in the equivocal and undecidable relation of biographical to poetical figure.[38]

Responsive to the structure of mourning, baroque allegory "revives the empty world in the form of a mask." Shelley's modern pastoral elegy displays the depleted figure of the poet to the emptied world, in a gesture that can be, and was, read as a provocation. The romantic cult of genius, which this poem is sometimes charged with fostering, is modern and melancholic. Like all the other pastoral conventions in *Adonais,* "the poet" is a resuscitated archaic figure that survives, precariously, into modernity in a way that points to its own exhaustion. In the manner of all such forms, it can appear by turns overwrought and undermotivated, too full and eviscerated, possessing the cultural gravity of the emblem, the bright hollowness of the commodity. But it is also a special case, referring to a particular if resolutely occulted empirical subject.

The yoking of poetic figure and occulted subject, which, scandalizing without settling anything, troubles the reception history of Shelley's poem, also serves to personalize the loss and the burden of survival that the revived archaic figure dramatizes. In the passage quoted, the figure of the elegist flamboyantly takes on that equivocal burden—a pressure of survivorship that could involve rejected or admitted culpability, redemptive action, shared contumely or death. But more often the poem exhorts "us" ("Come away!") to face this loss, in a manner that arrests and provokes. The precariousness of poetry and the "poet-function" in modernity becomes personalized in *Adonais*'s allegory on the death of Keats, binding the latter's poetry to the empirical subject, and readers to both, if in a particularly volatile and unstable way.

Adonais constructs a world in which the poetical remains of Keats could live on, posthumously. But its melancholic tactics ensure that romantic genius will have a Janus face. The artist whose fame and work live on into posterity is shadowed by what never came to live, what failed to thrive—figured by the lost "empirical subject" that has left behind only traces (the imprint on the back side of the mask, the marks left by the "living hand"). The biographical accident of Keats's early death affectively colors the poem's chastisement of a world that has outlived the arts it failed to succor, a world bound by its volatile and impossible attachments to what did not come to pass. This, I wish to argue now, is the meaning of *Adonais*'s exploration of the fate of the dead child, which speaks to the ethically binding power of the story of the one who died before his time.

The Dead Child

Adonais opens with an urgent address to the muse/mother Urania:

2

Where wert thou mighty Mother, when he lay,
When thy Son lay, pierced by the shaft which flies
In darkness? where was lorn Urania
When Adonais died? . . .

. . . .

3

O, weep for Adonais—he is dead!
Wake, melancholy Mother, wake and weep!
Yet wherefore? Quench within their burning bed
Thy fiery tears, and let thy loud heart keep
Like his, a mute and uncomplaining sleep:
For he is gone, where all things wise and fair

> Descend;—oh, dream not that the amorous Deep
> Will yet restore him to the vital air;
> Death feeds on his mute voice, and laughs at our despair. (10–27)

Urania's pride of place and the extensiveness of the poet's attention to her here (he addresses her over the course of five strophes) might lead us to anticipate her central role in what is about to unfold. Yet she quietly drops out of the action, only to make a belated, dramatic appearance midway through the poem. There is remarkable consensus among readers of *Adonais* that the Mother represents an "inadequate" or "naïve" instance of mourning that the elegist must resist, "transcend," or "overcome."[39] Reading this poem through the melancholy poetics of *Hyperion*—the poem that so impressed Shelley, and that, in Tilottama Rajan's terms, hews to an ethic of "worklessness" rather than working through[40]—might cause us to be skeptical of the oedipal and triumphalist narrative of mourning that underlies these critical accounts. None of these readings, moreover, fully account for the odd lag between the elegist's address and the Mother's entrance on the scene, between her initial unresponsiveness and her belated interruption of the work of elegiac mourning.

What accounts for that initial unresponsiveness? Possibly, the elegist simply decides to retract his call. In the passage quoted above, he equivocates and reverses himself: "Wake, melancholy Mother, wake and weep! / Yet wherefore? . . . let thy loud heart keep / Like his, a mute and uncomplaining sleep" (20–24). This poet has read Ovid, has read *Lycidas*, and knows from the start that even the Muse that Orpheus bore could not defend her son, that there is no turning around of death. But we're also invited to wonder whether he retracts his call because he knows she wouldn't hear it anyway:

> **2**
>
> Where wert thou mighty Mother, when he lay,
> When thy Son lay, pierced by the shaft which flies
> In darkness? where was lorn Urania
> When Adonais died? With veiled eyes,
> 'Mid listening Echoes, in her Paradise
> She sate, while one, with soft enamoured breath,
> Rekindled all the fading melodies,
> With which, like flowers that mock the corse beneath,
> He had adorned and hid the coming bulk of death. (10–18)

In this imagined scenario, Urania, "veiled" and self-confined in her bower (already and proleptically the bower of Adonis, that cordoned-off world that includes the equivocally suspended youth within its confines), battens on the rekindled "fading melodies" of her son's verse. Sliding from the apostrophic mode to that of third-person description, the elegist hints at a disenchant-ment with this Mother he imagines as so absorbed by the melancholic appeal of Adonais's verse that she's oblivious to his actual death; and perhaps also with the dead poet himself, the Mother's favorite, the author of verse at once dangerously seductive and fatally distracting.[41]

The elegist himself here obliquely charges the Mother with inadequacy, but as Sacks points out, elegiac chastisements in the form of "Where wert thou?" can work to turn outward the feelings of culpability that might other-wise be too close to home.[42] Urania's suspended state is at once peculiarly maternal and also exemplarily literary, and in either register, her "dreaming" condition points to the potential for blindsidedness. Maternal reverie—a form of caring that psychoanalysts say "holds" the child and is the very con-dition of its capacity for imaginative life—is indistinguishable, at some level, from negligence: Reverie is light (in)attention, the parent enamored with the idea of the child, with the idea of the child's own capacity for reverie, even as she pulls back from direct engagement with the actual child—even, we might say, as she and the infant enter into a mutual fantasy of the child's invulnerability to accident.[43] The verse connects this absorbed, negligent attention to the dynamics of poetic response. The Mother's receptivity to the mood of Adonais's verse comes with a forgetting of his personal fate; in this, she mimes the Keatsian poet, when for example the speaker of "Ode to a Nightingale" becomes absorbed in the cadences of a poetry "half in love with easeful death," until the thought of becoming a "clod"—the recogni-tion that "death" has bodily as well as figural reference—"wakes" him from his reverie. If on the one hand the poem seems to chastise the Mother as a certain kind of indulgent reader of Keats, a reader who like Keats's speakers indulges a dangerous and delusive melancholic proclivity, on the other, her absorbed listening to an "echoing" and repeating verse that distends time and plays with the lovely but hollow figure suggests an exemplary responsiveness to the modern, melancholic verse whose power and timeliness Shelley's poem recognizes and echoes.[44] These reflections, moreover, hint at a more general truth, which is that one's attachment to poetry, to the illusion of poetic voice (the "false surmise" that makes elegiac delusion emblematic of poetic experience itself), necessarily "forgets" the embodied poet's fate.[45] Urania responds to poetry that lives on, "still," suspended between life and death and forever re-animatable, like the embowered body of Adonis as poets have rendered it.

The good enough Mother is thus necessarily a fatally inadequate Mother, and the good enough reader is similarly unconscious, asleep at the very moment s/he is most responsive. After this brief appearance the Mother, who poses a *question* of "adequate response," is simply suspended: She hovers over the first half of the poem even as the poet seems to forget his appeal to her, just as she seemed to forget the vulnerability of her son. Her suspension functions for the elegist in the way a mother's distraction might function for any child: Dropping his call for her direct engagement with his task, he opens up a space for his own response. While she dreams, he makes his separate path to Rome and the dead Adonais, settling into his role as the impresario of a work of mourning that, by stanzas 18–21, has progressed to where he can notice the return of spring and a renewed, and less formally distanced, sharpness of grief: Grief expressed twice ("woe is *me*" [154, 183]), once in the context of an acknowledgement of the decay of his subject's bodily remains ("the leprous corpse touched by this spirit tender / Exhales itself in flowers of gentle breath" [172–73]), and then, of perhaps a sharper pang, brought on by the thought that "grief itself" may prove "mortal," that loss could be forgotten or worked through (183).

The Mother returns precisely here, to interrupt the progress of mourning and the potential fading of grief:

22

> *He* will awake no more, oh, never more!
> "Wake thou," cried Misery, "childless Mother, rise
> Out of thy sleep, and slake, in thy heart's core,
> A wound more fierce than his with tears and sighs."
> And all the Dreams that watched Urania's eyes,
> And all the Echoes whom their sister's song
> Had held in holy silence, cried: "Arise!"
> Swift as a Thought by the snake Memory stung
> From her ambrosial rest the fading Splendour sprung. (190–98)

She is "stung" to remembrance of what she has somehow known all along, the mortality of her son; or perhaps she is finally stung to register, belatedly, the elegist's formerly ineffectual, retracted call; or perhaps the poet is here stung to remember the maternal figure he had so urgently called upon earlier in this poem. Or perhaps the line suggests the interdependence of these delayed awakenings. Revived by a "Misery" generated out of her "dream," which was also her reading of Keats, or a "Misery" generated by the "dream" that is *Adonais* and, more nearly, the elegist's awakened "grief" at the thought that grief itself might be mortal, the Mother awakens to function as a setback. Her intransigent sorrow returns the poem to its beginning as once again a display of passion briefly challenges Death's power by effecting the convulsive, momentary reanimation of the exquisite corpse:

25

In the death chamber for a moment Death
Shamed by the presence of that living Might
Blushed to annihilation, and the breath
Revisited those lips, and life's pale light
Flashed through those limbs, so late her dear delight.
"Leave me not wild and drear and comfortless,
As silent lightning leaves the starless night!
Leave me not!" cried Urania: her distress
Roused Death: Death rose and smiled, and met her vain caress. (217–25)

The Mother's protest is, momentarily, a magically effective one, which turns time back to the hour of death. Worn grief—the possibility that grief itself will fade—becomes fresh grief; the fantasy of reversing death powerfully returns; the image of the corrupted dead is powerfully refused.

"Dreaming," the Muse misses the death of her son; belatedly awakening, she implores Adonais to return, not to life, exactly, but for a final leave taking. Like Bion's Venus before her, the Mother asks for just one last word, one last kiss:

26

"Stay yet awhile! speak to me once again;
Kiss me, so long but as a kiss may live;
And in my heartless breast and burning brain
That word, that kiss shall all thoughts else survive,
With food of saddest memory kept alive,
Now thou art dead, as if it were a part
Of thee, my Adonais! I would give
All that I am to be as thou now art!
But I am chained to Time, and cannot thence depart! (226–34)

This is a strangely modest fantasy: Why not ask for the dead one's more lasting return? The wish can only arise from a desire for closure, in the context of a death that for the Mother happened offstage. Yet the closing moment she asks for is one that would keep grief forever alive in the survivor "chained to Time." Generated from out of the work, the Mother arrives belatedly to bear a desire for that which is inassimilable to the work of mourning.

This scene evokes a haunting passage in Freud's *The Interpretation of Dreams* that centers on a dream of parental loss. Freud tells the story of a father, exhausted from having nursed his child during the illness that ultimately caused the latter's death, who falls asleep in the room adjacent to that in which his son's corpse is laid out. There he dreams that his son appears by his bedside, catches him by the arm, and says, "Father can't you see I'm burning." The father wakes to realize that while the old man hired to watch the body has fallen asleep, a candle next to the coffin has fallen over, lighting on fire the child's shroud and burning the arm of his body.[46]

Readings of this dream offered by Freud, Jacques Lacan, and Cathy Caruth all remark on this delay, in the first instance, of the father's awakening. Why does he dream this oddly, directly referential dream instead of responding immediately to the urgent crisis of the fire? Freud produces two answers to this question: first, that the dream responds to the father's wish for his child to be alive and speaking again, allowing the father to delay for a moment his waking to the knowledge of its death; and second, and redundantly it would seem, that the dream, like every dream, also answers a more universal wish—the wish of consciousness to keep dreaming, to stay asleep.[47] Perhaps so, but then for Lacan, a question that remains concerns the call that emerges from "within" the dream. If the father's wish is to keep dreaming, why then does he dream the call, coming from the son transiently restored to life, that wakes him—that forces him to awaken to the death he cannot assimilate, that he can only ever encounter "too late"? Lacan returns to the dream to see in it an instance of consciousness's foundational, traumatic encounter with the "real" as a missed encounter.[48] For Caruth, Lacan's reading bores into the dream's figuration of the ethical challenge of survivorship:

> The dream reveals how the very consciousness of the father as father, as the one who wished to see his child alive again so much that he sleeps in spite of the burning corpse, is linked inextricably to the impossibility of adequately responding to the child in its death. . . .
>
> Ultimately, then, the story . . . is for Lacan the story of an impossible responsibility of consciousness in its own originating responsibility to others, and specifically to the deaths of others.[49]

This evocative, moving story and its history of readings tug at *Adonais:* the logic of the Mother's perhaps culpable, perhaps inevitable "missing" of the moment of her son's death, her response delayed by a "dream"—her own, enmeshed in Keats's lulling verse, or Shelley's, that is, the "highly wrought" poem of *Adonais* itself, which ostentatiously allows her to sleep on; her subsequent awakening in response to "Misery," whose urgent call seems to come out of the "dream"; and her wish, after she grasps that death has happened, for the child's transitory return—a wish that discloses a melancholic intention to keep alive a "part" of the lost one in her breast, as a sign of the forever imbricated relation of the child who dies and the parent who survives.[50]

Indeed, one could argue that *Adonais* grasps and sharpens the structure of the narrative it predates. For Freud, Lacan, and Caruth assume, almost without remark, that the father who dreams of his child's return has in the first place "missed" the latter's death, even though the narrative suggests otherwise, that he was watching by the bedside, that the child, perhaps, died in his parent's arms. Yet Caruth describes the child as one whom the father "has let die unwitnessed": "The force of the trauma is not the death alone . . . but the fact that, in his very attachment to the child, the father was unable to witness the child's dying as it occurred."[51] The contrived delay of Adonais's Mother, who culpably yet inevitably misses the death of her son and whose subsequent longing is for "one last word," "one last kiss," from the already dead child who comes back solely to take leave once again, acknowledges and dramatizes the insight of Freud's story, that death always involves a traumatically missed event: One "misses" the living encounter with the reality of the *dead* child.[52] The child who appears in the dream Freud recounts, or the child enjoined to take one last leave from the Mother of *Adonais*, emerges from death's camp to address the survivor "one last" time: the only moment of leave-taking that *could* qualify as the last, since recognizing it as such could only happen belatedly from the other side of a death that has occurred; and it could only take place in an impossible landscape, in the gap between the parent's life and the child's death. At this moment, Caruth speculates, the parent, grasping and grasped by the dead child, is constituted as a parent "chained to Time," as a survivor whose "mode of existence" is "determined by the impossible structure of the response."

The Mother whose appearance is generated right here—just at the moment that the elegist is stabbed by the possibility that grief itself could fade—is not a figure of "inadequate" or "regressive" mourning except insofar as her refusal shadows and halts any narrative of successful working through loss. She is more accurately one half of a couple. A reader in the grip of biographical fascination might think of Mary Shelley, one half of the mourning Shelley couple, who after the deaths of their children bore a burden in part projected on her by the grieving father, himself ostensibly committed to moving on, of serving as the designated mourner, the one lost to grief, frozen in a locked relation to her dead child and dead to all appeals.[53] The Mother in the poem asks for the momentary, convulsive reanimation of the dead child, whose "last word," "last kiss," lodging in her breast, would make her the very figure of melancholy, or, in psychoanalytic terms, would transform her into the "dead mother," the mother so bound in private grief that she cannot respond to the appeals of the living.[54] This equivocal gift was in fact given to the Shelleys, when their child William was "reanimated after the process of death had actually commenced, and . . . lived four days after that time."[55] We might speculate that the occasion of this poem, the death of John Keats—unanticipated, "missed," and belatedly triggering the shocked apprehension of what has been lost—opens to that earlier, "terrible reprieve" and the frozen time between, in which the possibility that one could move on from loss was repeatedly refused by the mother who could not get over it, who, here, finally, is acknowledged to have carried the burden of a shared, impossible survivorship.[56]

In her bower, the Mother listens to the voice of one already dead, but this knowledge is suspended. Waking from this "dream," she grasps the death that the illusion of poetic voice had adorned and hid. What she asks for is one last convulsive revival of his figure, now in the context of an acknowledged death. She asks, that is, for yet another manifestation of a figural strategy especially connected to the allegorical poetic practice of Keats; but henceforth, when she re-enters the dream of reading, her experience will be of writing that has become an endlessly-iterable "one last word"—will be colored by the sharp awareness of this as the remains of the lost empirical subject. The melancholic formal structure becomes "personalized," the reader becomes vulnerable to being "stung" by the memory of death and the burden of an unnatural, even impossible survivorship that the poem links to the survival of a child and/or a contemporary, and that is tied to the survival of romanticism itself. Always when we read, we read the "remains," that which lasts posthumously after the time of writing. This poem proleptically tells the story of the posthumous survival of "Keats." But the triumphant narrative of the one who claims his rightful inheritance and place after death is shadowed by the catastrophe of the child that dies before its parental generation, disrupting an orderly handing-down of cultural capital and exposing both the annihilating power and vacancy of such inherited structures.[57] The stinging that attends the posthumous reading of Keats, and ultimately, of Shelley—the stingings of a remembrance that, once entertained, inevitably risks sentimentality, melo-drama, self-parody—has functioned historically to foster the survival of a critical, melancholic romanticism.

The poet abandons the Mother a second time, not, I would argue, because the poem successfully "transcends" her position, but because it acknowledges and absorbs her devastation. The conclusion of the poem again urges the reader to "go" to Rome, now more explicitly the locus of a past in ruins. Here we are shepherded to the grave of the child attended by a "sealed over" grief:

48

Or go to Rome, which is the sepulchre
O not of him, but of our joy: . . . .

. . . .

49

Go thou to Rome,—at once the Paradise,
The grave, the city, and the wilderness;
And where its wrecks like shattered mountains rise,
And flowering weeds, and fragrant copses dress
The bones of Desolation's nakedness
Pass, til the Spirit of the spot shall lead
Thy footsteps to a slope of green access
Where, like an infant's smile, over the dead,
A light of laughing flowers along the grass is spread.

50

And grey walls moulder round, on which dull Time
Feeds, like slow fire upon a hoary brand;
And one keen pyramid with wedge sublime,
Pavilioning the dust of him who planned
This refuge for his memory, doth stand
Like flame transformed to marble; and beneath
A field is spread, on which a newer band
Have pitched in Heaven's smile their camp of death
Welcoming him we lose with scarce extinguished breath.

51

Here pause: these graves are all too young as yet
To have outgrown the sorrow which consigned
Its charge to each; and if the seal is set,
Here, on one fountain of a mourning mind,
Break it not thou! too surely shalt thou find
Thine own well full, if thou returnest home,
Of tears and gall. From the world's bitter wind
Seek shelter in the shadow of the tomb.
What Adonais is, why fear we to become? (424–59)

"Go to the spot," he instructs: to the grave of the one who failed to thrive—
of a mute inglorious Milton, of a boy of Winander, of the infant of "The
Thorn," whose putative grave, covered with dancing flowers, we may approach when "she is [not] there," or of the child William of *Frankenstein*.

Pausing at these young graves, the elegist aligns himself with an expanded romanticism that now includes Gray, Wordsworth, and Mary Shelley in its circle of survivors of "hope" that has "gone before."

Romanticism descends to the future as a movement and a corpus. The remains stewarded for posterity shore up a national culture, even at a time of the threatened irrelevance of art. Shelley's poem is invested in this project. But it also suggests that project's lining, a romanticism that does not descend to its future but rather figures and seeks to create a modernity bound by volatile relations of attachment and responsibility to the possibilities it failed to succor.[58] *Adonais* works to secure the survival of the possibility of poetry into a modernity potentially indifferent and hostile to its power, in verse that will come to possess a posthumous sting of its own:

55

The breath whose might I have invoked in song
Descends on me: my spirit's bark is driven,
Far from the shore, far from the trembling throng
Whose sails were never to the tempest given;
The massy earth and sphered skies are riven!
I am borne darkly, fearfully, afar;
Whilst, burning through the inmost veil of Heaven,
The soul of Adonais, like a star,
Beacons from the abode where the Eternals are. (487–95)

3. Shelley's Pod People

A certain shape recurs in Shelley's verse—a beautiful, slumbering human form. In Canto 10 of *The Revolt of Islam*, Laon discovers such forms amidst the ruins of a maddened civilization:

XXIII
Sometimes the living by the dead were hid.
　　Near the great fountain by the public square,
Where corpses made a crumbling pyramid
　　Under the sun, was heard one stifled prayer
　　For life, in the hot silence of the air;
And strange 'twas, amid that hideous heap to see
　　Some shrouded in their long and golden hair,
　　As if not dead, but slumbering quietly
Like forms which sculptors carve, then love to agony.[1]

The stanza adumbrates three classes of being: the living, the dead, and the "as if not dead"—bodies suspended in and shrouded by their own nimbus, preserved intact within the wreckage. It is "strange" to find these hermetic figures here. They seem to insist on their radical extraneousness to human concern, on the way in which they simply do not matter—to the plot of this poem, to the scene in which they are posited. Yet that very insistence seems to place them in some relation—or charged nonrelation—to the overtly social landscape in which they slumber.

True aliens, these pod people only simulate the natural human body. They are also only "like" romantic works of art, whether conventionally understood as expressing and inciting human passion, or rendered by Shelley as "seeds" and "dead leaves" that slumber, dormant, until futurity unlooses their incendiary social potential. These are identified with motion, mutability, transference—the movement of trope and verse itself. In contrast, the perpetual dreamers of *this* passage, with their factitious, arresting glamor, resist metamorphosis, the poetic turn, and all the transformative practices and values we have come to associate with Shelley's poetry. They are thus related to a certain construction of "the aesthetic" as autonomous, enigmatic, auratic form. The stanza could thus be seen to pose the question of the relation of the aesthetic to the social field.

These beautiful dreamers live a posthumous life, beyond life and death but transcending neither. I want to suggest that they speak to a fantasy of the endurance of the poet and the poetic work, not as endlessly renewable, socially efficacious resources, but as forms radically closed to our concerns. They can thus be connected to an experience of Shelley's own poetry, which, however sympathetic we are with recent work that insists on the poet's commitment to social and political change, can strike us as most wonderful at its most difficult and hermetic, the point where it fails to yield to our reading. They can also evoke the exquisite loveliness of Shelley himself as he appears in the accounts of his contemporaries—as the prematurely arrested figure who never was of our kind.

In the pages that follow I want to look at the Shelley circle's posthumous constructions of "the Poet"—the one who walked among us like a mercurial visitant from another world, and, more rarely, the closed, immobilized but equally unearthly form that slumbers forever in the hearts of those who knew him. These constructions are cultic but not naïve, I would argue. They are informed by passionate, attentive readings of Shelley's poetic figures, including figures of the aesthetic as that which adamantly refuses to matter in terms of human economies of desire and exchange. Perhaps, Shelley's ruthless Witch of Atlas suggests, the artist is most loyal to human needs and desires when his art preserves at its core a resistance to our demands.

Shelley's Bones

In 1869, when Edward Trelawny, the friend of Shelley, was in his late seventies, William Michael Rossetti, born after the poet's death, began a series of visits to him. These visits resulted in Trelawny's expansion and republication of his *Recollections of the Last Days of Shelley and Byron*, as *Records of Shelley, Byron, and the Author*.[2] They resulted as well in Rossetti's delighted acquisition of a little piece of bone:

> He gave me a little piece (not before seen by me) of Shelley's skull, taken from the brow: it is wholly blackened—not, like the jawbone, whitened by the fire. He has two such bits of jawbone, and three (at least) of the skull, including the one now in my possession. I must consider how best to preserve it.[3]

Trelawny had these bones to give away because he was himself a relic—
the last survivor of the small circle who orchestrated Shelley's cremation after
his drowning in Italy. By the time Rossetti met him, he had been living for
some years off his stories of the poet's last days. Here is his account of his
first encounter with Shelley's skull, on the beach off the Via Reggia where
the drowned body had washed up:

> We were startled and drawn together by a dull hollow sound that followed
> the blow of a mattock; the iron had struck a skull, and the body was soon
> uncovered. Lime had been strewn on it; this, or decomposition, had the effect
> of staining it of a dark and ghastly indigo colour.[4]

Attended by Leigh Hunt and Lord Byron, and assisted by a host of Italian
officials, Trelawny proceeded to move the corpse onto a funeral pyre and to
repeat the ceremony that had been performed for Shelley's friend Edward
Williams the day before:

> After the fire was well kindled we repeated the ceremony of the previous day;
> and more wine was poured over Shelley's dead body than he had consumed
> during his life. This with the oil and salt made the yellow flames glisten and
> quiver. The heat from the sun and fire was so intense that the atmosphere was
> tremulous and wavy. The corpse fell open and the heart was laid bare. The
> frontal bone of the skull, where it had been struck with the mattock, fell off;
> and, as the back of the head rested on the red-hot bottom bars of the furnace,
> the brains literally seethed, bubbled and boiled as in a cauldron, for a very long
> time. . . . The only portions that were not consumed were some fragments
> of bones, the jaw, and the skull; but what surprised us all was that the heart
> remained entire. In snatching this relic from the fiery furnace, my hand was
> severely burnt; and had any one seen me do the act I should have been put in
> quarantine.[5]

The fire consumes the elaborate machinery Trelawny has mobilized to produce this spectacle on a recalcitrant, modern landscape. In the end, all that
stays with us is the boiling, fabulous body, with its unorchestrated energies,
utterly transfigured into something rich and strange—into the elusive, ungraspable figure of poetic genius.

Or almost utterly. There is the matter of the bones and the heart that
refuse to burn. These become "relics," parts to which accrue the magic of
the lost one—like manuscripts, locks of hair, portraits, biographical anecdote,
other things that originate in physical proximity to the dead person. Relics
can stand, or stand in, for the lost body itself, in the way a fragment can come
to stand for the projected shape of a lost work or corpus. The heart acquired

these latter values in the course of its afterlife, which began when Trelawny gave it at the cremation to Leigh Hunt, who begged it of him; Mary Shelley then wanted it, but the uncharacteristically unchivalrous Hunt wouldn't give it up until after some weeks of negotiation. The heart was then encrypted in a locked drawer of Mary Shelley's writing desk, folded in a page of *Adonais*, where it was discovered after her death and buried. Leigh Hunt, in the meantime, ever after mourned and eulogized its loss: "Cor Cordium," or heart of hearts, is the epitaph he put on Shelley's tombstone; "Let those who have known such hearts and lost them judge of the sadness of his friends," he writes in Shelley's obituary.[6]

Like Rossetti, who wondered "how best to preserve" his bit of bone, these lovers of Shelley had the passion of collectors and hoarders. But what of Trelawny, who snatched these remains from the fiery furnace only to give them away? He reminds us that the labor of the circle is twofold: to collect the pieces, and to put them back into circulation. An adventurer who gave up a career at sea to follow the poets, the preserver of their deaths and their relics, Trelawny knew that these traces are the stuff of biography—little bits of material that begin in proximity to the person but only come into their full value when disseminated. If the heart, exposed in its cage, looks especially plummy, worth burning oneself for, perhaps this is less because it represents the core or essence of the biographical subject than because it is the figure of circulation. Trelawny, who tracks the metamorphic career of Shelley's body as it is drowned, buried, disinterred, burned, encrypted, and buried again, liked to keep things moving. He keeps alive the "surprise" of the heart's spectacular appearance by passing it along; he keeps always a few bones in reserve, for the ever-renewed delight of the initiate. By these tactics he sustains the magic of the relic—its reference, not to the natural human body, but to the protean, otherworldly shape of the poet.[7]

A professional romanticist could well find an interest in the career of Shelley's bones somewhat embarrassing: Even during the nineteenth century such reliquarianism seemed to some a particularly excessive and dismissible manifestation of the romantic cult of genius. Yet Paul de Man's important essay "Shelley Disfigured" suggests that versions of this attachment may inform the very construction of Shelley's corpus and the entire history of his reception. In his essay on Shelley's "Triumph of Life," de Man identifies a poetics of disfiguration that repeatedly erodes and erases what it posits, that "warns us that nothing, whether deed, word, thought, or text, ever happens in relation, positive or negative, to anything that precedes, follows, or exists elsewhere, but only as a random event whose power, like the power of death, is due to the randomness of its occurrence."[8] Paradoxically, Shelley's literal death by drowning before finishing the poem has operated to give positive "shape"—the shape of a fragment—to a text that is better described as a performance of this negative knowledge. "What we have done with the dead Shelley, and with all the other dead bodies that appear in Romantic literature . . . is simply to bury them, to bury them in their own texts made into epitaphs and monumental graves . . . They have been transformed into historical and aesthetic objects."[9]

The cultic life of the dead Shelley might seem to be the most naïve and egregious of these monumentalizing strategies. Yet as de Man repeatedly demonstrates, it is not easy to disengage the valuative work of commemoration from the rigor of a reading. What "shape" circulates in these early accounts of Shelley? In Thomas Hogg's account of meeting Shelley at Oxford, his friend first appears as a "stranger," a visitant, who speaks with no natural voice and is animated by no natural life.[10] Here is Hogg describing Shelley sleeping:

> He would sleep from two to four hours, often so soundly that his slumbers resembled a deep lethargy; he lay occasionally upon the sofa, but more commonly stretched upon the rug before a large fire, like a cat; and his little round head was exposed to such a fierce heat, that I used to wonder how he was able to bear it. Sometimes I have interposed some shelter, but rarely with any permanent effect; for the sleeper usually contrived to turn himself, and to roll again into the spot where the fire glowed the brightest. . . . At six he would suddenly compose himself, even in the midst of a most animated narrative or of earnest discussion; and he would lie buried in entire forgetfulness, in a sweet and mighty oblivion, until ten, when he would suddenly start up, and . . . enter at once into a vehement argument, or begin to recite verses, either of his own composition or from the works of others, with a rapidity and an energy that were often quite painful. During this period of his occultation I took tea.[11]

Shelley is here possessed of the charge of the poetic figure, and not just any figure, but his own as described by de Man: He is a shape all light, subject to periodic occultation; or, more fatally put, an evanescent and fading form, continually metamorphosing, vanishing, going under. In the words of William Hazlitt: "His person was a type and shadow of his genius. His complexion, fair, golden, freckled, seemed transparent with an inward light, and his spirit within him

> —so divinely wrought,
> That you might almost say his body thought.

He reminded those who saw him of some of Ovid's fables."[12] And here is Trelawny, who in his *Records* describes his first encounter with Shelley, who simply disappears from a room of people: Trelawny asks, "Where is he?" and Jane Williams answers, "Who? Shelley! Oh, he comes and goes like a spirit, no one knows when or where."[13] In the logic of these biographical testimonials, the drowning of this figure is merely a repetition of a characteristic disappearance. In the account of the Genovese captain who reported seeing the spectacle of the *Don Juan* in turbulent waters: "The next wave which rose between the Boat and the vessel subsided—not a splash was seen amidst the white foam of the breakers. Every trace of the boat and of its wretched crew had disappeared."[14]

The "Shelley" who appears in the memoirs of those who knew him is always on the brink of being lost. Most characteristically, he is lost in books—the natural setting for a poetic figure. The first time Trelawny meets him, Shelley begins to read and translate Calderon: "Shoved off from the shore of common-place incidents that could not interest him, and fairly launched on a theme that did, he instantly became oblivious of everything but the book in his hand, . . . After this touch of his quality I no longer doubted his identity."[15] Trelawny's nautical figure suggests that Shelley's immersion makes him vulnerable to drowning. This is literally true: His inability to get his nose out of his book makes him a perilous sailor. But there's also a fatal logic at work here: Narcissus-like, the poet finds and loses himself in other scenes, in landscapes that do not support human life. He's always reading, and he always gravitates toward water, and no one likes to think of the combination, particularly Trelawny, who goes searching for him in a forest one day and stumbles upon an old man who guides him to an ominously Ovidian scene: "By-and-by the old fellow pointed with his stick to a hat, books, and loose papers lying about, and then to a deep pool of dark glimmering water, saying 'Eccolo!' I thought he meant that Shelley was in or under the water."[16]

This ability to be transported lends Shelley his charm, makes him a marvelous and wonderful figure, a man like no other, according to the recollections of his friends. He seems to have inspired in them the stabbing emotion that a lover of books feels when watching the reader, the obsessive scholar, the writer, when that person seems to carry a capacity for immersion beyond all limits: a love that is an amalgam of identification, protectiveness and dread, and, no doubt, envy and rage. Such a figure seems on the one hand to be in constant need of rescue: to be reminded to come home, to eat, and periodically, to be fished out of the fire or the water. And yet one intervenes at his and one's own peril: when Shelley is sleepwalking or seeing ghosts, or when he's out in a boat over his head, one can only hold one's breath, for the merest gasp might tumble him out of the poise that sustains him. So he is kept alive by constant vigilance—the practical measures and magical thinking of the circle that forms around this mercurial stranger who does not seem to have attached himself to life.

It's hard to imagine that Shelley, an expert in the allure of the vanishing figure, doesn't intuit this, that there isn't an element of performance in his obliviousness to the world. This is suggested by another anecdote Trelawny tells. One day, swimming in the Arno, Trelawny "astonished the Poet by performing a series of aquatic gymnastics, which [he] had learnt from the natives of the South Seas." Shelley asks, "Why can't I swim?" Trelawny replies, "Because you think you can't," and advises him to try.

> He doffed his jacket and trowsers, kicked off his shoes and socks, and plunged in; and there he lay stretched out on the bottom like a conger eel, not making the least effort or struggle to save himself. He would have been drowned if I had not instantly fished him out. When he recovered his breath, he said,
>
> "I always find the bottom of the well, and they say Truth lies there. In another minute I should have found it, and you would have found an empty shell. It is an easy way of getting rid of the body."[17]

On the one hand, this story tells the usual story: of the poet careless of his cage, always ready to leave this world. But on the other hand, how else could a man who can't swim captivate a man who learned his tricks in the South Seas than by this flamboyantly staged willingness to drown? How else could a man without the will to live provoke the dramatic interventions necessary to keep him afloat? Trelawny's Shelley is a little stooped from a life of being doubled over still surfaces, and it's not always possible to know if his Narcissus posture represents an extreme of self-forgetfulness or of ruthless self-absorption. And indeed, more than any positive image of Shelley as an ideal or ethereal figure, it's that undecidability—the undecidability of a pure self-reflex—that constitutes his charm.

The Shelley that circulates in these early biographies is the projected phantasm of his verse: the personification of a negative knowledge and an ungraspable poetics, or, in de Man's words, "the glimmering figure [who] takes on the form of the unreachable reflection of Narcissus, the manifestation of shape at the expense of its possession."[18] The posthumous creation of the circle that labored to give shape to the poet after his death, this glimmering figure is neither a naïve nor an escapable construction. It descends to haunt the most powerful of our modern readings of Shelley—for instance, de Man's: a haunting symptomized by de Man's gestures of figuration and his inordinate attachment to the figure that refuses to attach itself to any life supports whatsoever.[19]

Death arrests this evanescent form. In death Shelley reminds Leigh Hunt of a "spirit" "found dead in a solitary corner of the earth, its wings stiffened, its warm heart cold."[20] His description recalls the splayed skeleton found—or fabricated—by Trelawny:

> Two bodies were found on shore,—one near Via Reggia, which I went and examined. The face and hands, and parts of the body not protected by the dress, were fleshless. The tall slight figure, the jacket, the volume of Aeschylus in one pocket, and Keats's poems in the other, doubled back, as if the reader, in the act of reading, had hastily thrust it away, were all too familiar to me to leave a doubt on my mind that this mutilated corpse was any other than Shelley's.[21]

The stiffening of the glimmering figure into the determinate shape of the Poet recalls de Man's claim about the fate of Shelley's corpus, which "stiffens" into the rigidity of an historical and aesthetic object when read backwards through his death. Yet these descriptions of the poet's corpse suggest that "the aesthetic object"—the static, closed thing that comes to stand for art—may represent less a detour from the rigors of reading than the limit-case of a Shelleyan poetics. Shelley's dead body is the formal, fixed rendering of an infinitely redoubled strategy of figuration.[22] In death, Shelley's bones arrange themselves into the posture of the reader arrested in a moment of absorption, but too late to save himself from drowning; or, perhaps, of the reader already drowning—doubled over and lost in his book, or in the figure of the dead Keats—before death's random blow arrests him; or, even, of the reader halted before the "shape" of the dead Shelley, discovering herself already absorbed into his circle.

Live Burial

Hunt's image of Shelley as a stiffened ephemeron recalls the exquisite bodies tucked away in the ruins in the stanza I began by quoting. These bodies can in turn be linked to the encrypted form that colonizes the circle after Shelley's death, causing it to stiffen into an obdurate, breakable formation. The beautiful hermetic dreamers of Shelley's poems provide a way to think about the problems attendant upon reading or mourning Shelley. How does one get hold or let go of a radically arrested figure?

Pod people occur throughout Shelley's work, but they are strangely insistent in *The Witch of Atlas*, Shelley's great autobiographical poem of 1820. The glamorous Witch is herself a pod person. She spends her days in a cave and her nights in a fountain or well, where she folds into a chrysalis form, a barely animated effigy of herself, recalling her author's stints as conger eel or occulted sleeper:

XXVIII

This lady never slept, but lay in trance
  All night within the fountain—as in sleep.
Its emerald crags glowed in her beauty's glance;
  Through the green splendour of the water deep
She saw the constellations reel and dance
  Like fire-flies—and withal did ever keep
The tenour of her contemplations calm,
With open eyes, closed feet and folded palm.

During the poem the Witch moves out of the cocooning spaces of cave, fountain, and well of fire, to set out on travels that Stuart Sperry calls "a journey without goal or quest."[23] But like an otherworldly Johnny Apple-seed, wherever she goes she collects and sows forms that mime her own encapsulated beauty. Most strikingly, she creates a somnolent hermaphrodite that briefly accompanies her; then, in the last movement of the poem, she follows the Nile to the seat of human civilization, where she walks by night, "scattering sweet visions" and "observing mortals in their sleep." To the most beautiful of these she gives a "strange panacea" (LXIX). When such a one dies, she unwraps the shroud, throws the coffin into a ditch, and lays the body out:

LXXI

And there the body lay, age after age,
  Mute, breathing, beating, warm, and undecaying,
Like one asleep in a green hermitage,
  With gentle smiles about its eyelids playing,
And living in its dreams beyond the rage
  Of death or life; while they were still arraying
In liveries ever new, the rapid, blind
And fleeting generations of mankind.

Thus her sports leave behind deposits—figures evocative of poets lost in their creations, of works whose contents have withdrawn into inscrutable form, and of observers absorbed in some other scene than the social landscape they inhabit—all of which have in common a posture that, borrowing from Theodor Adorno, one might call aesthetic "comportment."[24]

The ubiquity of these withdrawn figures in *The Witch of Atlas* seems teasingly related to the text's almost complete lack of conversation, in 1820, with Shelley's ambitious, overtly political writing of 1819—a year that saw the completion of *The Cenci* and *Prometheus Unbound* and the composition of new works including *The Mask of Anarchy, A Philosophical View of Reform*, and "England 1819," all deeply engaged with post-Peterloo England. Indeed, we could speculate that *The Witch*'s abstracted forms serve to foreground a certain absence of relation: the absence Mary Shelley protested and Percy Shelley insists on in his dedicatory stanzas "To Mary (On her objecting to the following poem, upon the score of its containing no human interest)," where he asserts that his poem tells no story and has no pretensions to an audience—it is like the kitten's objectless *jeu*, and the ephemeron that lives only for a day (I–II).[25]

In her notes to Shelley's *Posthumous Poems*, Mary Shelley returns to the scene of this disagreement. At the time, she explains, she was urging Shelley to write on "subjects that would more suit the popular taste than a poem conceived in the abstract and dreamy spirit of *The Witch of Atlas*":

> It was not only that I wished him to acquire popularity as redounding to
> his fame; but I believed that he would obtain a greater mastery over his own
> powers, and greater happiness in his mind, if public applause crowned his
> endeavors. . . . But my persuasions were vain, the mind could not be bent from
> its natural inclination. Shelley shrunk instinctively from portraying human
> passion, with its mixture of good and evil, of disappointment and disquiet. Such
> opened again the wounds of his own heart; and he loved to shelter himself
> rather in the airiest flights of fancy, forgetting love and hate, and regret and
> lost hope.[26]

The context of *The Witch of Atlas*, she suggests, is not the work of the year that preceded its composition but the professional and domestic disappointments that ushered in, plagued, and followed that burst of productivity. She's thinking no doubt of Shelley's failure to command any audience at all with his writing. By the time of *The Witch*'s composition, *The Cenci* had been rejected by Covent Garden, and Ollier and Hunt were remaining silent on all the other pieces. And she hints at the private losses that marked this time: the death of William, the second of their children to die in Italy; her own subsequent depression; the death of at least one other Shelley baby and a further hardening of the couple's estrangement.[27] Mary Shelley identifies Shelley with his Witch: Like her, he cordons off an arena of "airy fancy" within which to sport, rather than engaging "human interest." And she suggests that the mercurial play of poet, work, and poetic figure exists in some relation to the sealed-over wounds of the heart.

Mary Shelley may not be right about this urbane poem, which could be said to have an uncharacteristically strong sense of audience. But she is suggestive about the Witch herself, who exists in a pointed, even comic lack of relation to human passionate life. The Witch's first act is to bolt from the creatures who orbit in the "magic circle of her voice and eyes" (VII): She must leave, she tells them, because she is not of their kind, and not being mortal herself, she doesn't want to get attached to them only to have to suffer at their deaths (XXIII). Her problem with commitment, however, is nowhere more striking than when she abandons the "fair Shape" she herself has created out of a "repugnant mass" of "fire and snow" (XXXV):

A fair Shape out of her hands did flow—
   A living Image, which did far surpass
In beauty that bright shape of vital stone
Which drew the heart out of Pygmalion.

XXXVI
A sexless thing it was, ...

. . . .
   The countenance was such as might select
Some artist that his skill should never die,
Imaging forth such perfect purity.

We've been reading long enough to feel a plot coming on—a version of the Pygmalion myth. This *is* a Shelley poem: *Shouldn't* the Witch poesy be destined to fall in love with her creation, to love it perhaps "to agony"? Yet by the end of the stanzas quoted, this possibility has been closed off. The Image is a "sexless thing," and its beauty has become the preoccupation of a new artist. For the Witch herself, the Image is less an object of fixation than a way to keep moving: She peremptorily commands it to "Sit here!" in her boat (XXXVII); at her command "Hermaphroditus" (the only time it is named) it spreads its wings and flies her upstream, where she and the poem abandon it (XLIII).

Indeed, the force of Shelley's story could be said to reside in its polemical resistance to the solutions of Pygmalion. Repelled by the "hardness" of the women of his state, the first ever to turn to prostitution, Pygmalion throws himself into his art; only when he sees and falls in love with the woman in the marble does he come to know his own desire, which the gods then fulfill.[28] His art is thus a form of therapy, a "working through" blocked impulses until desire comes to be known and to speak, and his story belongs to a popular class of narratives of human interest—stories of the heart's efforts to know and close with its objects. It is thus "romantic," at least in terms of popular accounts of that aesthetic: The tale casts the work as expressive of the genial artist's desires and suggests its power to effect the integration of the person and the overcoming of social antagonisms through its awakening of sympathy and love.

If in the Pygmalion story the aesthetic object serves the interest of the human subject, in the Witch's story the created form is impervious to human needs and aims. The impediment is perhaps in the object itself. The proper name "Hermaphroditus" refers us back to another tale from *The Metamorphoses* in which latency proves to be destiny. Already bearing the stitched together names of his famously libidinal parents Hermes and Aphrodite, Hermaphroditus, at fifteen years old, has no interest in awakening to sexual desire. The plot turns on his refusal of the nymph Salmacis, whose pool Hermaphroditus visits. Struck by his beauty, she propositions him; he rebuffs her advances; she retreats into the woods but stays to observe him; he, "as if no one were looking at him," strips and bathes in her pool; incited by his beautiful form, she jumps into the pool after him and clings to his body. When he resists her, she calls to the gods to allow her never to be parted from this youth: and so he becomes "the Hermaphrodite"—an enervated half-man, half-woman. That is, it becomes a fallen, fixed version of what he was, in a doom he may have even invited: a creature forever before or beyond sexual life.[29]

When Shelley imports this story to *The Witch of Atlas*, he suggests that the creator creates wo/man, not in her own image, but in the image of the Image. If Pygmalion falls in love with the human form he sees in the marble, the Witch's Shape is arresting for the way the marble—the formal, material dimension, the dimension of "Image" and "countenance"—swims up into the supposedly living thing.[30] One is caught up, not by a promise of intimacy, but by an apprehension of the radical alterity of this apparitional form to human desire.[31] The Witch's creation thus points to an "abstracting" tendency of Shelley's art, which critics have historically linked to his preoccupation with the "ideal" but which seems better described by, say, de Man's account of the poetry's strategies of "figuration." The hermaphrodite and all the beautiful slumbering forms of *The Witch of Atlas* are adamantly unsubjectable: They refuse to satisfy, and they unmask the ruse by which a factitious, formal thing could be said to do so.

And yet—like Ovid's Hermaphroditus, whose flaunted unavailability incites the nymph Salmacis, and like the beautiful slumbering figure Shelley admired in the Villa Borghese,[32] the Witch's Image is lovely, "surpassing" the beauty of Pygmalion's statue, and surely capable of becoming the object of someone's fascination if not passion:

XL

And ever as she went, the Image lay
  With folded wings and unawakened eyes;
And o'er its gentle countenance did play
  The busy dreams, as thick as summer flies,
Chasing the rapid smiles that would not stay,
  And drinking the warm tears, and the sweet sighs
Inhaling, which, with busy murmur vain
They had aroused from that full heart and brain.

Indeed, the Image is here the very figure of fascination: of consciousness playing about the countenance, creating and imbibing delicate and evanescent traces of an unfathomable affective life. This sweetly and gently monstrous countenance holds us if it fails to hold the Witch, and it does so in a way that evokes what could be said to be an ur-scene of attachment, the experience of watching the baby sleep: watching the closed, fleetingly and delicately animated face of the creature to whom it is one's destiny to become attached as it is given over to what the psychoanalysts call "hallucinatory satisfaction," its "dreams"—neither belonging to it nor exterior to it, and indistinguishable from one's own fascination—sporting over its metamorphic countenance. In this setting, the observer's love could take the form of wanting to preserve forever this fragile dream of perfect self-sufficiency; to ward off permanently the creature's awakening to a consciousness of dependency and loss, the cost of its entry into human desire, human interest, and human exchange. The purest idolatry, such love would defend the primitive magic of the image from its erosion by life.

Human beings never willingly give up on a libidinal position, Freud tells us; artists least of all.[33] D. W. Winnicott even contends without reference to clinical evidence that artists, as a class, are "ruthless" because they simply refuse the guilt that comes with the depressive position.[34] It is possible to see what critics call the Witch's "limitations"—her failure to form attachments and respond empathically to a rich, complex field of human passions—as a beautiful refusal to lose. If under the regime of "the rage of death or life" archaic dreams must be forgotten in order that generation after generation of human subjects and their labor can be efficiently cycled into the liveries of various work masters, the Witch's sport would seem to refuse and foil that killing productivity—particularly when, moving from form to form "like a sexless bee" (LXVIII), she takes the most beautiful out of circulation to deposit and abandon them in secret crypts. Her carelessness, her ruthlessness,

her refusal of grief, her penchant for airy flight and her somnambulistic returns to the eerie loveliness of the abstracted human form—all derive their
logic from her "defense" of poetry.[35]

Thus the poem articulates a fantasy of the poet, the work, and the baby,
not as sites for regenerative exchange, but as repositories that preserve magical, archaic things from a devastating human interest. This is a fantasy shared
by psychoanalytic theory, which, like Shelley's circle, and like romanticism
in its highest and lowest forms, sometimes casts the artist—the one who is
arrested before growing up—as a magical throwback to another dispensation,
making good on our losses. In the terms of this fantasy, what we might want
is not to be engaged by poetry's appeal to our passions, but rather, to preserve
poetry's strange distance from human interest—to reassure ourselves that
magical, hermetic poetic figures exist among us, slumbering in secret as we
live out our days, entering our dreams by night, keeping alive the possibility
of a ruthless, magical refusal of loss.

At the end of *The Witch of Atlas* the poem's somnolent forms lie suspended,
"age after age," amidst a world that "rages" around them. *This* world is also a
world of dreamers—misers, priests, kings, and lovers whose dreams, as a result
of the Witch's pranks, become parodic and utopic, unmasking "reality" itself
as a collective dream. The Witch finally and capriciously becomes the muse
of an interventionist poetry. Yet still the figures she has encapsulated slumber
on, in significant noncommunication with even this transformed social field.
The poem's ending suggests the insistent and perhaps founding obduracy of
"the aesthetic" to even the most admirable political visions; and it implies
that art may be most loyal to humanity's dreams when it preserves, encrypted
within it, a resiliently inhumane impulse—a ruthless refusal to speak to what
we may only imagine are our concerns.

Coda: The Exquisite Corpse

In real life, of course, if out of idolatrous love you respect too much the
capacity for hallucinatory satisfaction of babies, poems, or poets, they fail
to thrive. It seems likely that both Mary and Percy Shelley suspected that
this was the fate of the Shelley babies who died in Italy; it was arguably the
fate of the stillborn poetry. And, psychoanalysis tells us, if a loved object
dies before the work of attachment, which is also the work of letting go,
is completed, the outcome is not the "working through" of mourning but
a refusal to recognize loss: the magical incorporation of the object in the
form of a blocking imago, in a move of "hallucinatory satisfaction." Thus

the countenance of the sleeping baby who needs for nothing mirrors the exquisite corpse buried alive in the heart of the one who cannot grieve.[36]

The Witch of Atlas was composed a year and two months after the death of William Shelley, the second of three Shelley children to die in Italy; the year anniversary of his death was marked by the death of the third, Shelley's "Neapolitan charge."[37] The poem's embryonic, unawakened forms conjure these babies who can neither be restored to the living nor be put to rest, as well as the parents who can neither face their continued insistence nor let them die, nor puncture each other's hermetic isolation, nor independently heal the wounds of their separate hearts—in part because each holds the key to the other's sorrow. They speak to a fantasy of the body beyond sex and the engendering of life and death; and of the body that leaves encrypted babies everywhere, in the shape of quasi-aesthetic objects buried in textual graves. And they speak of the cryptic poem itself, with its aggressively flagged lack of relation to the heart's secrets.

It's possible to feel the pressure of these domestic circumstances in a cluster of poems from this period, including *Epipsychidion* and *Adonais*. In these poems, as well as in most biographical accounts of the Shelley marriage, the couple's stuck formation would seem determined by Mary Shelley's stuck mourning: She is the commissioned mourner, while he suffers indirectly when her "coldness" lays him to sleep; he could revive, he suggests halfheartedly, if only something could slake her wound.[38] But what would it take to slake the mother's wound? She herself tells us in *Adonais*. Urania, the last to visit the corpse of her youngest born, makes an appeal to him and, indirectly, to Death (XXV):

"Leave me not wild and drear and comfortless,
As silent lightning leaves the starless night!
Leave me not!" cried Urania; her distress
Roused Death: Death rose and smiled, and met her vain caress.

XXVI

"Stay yet awhile! speak to me once again;
Kiss me, so long but as a kiss may live;
And in my heartless breast and burning brain
That word, that kiss shall all thoughts else survive
With food of saddest memory kept alive,
Now thou art dead, as if it were a part
Of thee, my Adonais! I would give
All that I am to be as thou now art!
But I am chained to Time, and cannot thence depart!

The mother asks for one last word and one last kiss—one breach of death's seal, one instance of mutually avowed attachment—in order that she may get on with her grieving.[39]

The Shelley babies in fact died in their mother's arms. But the scene anticipates Mary's experience of the loss of Percy, which had no last breaching moment; rather, the report of the mutilated corpse, the heartless breast, and the burning brain came to her from afar, to stiffen a pointed lack of relation. That report was Trelawny's, of course. After Shelley's death the circle transformed from a volatile dynamic to a formation demanding constancy and allegiance, a change blamed on Mary Shelley by Trelawny among others; historically, biographers have preferred his and Hogg's "lively" Shelley to Mary and Lady Shelley's "idealized" one.[40] But the mercurial visitant and the stiffened form are each true, although to different experiences of loss. Trelawny, who thrusts his hand through the wall of the poet's body and delivers it of its previously enwombed form, gives birth to a Shelley possessed of a great heart, and purchases his own mobility in the process. This is the scene that Mary Shelley misses, and so she fails to escape the role of the commissioned mourner, forever constant to and immobilized by the encrypted, wounded heart and exquisite corpse.

4. Late Coleridge

John Keats and Percy Shelley died young; Samuel Taylor Coleridge, born a generation earlier, outlived them. And yet Coleridge belongs among the prematurely arrested figures of British romanticism, as Hazlitt's account of him suggests: "All he has done of note he has done long ago; since then he has lived on the sound of his own voice."[1] These final chapters of this study have as their subject "late Coleridge"—the Coleridge who survived the first generation of romanticism and his own promise, haunting the world of London as a posthumous soul. The present chapter traces Coleridge's performance of, and thinking about, a thinking that is not productive in ordinary terms. Arrested and arresting, this thinking, which, following Coleridge, I will call "work without hope," occurs on this side of aim, intention, publicity, even relation.

The chapter after this will speculate about the social value of such thinking. "Coleridge the talker" became a fixture of his London world: What accounts for the celebrity status of this thinker, whose thoughts, almost everyone protested, proved resistant to absorption, translation, and historical recovery? Writing on Charles Baudelaire, Walter Benjamin describes Baudelaire's emergence at a moment when one kind of contract between poet and audience has expired and a new one has yet to be forged: for Benjamin, Baudelaire's idiosyncratic persona and sui generis status have in part to do with his emergence at just this moment, when the relationship between the poet and his audience is being renegotiated.[2] Thomas De Quincey also describes Coleridge's relation to his audience as an unusual form of "contract": "It was a silent contract between him and his hearers that nobody should speak but himself."[3] De Quincey's comment suggests what is striking about the phenomenon of late Coleridge: An expenditure of intellect that can seem radically at odds with any sense of address or object, with any normatively construed social aim, nonetheless enters into "contract" with a social world.

Late Coleridge, I will argue, becomes a figure of intellection unconstrained by norms, including the pressures of social relation itself.

"Limbo"

If early in his career Coleridge wrote the poetry of enchantment, late Coleridge explored the dispiritedness of limbo, that borderland state—neither salvation nor damnation, life nor death—where souls wait, forever, for nothing. The lines that appeared as the poem "Limbo" in the 1834 *Collected Works*, lifted from a notebook entry of 1811, comprise his best-known charting of this terrain:

Tis a strange Place, this Limbo! Not a Place,
Yet name it so—where Time & Weary Space
Fetter'd from flight, with night-mair sense of Fleeing
Strive for their last crepuscular Half-being—
Lank Space, and scytheless Time with branny Hands
Barren and soundless as the measuring Sands,
Mark'd but by Flit of Shades—unmeaning they
As Moonlight on the Dial of Day—
But that is lovely—looks like Human Time,
An old Man with a steady Look sublime,
That stops his earthly Task to watch the Skies—
But he is blind—a statue hath such Eyes—
Yet having moon-ward turn'd his face by chance—
Gazes the orb with moon-like Countenance
With scant white hairs, with fore-top bald & high
He gazes still, his eyeless Face all Eye—
As twere an Organ full of silent Sight
His whole Face seemeth to rejoice in Light/
Lip touching Lip, all moveless, Bust and Limb,
He seems to gaze on that which seems to gaze on Him!

No such sweet Sights doth Limbo Den immure,
Wall'd round and made a Spirit-jail secure
By the mere Horror of blank Nought at all—
Whose circumambience doth these Ghosts enthrall. . . .[4]

This "strange Place" / "Not a Place" can be connected to the mental theater of the bookish opium-eater who, in 1797, experienced images wondrously arising in the mind "as things."[5] But years later, the wonder is gone: Images continue to make their appearances on the stage, but as shades that "flit" purposelessly across a barely delineated, crepuscularly lit proscenium. Here, where time barely moves and "Lank Space" loses dimension, nothing secures or animates the disenchanted mind.

Out of this unpromising landscape, however, emerges the arresting image of an old man—blind, "moveless," luminous, captivating. The image is grounded in nothing: It appears as the elaboration of a rejected simile, as what the ghosts of limbo explicitly do not resemble. The poet is looking for a fit figure for meaninglessness, but words and images *will* mean, will always have too close a link to the familiar and known. The old man is thus invoked as a figure of the figure that comes to mean too much, although, the verse insists, his apparent meaningfulness is an effect of *mere* seeming, mere simulation, mere mimicry: the old man looks like he's looking at the moon, which seems to be looking at him, and together the whole composition is what the moon on a sundial, which looks like human time, looks like. Finally, the image is canceled again at the beginning of the next strophe: "No such sweet Sights doth Limbo Den immure."

The moment nevertheless feels like grace, a positive generated out of these multiplied negatives. In an 1828 letter to Aleric Watts in which he enclosed the passage, Coleridge calls these "some of the most forcible Lines & with the most original imagery that my niggard Muse ever made me a present of."[6] "Lovely," a "sweet Sight," the vision of the old man momentarily stops the mind's restlessness, illuminating the crepuscular landscape and transiently effecting an escape from the immuring walls of limbo den. For a moment, an apparently canceled possibility appears—that which is not limbo, not like limbo, and not like anything familiar, as for example human time, either.

Yet the image that moves its creator out of limbo's walls, themselves circled round by "blank Nought at all," is the very picture of captivity: the body rendered as an enclosed, mute, self-sustaining system, lip touching lip, an eyeless face all eye, the whole face become a sealed, blind organ, and this blank organ, in turn, perfectly held by the blindly mirroring O of the moon. The incantatory repetitions of the verse and the formal repetition of the shape of the O suggest that these redoubled noughts produce something overfull, something that "looks like" and sounds like and even feels like plenitude. The turn is in part effected by a shift in view: If the lines preceding the emergence of the figure of the old man attempt, through the imperfect medium of language, to describe the place/not place from inside, the figure itself presents the spectacle of the immured world from the outside. Staged and seen from a spectatorial distance, radical solitude becomes fascinating, "sweet." The blind man does not look, he only looks like, and because he cannot see himself (in this sense, of course, we are all "Blind"), he cannot know that it looks like he is looking and being looked back at. But we see him held by the moon he cannot see, obliviously bathed in its light, caught in a system of mirroring nonlooks that nonetheless seem protectively to hold his solitude.

One can be touched by light and not know it. Indeed, this may be the only grace that comes to limbo, and perhaps it doesn't matter that the conversion experience is purely formal and aesthetic. The sweetness of the image comes not from the hope it offers. By definition, there can be no hope in limbo, and the image scrupulously offers no alternative time or space, gestures toward no future, proposes no truth. Its value derives rather from its status as a rare gift from the muse—a moment of grace in which self-immurement is transfigured into something "lovely," beautiful, perhaps, by virtue of its very refusal of the lures of meaning, of participation in any telos, of any notion of purpose or use. The image is what hope or promise would look like if it weren't propelled toward some future fulfillment in human time; or what precocity would look like if it were never realized but remained forever suspended, pregnant, "still"; or what social dynamics would look like in the absence of an expectation of exchange—like perfect, arrested, nonrelational reciprocity.

The image recalls Wordsworth's evocative lines in "Tintern Abbey": "These forms of beauty have not been to me, / As is a landscape to a blind man's eye" (24–25).[7] The compounded negatives make us wonder: how/what does a blind man see? Not/Nought at all? Or does he see like Wordsworth, the poet of the conjured absent possibility? Like Milton or Homer, whose famous marble busts Coleridge's blind, luminous, statue-like figure calls up? Like Coleridge himself, the round-faced, large-eyed, prematurely old sage of Highgate—collapsed, self-immured, yet wonderful, touched by grace? The blind man of limbo is "like" many things, including "late Coleridge"—the writer whose genius is to see as a blind man and make the canceled, negated possibility appear; the "old man eloquent," translated, when he steps into the theater of the other's look, into the charismatic limit-case of a thinking that is at odds with life as we know it—unrenderable into any common language and unsuited to any common use.[8]

Seeing with the Negative Eye

Or, in more Coleridgean terms: The figure of "Coleridge" lends outness to the idea that an attachment to thinking may be bound up with a radical refusal of relation—and, perhaps, to a certain negativity haunting thought itself—and allows these to be partially recuperated, "positivised," in the figure of Genius. In the remainder of this chapter I want to explore late Coleridge's own thinking about thinking, following a strain of his abstruse research that he himself called "work without hope."[9] If this work, which movingly traces dynamics of precocity and collapse, fascinates in part by its obvious relevance to its famously lapsed author, it also allows us to link these dynamics to the attachments the mind forms to thinking itself, and to link "thinking itself" to working without an object. Coleridge's late work pursues a set of preoccupations that resonate with those of contemporary critical theory. But what he calls his "abstruse research" also explores intellection in ways that suggestively anticipate contemporary psychoanalytic accounts of thought's pathological and necessary link to what André Green and others call "the work of the negative"—work propelled by and proceeding in the shadow of a radical and inevitable disappointment in objects. It performs that exploration as a kind of maverick "work" that obliquely refuses or eludes demands of efficiency and instrumentality, in the face of the increasing rationalization and professionalization of even intellectual production during this period.

Limbo is a landscape one backs into, Coleridge suggests, in the notebook entry that eventually blooms into the passage quoted above. He has been reading or recalling John Donne's "The Flea," and the poem that becomes "Limbo" germinates when he begins to imagine Donne's eponymous hero dying a hero's death, becoming secreted in a "dry Potticary's bladdery hide," and by this means crossing "unchang'd" into limbo den, where the flea becomes a kind of minim Dante, the only "true *Something*" amidst the ghosts:

> The sole true *Something* this in Limbo Den
> It frightens Ghosts as Ghosts here frighten men—
> Thence cross'd unraz'd and shall, some fated Hour,
> Be pulverized by Demogorgon's Power
> And given as poison, to annihilate Souls—
> Even now it shrinks them! they shrink in, as Moles
> (Nature's mute Monks, live Mandrakes of the ground)
> Creep back from Light, then listen for its Sound—
> See but to dread, and dread they know not why
> The natural Alien of their negative Eye.
>
> Tis a strange place, this Limbo. . . . (*CN* III:4073)

Donne's flea is a gregarious, even promiscuous creature, image and vehicle of human intercourse. But once crossed into limbo, bleached of its animating flea-ness, this "*Something*" has reversionary, negative effects—effects, at this pivot of the poem, on the soul's eye, which becomes light-phobic, but also, perhaps, newly capable of "sounding" the strange place in which it finds itself.[10]

The lines chart a reading dynamic we've encountered before in Coleridge, in which his moved response to another poet's work ultimately precipitates his own collapse into and exploration of a blank or void psychic landscape.[11] We could speculate that *this* passage perpetuates and extends the original poisonous reading-effect, since according to its own logic it must itself be the Demogorgic druggist that dispenses tincture of flea—Donne's flea suspended in Coleridge's medium—to the souls who become subject to the effects of the dose. "Even now" (that is, "in the very moment of this reading"), "it shrinks them"—shrinks us? Locates us, "now," in limbo?

But how would this reading-effect work? My account—which invokes the scenes of the literary man with his book, the literary critic with hers— perhaps goes too far in securing the passage, the unsettling force of which would seem to be linked to the impossibility of knowing where one stands in relation to its spaces and figures: for example, to "they," the souls of the stanza just quoted. Annihilated, "they" become links in a chain of tropes— shrunken souls like moles like mute monks like live mandrakes—that, in contrast to Donne's congenial flea, each conjure an extreme of insularity. Poised between the dark and the light, captivated by what they dread, not quite "*Something*," Coleridge's creatures call up in advance of their naming the atavistic, secreted part-objects of psychic experience—reluctant fetuses, unexpelled feces, maternal phalluses—as well as unsaid or unwritten or un- published words/works, as well as retentive psyches or bodies that immure their horrors and treasures, revealing to the world only that something is not coming to light.[12] But who are "they" to the poet or us? *They* are shrunken by what the poetic speaker and *we* might be incorporating, "even now." Are "we" or "he" "them," or "like" them? If we shrink back from identification with these not-*somethings*, we perhaps betray our affinity with what we dis- avow. But even if we choose to embrace these abjects, or, less generously, to decide they refer to their famously self-obstructed creator, the grammatical construction makes such identification impossible. We find ourselves neither "here" nor "there," poised between identification and disavowal, arrested, with these blind figures, in limbo/"Limbo"—located, not in some determi- nate place, but in this fissured "not a place." That is, we become borderline.[13]

This moving late verse takes the measure of a psychic landscape inhabited by the lapsed soul. But its appeal is not confessional or otherwise subjective. It neither seeks to unlock the "I"'s reserves nor to solicit a sympathetic "you," nor does the terrain it explores seem to be or belong to the deflated speaker, who inhabits it as partially and unpredictably as does the reader. Rather, the landscape of limbo is dominated by the ghostly secreted object. Far from inciting or expressing sympathy or desire, limbo's withdrawn objects negativize aim: They hold and are held in abeyance, and in this manner they define the perimeters of a den whose boundaries can only be known by what the blind soul touches up against and "shrinks" from. "Limbo" opens out in the shadow of an absent, foreclosed object, whether we understand that object as addressee or destination. The poet or the reader "moved" or "touched" by the poem must learn to read blindly, shrinkingly, with a negative eye, taking the measure of spaces and objects that can only be known inductively by what they do not reveal of themselves.[14]

"Limbo" concludes with the apparent stabilizing of inside and outside:

No such sweet Sights doth Limbo Den immure,
Wall'd round and made a Spirit-jail secure
By the mere Horror of blank Nought at all,
Whose circumambience doth these Ghosts enthrall.

. . . .

A lurid Thought is growthless dull ~~Negation~~ Privation
Yet that is but a Purgatory Curse
Hell knows a fear far worse,
A fear, a future fate. Tis *positive Privation Negation!* (*CN* III:4073)

The poem appears to stop when the "not" of its repeated gestures of foreclosure is itself projected onto the outside, where it comes into view as the hyperbolically dreadful and enthralling "blank Nought at all"—defined variously, in Coleridge's drafts of the poem, as "positive Negation," "positive Privation," "aye-unepithetable Negation."[15] The equivocations suggest that there might be something strategic and productive about this tautological psychic structure: Perhaps one secures oneself, holds onto one's privation, out of fear of (a projected, trumped up) Privation; perhaps one projects "the negative" onto the outside in order to have a reason to "shrink" into an enthralling inner blankness—in order to hold on to one's insularity. The end of the poem seems designed to allow the poet to subside, to reclaim a securing space on the border of a conjured horror, and to end, once and for all, the work. But working without hope is strangely productive: The closing of limbo becomes the spur to new "work" in the form of another poem—or another turn of the same poem—that follows immediately in the notebook and whose subject is, once again, the "unepithetable Negation" that "borders" "here."[16] The stops and starts of "Limbo" suggest for the one enthralled by Nothing, this attachment can itself become an illimitable intellectual project.[17]

"Work without Hope," or the Work of the Negative

His motto is, to be everything or nothing.

William Hazlitt, "Mr. Coleridge"

The notebook entry that includes the lines later published as "Limbo" was written in 1811 in the aftermath of Coleridge's shattered reaction to Basil Montague's report that Wordsworth had "no Hope of him," a phrase Coleridge repeated in his many rehearsals of and complaints about the incident.[18] Given that Wordsworth had merely articulated assessments that Coleridge himself had been voicing for years, the extremity of the latter's reaction might seem disproportionate, but it's also predictable: Wordsworth's expressed withdrawal of his hope for his friend merely provoked an especially catastrophic instance of a mode of collapse that punctuated Coleridge's life—the collapse of a fragile structure of being "full of promise," in which one's capacity to be a dazzling world unto oneself is linked in complex ways to being the bearer and object of the impossible hopes of others. If from moment to moment the grounds for these crashes mutate and shift (finances, marriage, interest in Sara Hutchinson, and especially, projects uncompleted or unbegun) the pattern suggests that any local setback taps into a more absolute and devastating sense of failure. Coleridge recognized these rhythms and others, most notably Hazlitt, thought about them as well: The great hopes he inspired in himself and others seemed intimately linked to his losses of hope, his failure to produce the great work, his expenditure of himself instead in fruitless, ceaseless talk, abstruse research, and unpublished writing.[19]

What I am calling in this chapter "late Coleridge" refers to this post-hope expenditure, which, depending on how one looks at it, potentially includes everything Coleridge produced after the heady period of the first edition of the *Lyrical Ballads*, or alternatively, after the crash of 1802 that led to his convalescent trip to Malta in 1803.[20] (The first volume of Richard Holmes's biography of Coleridge ends with the departure to Malta and Holmes's speculations about how Coleridge's reputation would have been different had he died at this point—as though, like Hazlitt, Holmes acknowledges a certain posthumous character to the Coleridge who survived well into the century.[21]) Although the quantity of this late work is by no means lacking, its quality—its patched together, fragmentary, generically hybrid character, and in many instances, its fugitive life in private notebooks, letters, others' reports of lectures and talk—raise questions that concern, in various ways, the idea of the object. If this is "work," what is its object? To whom, if anyone, is it addressed, and what purpose or aim, if any, does it serve? How are we to define, name, and/or draw the boundaries of the "objects" that constitute the late Coleridge corpus? In what way could a text like "Limbo"—either as originally published in 1834 (perhaps, but not certainly, under Coleridge's oversight), or as the much longer poem or compendium of poems that make up the notebook entry referred to as *CN* III:4073—be said to have integrity as a "work of art"?[22]

Following the psychoanalyst André Green, I want to link Coleridge's late work—his copious, brilliant, guilty productivity as well as his analyses of this expenditure—to what Green calls "the work of the negative"—the rubric under which Green places a cluster of phenomena that have come to preoccupy psychoanalytic theorists of our own time, and which all involve disorders of work or productivity symptomatic of a troubled relation to objects. These include melancholia, characterized as a failure to work through the loss of the object; borderline states, which are especially resistant to psychoanalytic treatment because of the subject's cathexis of and identification with blank states and withdrawn or dead objects, the apparitional "projects" of which Green calls "negative hallucinations"; and "negative transference," a vicissitude of the analytic relation marked by the analysand's tendency to become attached to what is lacking in the analyst, that leads to "analysis interminable"—analysis as constant, untransformative work. Although Green carefully discriminates the registers and effects of these various manifestations of the negative, they cumulatively map a psychic landscape dominated by a dead or occluded object, in which the analysand's incessant analytical work is intractably bound up with the project of maintaining the (non)attachment to what is decisively unavailable and withdrawn. Coleridge sometimes employs the suggestively technical language of "negativity" to describe this sort of work (as with the "negative Eye" of "Limbo," for example), but he also names it "abstruse research" and sometimes calls it "work without hope," the title of a poem that ends, "Work without Hope draws nectar in a sieve, / And Hope without an object cannot live" (*PW* 447). A sieve gathers nothing, of course, or, perhaps, taking a hint from Coleridge's orthographic habits, Nothing.[23]

"Work without hope" is Coleridge's term for a crashed mode of precocity or genius, one that acknowledges the connection he and contemporaries make between the wonder and promise of his intellect and his equally impressive failure to produce the great literary or philosophical work, his apparent diversion of his talents into, at best, laying ostrich eggs in the sand. A notebook poem composed a bit earlier than "Limbo" suggests an aetiology for these swings between "being everything" and "being nothing," and will return us to Green. Here are the verses:

Life wakeful over all knew no gradation
That Bliss in its excess became a Dream;
For every sense, each thought, & each sensation
Lived in my eye, transfigured not suppresst.
And Time drew out his subtle threads so quick,
& with such Spirit-speed & silentness,
That only in the web, of space like Time,
On the still spreading web I still diffused
Lay still commensurate—

(In the first draft of the poem, a version of this strophe continues with the lines:

For Memory & all undoubting Hope
Sang the same note & in the selfsame
Voice, with each sweet *now* of
My Felicity, and blended momently,
Like Milk that coming comes & in its
easy stream Flows ever in, upon the
mingling milk, in the Babe's murmuring
Mouth/ or mirrors each reflecting each/—)

What never is but only is to be
This is not Life—
O Hopeless Hope, and Death's Hypocrisy!
And with perpetual Promise, breaks its Promises.—

The Stars that wont to start, as on a chase,
And twinkling insult on Heaven's darkened Face,
Like a conven'd Conspiracy of Spies
Wink at each other with confiding eyes,
Turn from the portent, all is blank on high,
No constellations alphabet the Sky—
The Heavens one large black Letter only shews,
And as a Child beneath its master's Blows
Shrills out at once its Task and its Affright,
The groaning world now learns to read aright,
And with its Voice of Voices cries out, O! (*CN* II:3107)

The state described in this poem's first stanza would seem very different from that of "Limbo": the daydreaming subject experiences bliss and plenitude, not blankness and privation. Yet out of this excess of felicity comes the devastating shift of perspective of the second stanza and the blank universe of the last. The turn seems to come out of nowhere—literally, the gap between passages: On the far side of this vacancy, "undoubting Hope"—a sense that gift will inevitably succeed gift—gives way to hopelessness.[24]

The canceled lines from the poem's first stanza invite us to connect this collapse to the vicissitudes of infantile experience as reconstructed by psychoanalytic theory. The reverie evoked in the poem's first lines slides, in the canceled passage, into an account or memory of infant satisfaction, as though the infant, experiencing or hallucinating its diffusion within the holding environment of arms and breast, has returned to life in the mentally drifting adult.[25] The passage reminds us that reverie is said by psychoanalysts to originate in the baby's reaction to the mother's absence of mind (her own reverie, which "holds" the baby) and then to her actual absence: These absences open up spaces for the baby to hallucinate for itself the satisfactions it associates with her presence. The only truly happy ending to the baby's story, however, comes when the mother reappears "on time"—just soon and just late enough to deliver a relatively nontraumatic lesson about the power and efficacy of hope, on the one hand, and the contingency of desire, on the other.[26] Retrospectively, the advent of the mother can be understood as redeeming a promise to return; conversely, with her reappearance, the baby's power to invent and conjure, that which constitutes its "promise" as a creative human subject, is also fulfilled. Thus "promise" or "hope" may always emerge within a relational structure: One's sense of being promising, of possessing hope or promise, derives from being the object of the other's hopes and the recipient of the other's promises. Furthermore, "promise" may only be a meaningful term in the context of a messianic narrative structure involving the delayed advent of the other, whose appearance allows a promise or debt to be redeemed. A corollary, then, to these propositions, is that "promise" enables one to become attached to the idea of the future, to life itself.

But, a psychoanalyst like Green might remind us, many things can go wrong with the baby's waiting. Indeed, the possibilities of a missed encounter are so numerous it might seem that a happy outcome could only come by the happiest chance: The infant can be made to wait too long, or not long enough, or it can wait for a maternal object too narcissistic, depressed, abstracted, or "blank" to mirror back its delight on her return.[27] If something goes wrong with the waiting, the result is what could be called a disorder of "promisingness." On the one hand the baby might become a tiny philosopher/artist, learning to perform a desperate, precocious imaginative and intellectual aliveness in an attempt to awaken and/or satisfy a narcissistic or averted or "dead" object; or it might attempt to forego the disappointments attendant upon objects altogether by creating and retreating to a rich mental landscape that holds out the promise of an indefinitely sustained, hallucinated satisfaction. Alternatively, it might "die," becoming pathologically attached to lost or foreclosed objects, the things it "has not got," or experiencing both inner and outer landscape as blank, void, or even hallucinating that void as a negative apparition.[28] I set these out as discrete possibilities, but the first modes of filling the self—the modes of precocity, or, we could almost say, the modes of genius—always threaten to collapse into a sense of the self and world as empty, which might in turn produce recourse to the enlivening dose of thinking, imagining, reading, or opium.

Thus even in bliss the precocious are never far from limbo. In contrast to the damned, commanded to "abandon all hope," they experience abandonment: They wait, suspended, but for nothing, without expectation of transformation or salvation. As Virgil explains to Dante, "Cut off from hope, we live on in desire."[29] Or, in the words of Green, describing the infant's too-protracted waiting for the mother: "There is no longer any measurable time. There is only infinite waiting, eternal waiting in hopelessness and despair."[30] Or in the words of this poem: The subject who would batten indefinitely on his own gifts in fact waits for "what never is but only is to be," for forever-deferred fulfillment—even death seems a forever suspended horizon. Such a subject waits, but for Nothing, which on rare pathological or poetic occasions appears.[31]

These reflections resonate with what we know of the biographical subject, "late Coleridge," whose rehearsed forms of distress chime with some of the current preoccupations of psychoanalytic theory. I hope it is clear, though, that my intention is not to bring psychoanalytic forms of attention to a symptomatic text, but rather, to trace the way Coleridge's thinking here opens onto dimensions of our own intellectual landscape. In *Looking Away*, Rei Terada contrasts the delicacy and brilliance of Coleridge's anatomizations of what he called "spectra"—idiosyncratic, transitory, and marginal sensory phenomena—to what she sometimes suggests is his more limited thinking about "spectres," the hallucinatory shapes that come in dreams and vivid daydreams and that, she argues, present him with the "givenness" of appearance in a way that blocks speculative license: Most often, she observes, he attributes the genesis of this last class of phenomena to gastric distress.[32] This is a fair enough account of moments in Coleridge's thinking, but I would argue that at other moments he pursues hallucinatory forms—as here, the negatively appearing O—with the attention and nuance that Terada appreciates in his tracing of spectra: and indeed, this draft poem provides an account of the hallucinated O as generated *out* of the dynamics of the pleasurable, private free play he associates with spectra. (It also suggests that the negative hallucination or "spectre" itself derives from and manifests a protest against the givenness of appearances, just more stridently than does the play with spectra.) Terada argues that Coleridge's pursuit of spectra, if it occurs in local and private registers, opens onto tensions inherent in modern phenomenological thought; I would argue that his thinking about the negative similarly opens onto exemplarily modern concerns, including but not limited to those absorbing one strain of contemporary psychoanalytic theory.

I will return in a moment to my reasons for emphasizing *psychoanalytic* theory in this inquiry. That emphasis, however, does not mean to obscure the "metaphysical" character of this verse sequence, or more generally, of Coleridge's concerns with an order of things at once linguistic and existential. The verse sequence gives an impression of self-revelation even as it involves the progressive attenuation of the "I," which appears as a fragile, permeable structure in the first stanza, disappears as a rendered consciousness in the plaint of the second, and vanishes more entirely in the final stanza's pointedly nonsubjective account of the relationship of heavens and world. As the "I" falls away, the poem's orthographically distinctive abstractions—Life, Hope, Promise, Death, Hypocrisy—become charged with affective intensity and agency. We can speculate that the emergence of these powerful, ungrounded, strangely autonomous words and letters prompts the poem's final turn to its dramatized scenes of disturbed reading, in which the stars, normally the marshaled and fixed alphabetic elements of legible constellations, "start" from these moorings and instead signal to each other some knowledge withheld from an imputed, insulted reader/world; when the latter "turns" elsewhere, it is only to encounter an instaurated signifier of nonmeaning or Nothing, a blank/black O against the night sky.

This could of course be just another way of calling the poem "pathological": We can understand the spying, confiding eyes of heaven and the subsequent apparition of the O as "projects," subjective objects ejected into the world, where they take on a persecutory function; or we can think of the child's/ world's O, its inner blankness, as following from its incorporation of and identification with a "dead" and/or persecutory external object.[33] In either case, the poem ends with an equivalency of inside and outside—the world/child's O expressing both an inner emptiness and a meaningless cosmos—that mocks the fullness of the "each reflecting each" of the first stanza, and suggests the devastating withdrawal of cathexis from the world and self that characterizes the interpretive disorders of the psychoses and borderline states.

But Coleridge's precocious genius also opens up a terrain out of which our modern intellectual landscape emerges. Like "Limbo," this is a metaphysical poem in part because its logic is deeply and familiarly engaged with the conceits of Renaissance poetry, especially the work of Du Bartas, Crashaw, and Spenser.[34] If these earlier poems instruct the "eye" to read in the world and/or the allegorical text evidence of God's truth, this one inverts the lesson. Out of this inversion comes a language of quasi-personified abstraction that is modern allegory—a language that "points" but the reference of which is not meaning but exhaustion and vacancy; and a poetic voice—a "voice of voices"—whose negativity and powerful truth-effects, freed from any particularized subject-position, anticipate a range of modern and postmodern "projects" that connect the work of the negative to the work of thought itself.[35] Recent psychoanalytic thinking about the work of the negative sometimes casts intellectualism *as* a kind of pathology, as did Coleridge and his peers, who linked his penchant for "abstruse reasoning" to his failure to live up to his promise. In these accounts, the compulsion to think, to imagine, to self-analyze—what Coleridge's world named his "Genius"—is compensatory and defensive, the other face or lining of blankness or deadness.[36] At the same time, though, Green traces strains in both the Freudian and philosophical traditions suggesting that certain pathologies may merely bring to view a negativity that founds ideation *per se*—a negativity that comes to preoccupy and structure strains of philosophical and psychoanalytical speculation that derive from the German idealist philosophical tradition Coleridge imported to England. The phrase "the work of the negative" of course (and as Green points out) comes from Hegel and this lineage. Green's own work, moreover, ultimately argues that "negative hallucination"—the apparitional gap or void, which, together with its companion phenomenon, the hallucinatory experience of satisfaction, comprise the infant's first experience with the idea—is the theoretical concept necessary for any theory of representation: "It is the blank which constitutes any chain of thoughts."[37]

If I am privileging contemporary psychoanalysis here, this is because its insights resonate with the strain of Coleridge's thought that I am attempting to trace and that connects intellectual inquiry, including the philosophical pursuits that preoccupied him, to the vicissitudes of drive life. This strain of thought allows us to make connections between the pathological and the normative, by bringing home the inevitability of disappointment with objects and suggesting ways of thinking about the negative side of an ego-structure that necessarily derives from failed as well as happy attachments.[38] "Work without hope" names Coleridge's thinking about the attachments that the mind develops to thinking itself in the shadow of a decisively withdrawn object. I will suggest now that Coleridge's particular genius is to think about this thinking, not with the speculative, systematizing distance of the theorist, but as a blind man. "Abstruse reasoning," an intellectual language without purchase on the object, is the analytical discourse he invents to take the measure of the border spaces from the position of a denizen.[39]

Abstruse Research

That the lover of ideas—the baby hallucinating its satisfactions, the philosopher, the disappointed lover, the literary man—transfers his devotion onto the *idea* of the object in the absence of or uncertainty about the "real" object is a truth that well predates Kant and Freud, and in fact, Coleridge's "Constancy to an Ideal Object" helpfully works through this lesson. The poem addresses a "yearning Thought," "the only constant in a world of change," that "liv'st but in the brain." "She," the poet explains, exists independently from this "thought" that represents and supplants her as ideal object: "well I see / She is not thou, and only thou art she." The substitution has both costs and benefits. The speaker, who makes this transfer of affection from "she" to Ideal Object, gives up hope for desire's fulfillment: the Ideal Object is only *like* some "dear embodied Good," some "living Love"; no "hour" will "breathe on [it] with life-enkindling breath / Til Hope and Despair meet on the porch of Death." But by relinquishing this promise he retains control of his object and purchases his and its constancy: Unlike the mutable "she" it never changes—if it cannot fulfill, neither can it disappoint, desire.[40]

Coleridge's late work, however, more often describes a further torsion of the object: the ideal object mutated into, or recognized as, a barred or foreclosed object of "Hope." Here is Coleridge on that subject:

So much sorrow behind and before and around, no one wish of the very Heart, which even the Reason, that keeps drowsy watch in a Day- dream, can suffer to pass into Fancy, and to become the Material of a momentary Fabric of Pleasure—when every thing, that could give Happiness, presents its idea so closely interbodied with the immediate reflection of its impossibility, (& not a mere negative Impossibility but with the Reflection that it is made impossible by the actual presence of a positive, & sore heart-wasting CONTRARY) that the voluntary Mind shrinks from all, it would endure all things to attain, as from a debt of Misery, as from a stern Creditor knocking at the door, who must be admitted, some time or other, but oh! not today—in this drear desolation of the happy Soul is Hope utterly exterminated?—Woe is me! No!—A Kettle is on a slow Fire/& I turn from my Book, & loiter from going to my bed, in order to see whether it will boil/—& on that my Hope hovers—on the Candle burning

in the socket—or will this or that person come this evening—if he come at
all, it must be within an hour—who when he comes neither gives me the least
pleasure nor does me the least good, as I well know, & have not the dimmest
expectation that he will/or if I can by any wretched *usury* against myself,
borrow half an hour's comfortable sensation [to be repayed in pain] at a 10,00
per cent interest. (*CN* II:2839)

Like the earlier "Constancy to an Ideal Object," this passage might seem
to be about a predicament that in plainer language could go, "I love Sara
Hutchinson and I'm married to Sarah Coleridge." But here the lover, like
Green's baby, has waited too long: The protracted nonavailability of the actual "she," the eroding guilt for the desire itself, have led him to transfer his
attentiveness to the vigilant barring of the ideal object from consciousness.
And so he comes to inhabit a landscape dominated by what he "has not
got"—the idea so fully "inter*bodied*" with its "heartwasting contrary" that it
cannot even be entertained in wishfulfilling daydream.[41]

Yet even as the mind shuts out the desired object, hope persists on this
side of the door, dispersed into multiple scenarios that have in common a
bare formal structure of expectation and unfulfilling outcome. If the ideal
object never disappoints, defending oneself against its advent would seem to
consign one to repeated disappointments. That Coleridge's attachments tend
always to settle on what he "hasn't got," however, suggests a compensatory
logic at work in his object choices, and indeed, the situation he describes is
not without its charms. Indefinite postponement of the big creditor opens a
space where hope "hovers" over, potentially, every little transaction, in a way
that protects one from surprises and, as a kind of bonus, causes one's den to
become a mildly enchanted space, a version of the romantic domestic interior
described, for example, in the opening of "Frost at Midnight": a writer's
world, full of auguring familiars that might include fire, book, and awaited
stranger, and that support the mildly enthralling, addictive amusements—
what Coleridge elsewhere calls "pastimes or kill-times"—that divert the
blocked intellectual who marks time in the face of a dreaded, unconfrontable,
repeatedly postponed deadline (e.g., staying up too late, scanning the landscape for signs, making and breaking pacts with oneself, expecting and getting
rid of visitors, thinking, reading, opium-taking, and notebook-writing).[42]
Constancy to an ideal and foreclosed object, then, may provide cover, allowing one to shrink like a mole or monk into the confines of one's limbo den,
to occupy a closeted literary landscape—an opaquely referential system of
charged signs—and to live the strangely productive life of the literary man.
This is a constrained and dearly bought privacy and freedom, but a certain
freedom nonetheless.[43]

The baby falls in love with thinking when its first attachments fail; a man addicted to thinking may form impossible attachments in order to install himself in the situation of perpetual waiting, so that he can work without hope—that is, keep working, interminably, in the only way he knows how. These are the conditions out of which arises the rich conceptual landscape of the notebooks. In a manner typical of the entries of this period the note withholds proper names, but not so as to keep anyone with any familiarity with Coleridge from supplying them. The suppressions thus appear more symptomatic than efficacious, a shrinking from naming names that generates the semantic invention of "abstruse reasoning," a discourse not quite philosophical, not quite confessional, not yet psychoanalytical. This language can feel prototechnical: Latinate abstractions ("contrary," "Reflection," "positive," "Negative," "interbodied") repeated in entry after entry, begin to take on a particularity of meaning within a (as-yet-unfolded or unsystematized) philosophical or psychoanalytical frame of reference. At the same time, its effects are poetic and allegorical in that words become "like things"—overt figures like the Creditor, and orthographically distinguished elements like Hope, Misery, CONTRARY, Happiness, Pleasure, Kettle, Fire, seem animated by reference to a deflected or barred affective life.[44]

Work without hope opens up and proceeds in cryptic spaces—the "touched" mind and soma of the thinker, a field of eerily diffused feelings and animated, unruly ideas. Here is another notebook entry that begins as an address to an imagined friend on the possibility of domestic happiness, and concludes with a reflection on the impossibility of this writing to address *any one*:

> I trust, you are very happy in your domestic being; very—because, alas! I know that to a man of sensibility, & more emphatically, if he be a literary man,—there is no medium between that and—The secret pang that eats away the Heart.
>
> The sole Hope being an Idea,/wch in all our general associations (which must needs either overpower, or perplex and overgloom any partial or accidental association) is a form of Despair, relatively to others—& if contradictatorily, unnaturally, made the substance of Hope, the tertium quid of the combination frightens the Heart with Guilt in its approach—Hence even in dreams of Sleep the Soul never *is*, because it either cannot or dare not be, any ONE THING; but lives in *approaches*—touched by the outgoing pre-existent Ghosts of many feelings—It feels for ever as a blind man with his protended Staff dimly thro' the medium of the instrument by which it pushes off, & in the act of repulsion, O for the eloquence of Shakespeare, who alone could feel & yet know how to embody these conceptions, with as curious a felicity as the thoughts are subtle. As if the finger which I saw with eyes Had, as it were, another finger invisible—

Touching me with a ghostly touch, even while I feared the real Touch from it. What if in certain cases Touch acted by itself, co-present with vision, yet not coalescing—then I should see the finger as at a distance, and yet feel a finger touching which was nothing but it & yet was not it/the two senses cannot co-exist without a sense of causation/the *touch* must be the effect of that Finger, I see, yet it's not yet near to me, and therefore it is not it; and yet it is it. Why, it is it in an imaginary preduplication. . . .

How few would read this Note—nay, *any one?*/ and not think the writer mad or drunk! (*CN* II:3215)

The body of the note seems to set out to answer the question implicitly posed by the first address: Why is it that for the literary man it is all or nothing—perfect domestic happiness or complete despair? But it pursues its aim by indirection, veering into a by-now-familiar theater of enthrallment and dread inhabited by a shrinking, disintegrated subject (if a subject is still a subject when it is not any "ONE THING") and a shadowy or negative object, the abjured idea that animates and organizes "outgoing pre-existent Ghosts of many feelings." Here, the soul measures the confines in which it exists by touching up against or being touched by the ghosts of these ejected "feelings" and retracting from them in dread—like a mole or mute monk or mandrake, or like the blind man, who feels "with his protended Staff dimly thro' the medium of the instrument by which it pushes off, & in the act of repulsion." As in "Limbo," the figure of the blind man suggests sexual desire displaced, negativized, short-circuited but in a manner that diffusely eroticizes somatic/mental life: A prosthetic "staff" encounters its terrain through "the act of repulsion" by which it "feels" the "Ghosts of many feelings."

"O for the eloquence of Shakespeare, who alone could feel & yet know how to embody these conceptions," the writer breaks in, as if to suggest that "feeling" these things is generally inimical to knowing how to "embody" them; perhaps only the dramatic genius of Shakespeare can give "body" to something like "negation." The repetitions of "feel" in the passage—"touched by the outgoing pre-existent Ghosts of many feelings"; "It feels for ever as a blind man"; "O for the eloquence of Shakespeare, who alone could feel & yet know how to embody these conceptions"—start to suggest a kind of equivalence or slide among meanings of "feel" and "feeling": a somatic "feeling" that comes from touching or being touched; an affective response; a nascent or not-quite-articulated "understanding." Shakespeare "feels . . . conceptions," reminding us that what the dissolving, sensitized soul of the literary man touches up against, in this space, is the idea. If it is Shakespeare's genius to "embody" these feelings—the feelings one has at the approach of an enthralling, dreaded idea—it is perhaps the genius of late Coleridge to write about them in the language of disembodiment and abstraction. This is the language of "abstruse research"—"abstruse," that is, "recondite," "hidden," deriving from "ab-," away, and "trudere," "to push."

Elsewhere, Coleridge celebrates language for giving "outness" to things.[45] But some things, late Coleridge suggests, are belied by the outness of language. His abstruse forays into the vicissitudes of mind's devotion to the foreclosed idea develops a language that defines its subject by pushing away from it in repulsion, like the blind man with his staff, or like the ghostly finger that succeeds it in the paragraph. This latter image recalls various experiments Coleridge and Thomas Wedgwood performed in the 1790s to test the accuracy of sensory perception, all of which involved fingers, eyes, and objects. (For example, when one crosses one's fingers and shuts one's eyes, one's fingers are apt to register a single object as two objects; the eyes, opened, correct the impression. If one holds up one's finger and focuses on an object beyond it, however, the eyes themselves register a second, ghostly finger; in this case, the eyes themselves are at first unreliable until corrected by a shift in focus.) If Wedgwood thought he was deploying the methods of empiricist science to test associationist theory, to Coleridge the experiments spoke to the necessary intervention of the idea in the mind's ability to organize sense data: The eye, opened or re-focused, became for him the analogue of the conception that corrects the potential misleading experience of the sensible world.[46] In this notebook entry, however, it is as if the blind man of the first part of the paragraph opens his eyes in the second, but instead of coming into a position of full speculative mastery, he finds "the finger" split between the positive referent he "saw with eyes" and the ghost finger that continues to touch him "with a ghostly touch."[47]

This ghost finger—"not it; and yet it is it"—has its analogues in Green's *The Work of the Negative*: the Wolf Man's dream/hallucination of a severed finger, recounted and analyzed by Freud, becomes an important impetus for Green's speculations about negative hallucination, speculations that wind to a close with this reflection on the negative images of hands that mark the walls of the Patagonian Cueva de las Manos:

> There is no more vivid example of this than the negative hands found on the walls of Neolithic caves. A hand which is drawn never gives the same sensation of its prehensile power and the elusive nature of its grip, of the lure of perception and of the mark which the latter leaves on our body at the point where it perceives.[48]

Although Green's own work on the negative is propelled by his explorations of failures of relationship in their most extreme form, his insights extend more broadly to intellection itself. For disappointment attends the condition of being human, of having one's survival dependent upon the care of others who are inevitably preoccupied with things other than oneself, and it is disappointment—in the first instance, stemming from the withdrawal of "touch," the somatic pleasures that comprise the holding environment—that presses the infant into thought, into the "grip" of what is no longer present. While it appears primary and immediate, then, "perception"—the appearance of the "real finger"—in fact involves both the positive idea of the finger and the negative absence or blank that makes perception possible; it derives from drive life and the alluring relations of touch. This is what Coleridge's thinking in this passage blindly grasps: the lost touch that haunts and propels the abstruse movements of thought.

The passage, which approaches an understanding of what Green, following Winnicott, might call "the negative side of relationships,"[49] on the one hand limns a mind drawn to an extreme of insularity and deprivation, a subject that abjures the feared "real" touch in favor of intimacy with the "not it" and the endless repetition of scenes of failed or missed encounter. This drift structures the passage itself, which begins with an imagined address to a friend and ends with the question of whether "any one" would be capable of a relation to this thinking or this thinker that was not a stance of spectatorial distance and dismissiveness. Yet that last strangely performative final aside—"nay *any one?*"—at the same time obliquely and improbably conjures some imaginary audience, now explicitly not the original addressee and whose particular advent cannot be anticipated, that will wonder and "think" on the writer. Which is to say that on the other hand—that powerfully seductive "negative hand"—the literary man "touched" by these ghostly fingers, possessed of the rare gift of carving out a hiding place for thought on the far side of social demand, comes into view here as the recipient of a kind of grace. If one moves outside the den, as Coleridge does here in his last aside, what comes into view is the charismatic figure of late Coleridge: "mad or drunk," touched by the gods, who presents to the world the spectacle of a thinking unaddressed to "*any one.*"[50]

The Black Hole of Genius

At the end of "Constancy to an Ideal Object," the poet asks his addressee, the Ideal Object, "And art thou nothing?":

And art thou nothing? Such thou art, as when
The woodman winding westward up the glen

> At wintry dawn, where o'er the sheep-track's maze
> The viewless snow-mist weaves a glist'ning haze,
> Sees full before him, gliding without tread,
> An image with a glory round its head;
> The enamored rustic worships its fair hues,
> Nor knows he *makes* the shadow, he pursues!

"Such thou art" suggests a measure of explanatory confidence, belied, however, by the poetically satisfying but curiously inapropos analogy that follows. The lines describe the phenomenon of the Brocken specter—the shadow cast by a backlit figure onto alpine mists—which Coleridge had attempted to experience during his stay in Germany. The analogy between the earlier "thou" and this "image with a glory round its head" feels intuitively right: Each is an image-ideal, and the second figure illustrates what the speaker already "knows" about the first—that it is virtual, a projection. Yet the analogy is at the same time unfitting: If the "ideal object" is a "constant in a world of change," the Brocken phenomenon is a notoriously transient and unstable apparition (one can neither count upon its appearing at all, nor prolong its endurance beyond the light/mist conditions that make it possible); if the poet "knows" the virtual character of his ideal "thou" ("well I see / She is not thou"), the credulous rustic doesn't "know" he creates the image he perceives; and while the ideal object is the mental image of a desired "she," the Brocken specter is a self-projection.

The analogy, however, registers the ways in which the poem has by now veered from its initial confidence in the constancy of its ideal object. That first apostrophe—to a "yearning Thought"—already suggests the deceptive conflation of the constancy of a *mind* fixed on its object and that of the object itself, whether or not the latter takes the form of an embodied or virtual appearance. By the end of the strophe, the "Thought," in its character as the ideational *object* of thought, like anything else that "beat[s] about," seems to have veered or vanished, with the poet only able to imagine its absence: "the peacefull'st cot. . . . Without thee were but a becalmed bark, / Whose Helmsman on an ocean waste and wide / Sits mute and pale his mouldering helm beside." In the space between the strophe's first apostrophe and its final lines, the paean to a yearned-for object has torqued into thought's exploration of the phenomenon of its constancy to the Thought, a shift and loss of course that finds its image in the helmsman unmoored.[51] The only "constant" here could be said to reside in the bent of this particular mind, which invariably pursues the object to its absence or vanishing point.

"And art thou nothing?" precipitates out of this turn. The strophe introduced by the question arguably snatches a qualified affirmation out of the maws of despair. Unlike the rudderless helmsman, utterly adrift, the figure of the woodsman can at least attach his yearning to a *transient* glory, the image that temporarily captivates and orients him. The poet here keeps a certain distance from this figure, exposing what the rustic doesn't know: that the "image with a glory round its head" is the woodsman's own projected form. The poem thus sets up a distinction between naïve and the sentimental, in Tilottama Rajan's terms, or between a mystified credulity, on the one hand, and a critical, philosophical grasp of projective mechanisms on the other.[52] Yet the poem seems to affirm and celebrate both postures—both the rustic's unself-conscious pursuit of this "glory" and the philosophical mind's appreciation of the human imagination's participation in the creative "making" of its glorious objects.

Coleridge's note to the poem at once supports and complicates this account. The note points the reader to a passage from *Aids to Reflection* that deploys the Brocken phenomenon as an image of the possible relations one might have to the idea of Genius: "The beholder either recognizes [Genius] *as a projected form of his own Being, that moves before him with a Glory round his head,* or recoils from it as from a Spectre." Given that the note presses this observation into service as a gloss to "Constancy to an Ideal Object," one might expect the distinction it offers—between the one who "recognizes" and the one who "recoils"—to map neatly onto the poem's distinction between thinkers like the poet and the reader, who grasp both *this* mechanism of projection and, more generally, the virtual status of "ideal objects" including ego-ideals, and the rustic, who doesn't get that he is looking at a projected form of his own being. Yet this rustic does not "recoil" from the Brocken apparition as from a specter, but rather "worships" and "pursues" what he thinks is real. In this sense the naïve rustic is as happy a positivist as the beholder who recognizes Genius "as a projected form of his own being, that moves before him with a Glory round his head," or the philosopher who celebrates the imagination's power to "make": None recoil in dread from the image, which, however its status is understood (or misrecognized) serves to beatify the self. In contrast, it might be the lot of a particular *cast* of Genius to see, at the very core of the image, "Nothing," the black hole that allows self and world to appear, and to recoil in dread; or, taking a step outside the den, to recognize itself in this absence or shadow surrounded by aura, in this resonant blank that solicits the projections of others.

—+—

When I set out to write the essay that ultimately evolved into this chapter, my plan was to investigate the social meaning of Coleridge the talker. I was interested in the odd celebrity of this figure who famously collared people in the streets of Highgate, at dinner parties, and in lecture halls and talked on and on, to apparent reactions of delight and wonder. I wanted to ask what made so many people eager to listen, often for hours, to talk they almost universally professed not to understand. Eventually I did come to write on this subject, in what became the final chapter of this book. In a nutshell, my answer to my own question is that in a society increasingly rationalized, increasingly given over to standards of efficiency, productivity, and function, late Coleridge allows his world to imagine a mode of intellectual activity that cannot be put to use. And, of course, to put that imagined mode of intellection to use, for what has proven more culturally useful than the romantic conception of Genius?

But the process of arriving at this answer, which involved the long detour that is *this* chapter, has suggested to me that the true genius of late Coleridge may be to engineer his reader's backing of herself into a hole—the strange place / not a place of intellectual work. Struggling with this language, blindly feeling one's way into the conceptual landscape it opens up, one feels "touched": a little mad, a little drunk, perhaps, brushed by the ghosts of ideas that seem, precociously, to gesture toward our own preoccupations; and moved by the charged, charismatic, strangely exemplary figure of the one who works—incessantly, productively, and unproductively—without hope. Engaging late Coleridge, one finds oneself taking the measure of the spaces of our own social and political landscapes, including our academic institutions in which professionals read, analyze, teach, write books, attend conferences, and otherwise do our work, cleaving to notions of productivity in a culture that values output and seems increasingly to devalue our labor. In the process of doing this work, however, one can come to find oneself without speculative purchase, working from the position of the denizen, working without hope. And then, one has to draw the line—this can only be madness, drunkenness; let us weave a circle round him thrice.

5. Coleridge the Talker

In the spring of 1819, while walking from Hampstead towards Highgate, John Keats happened to bump into Samuel Taylor Coleridge on Mansfield Lane. He reported the incident in a letter to George and Georgiana Keats:

> Last Sunday I took a Walk towards Highgate and in the lane that winds by the side of Lord Mansfield's park I met Mr. Green our Demonstrator at Guy's in conversation with Coleridge—I joined them, after inquiring by a look whether it would be agreeable—I walked with him at his alderman-after-dinner pace for near two miles I suppose. In these two miles he broached a thousand things—let me see if I can give you a list—Nightingales, Poetry—on Poetical Sensation—Metaphysics—Different genera and species of Dream—Nightmare—a dream accompanied by a sense of touch—single and double touch—A dream related—First and second consciousness—the difference explained between will and Volition—so many metaphysicians from a wont of smoking the second consciousness—Monsters—the Kraken—Mermaids—Southey believes in them—Southey's belief too much diluted—a Ghost story—Good morning—I heard his voice as it came toward me—I heard it as he moved away—I had heard it all the interval—if it may be called so. He was civil enough to ask me to call on him at Highgate.[1]

And here is Coleridge's account of the same incident, as reported in *Table Talk*:

> A loose, not well dressed youth, met Mr Green and me in Mansfield Lane—Green knew him and spoke. It was Keats—he was introduced to me, and stayed a minute or so—after he had gone a little, he came back, and said, "Let me carry away the memory, Coleridge, of having pressed your hand." There is death in his hand, said I to Green when he was gone. Yet this was before the consumption showed itself.[2]

If there's a comic disparity between these two renderings of the same event, this is because each man describes, not life, exactly, but the intrusion of an iconic person into the register of the mundane. Keats's Coleridge is the Coleridge of legend, who inhabits the suburban world of Highgate as a visitant whose true place is timeless and boundless; his mode is dilation and he talks for hours. While Coleridge's Keats—the loose neckclothed boy of the reviews—is, precisely, bound, within the telescoped span of a tragically brief life; his mode is compression, and so he can only stay for a minute or so. Yet for all their differences, these two figures of British romanticism have much in common, which accounts, perhaps, for the odd fellow-feeling that comes through in both anecdotes. Personalities whose distinctiveness lies in being possessed of no fixed identity; self-absorbed yet selfless; wounded by the press and defended by the circles they mobilized and magnetized through a charm figured forth in an unearthly countenance, matchless speech, and an unusual capacity for becoming caught up in thought; men whose reputations, in a media culture, owed much to local and untranslatable performances— Coleridge and Keats, each in his way, served as a kind of spirit of the age.

Here, that spirit has something almost uncanny about it: Keats, already launched into his posthumous life, meets Coleridge, the ancient-mariner-like survivor of his own youth. Keats and Coleridge were temporally out of joint, although not necessarily in the heroic sense of being ahead of their times: Rather, each suffered from premature exhaustion, failing to arrive at a future that would redeem an early promise and an investment of hope. This chapter is an exploration of Coleridge's late career as a talker. Coleridge and his contemporaries tended to cast his prodigious talk as waste and failure. Yet this failure often converted to wonder when Coleridge the talker, who seemed to perform a genial thinking without limits or obvious issue, appeared to a melancholy age as the incarnation of a lost and archaic spirit. Serving to bind a modern intellectual culture to what it has ceased to accommodate, the figure of Coleridge the talker, I want to suggest, opens to the posthumous survival of romanticism itself.

"As if we were not *consubstantial*"

It is in contemporary anecdote more than in *Table Talk* that we most feel the spell of Coleridge the talker. Here is Henry Nelson Coleridge, describing a visit to the British Gallery in July of 1831:

> Mr. Coleridge was in high spirits, and seemed to kindle in his mind at the con-
> templation of the splendid pictures before him. He did not examine them all
> by the catalogue, but anchored himself before some three or four great works,

telling me that he saw the rest of the Gallery *potentially*. I can yet distinctly recall him, half leaning on his old simple stick, and his hat off in one hand, whilst with the fingers of the other he went on, as was his constant wont, figuring in the air a commentary of small diagrams, wherewith, as he fancied, he could translate to the eye those relations of form and space which his words might fail to convey with clearness to the ear. His admiration for Rubens showed itself in a sort of joy and brotherly fondness; he looked as if he would shake hands with the pictures. What the company, which by degrees formed itself round this silver-haired, bright-eyed, music-breathing old man, took him for, I cannot guess; there was probably not one there who knew him to be that Ancient Mariner, who held people with his glittering eye, and constrained them, like three years' children, to hear his tale.[3]

The anecdote is typical of contemporary accounts: Introduced into the space of modern London, Coleridge, talking, brings about a transformation of social relations. Here, museum-goers following the catalogue's orchestrated progress through the gallery are halted and reoriented, like the captivated auditors to Coleridge's own ancient mariner. The scene has the mute, luminous, iconic quality of memory or dream, the image of an unremembered speech "translated to the eye." Coleridge talking is most often a dumbshow: Coleridge surrounded by rapt listeners, producing talk that cannot be transported out of the charmed circle.

Contemporary accounts of Coleridge's post-Malta London life bring home his urbanity and modernity: Coleridge lecturing, of course, at Almack's, the Surrey Institution, or the London Philosophical Society, but also "sounding on his way" in Highgate and Hampstead or on the Strand, gathering crowds in the National Gallery, receiving visitors at the Gilmans' and dining out at Lamb's. They also remind us that early mid-century British print culture was a small world. The circles that gathered at the Gilmans' at Highgate, the names recorded in *Coleridge the Talker*, Seamus Perry's *Interviews and Anecdotes*, and Carl Woodring's introduction to *Table Talk* are familiar to scholars of the printed literature of the period: Lamb, Wordsworth, Southey, Hazlitt, Crabb Robinson, De Quincey; or, in the next generation, Sarah and Henry Nelson Coleridge, Byron, Carlyle, Irving, Fenimore Cooper, the men who became "the Apostles," Mr. Keats.[4] Clearly, the cachet of hearing Coleridge talk, as Peter Manning points out, has to do with a modern appreciation of the difference between print and unrepeatable local performance. Local and interpersonal performance, reported and circulated in a way that boosts authorial reputation, is a distinctive feature of modern commodity and celebrity culture; as Manning and others have noted, it's a culture Coleridge played to and manipulated.[5]

But Coleridge also functioned as a node of irritation or point of resistance in this world. Writing of Coleridge's lecturing, Manning comments, "Coleridge the lecturer simultaneously furnishes a paradigmatic instance of the poet as commodity producer in a market economy and . . . exposes the limits of the argument": Coleridge's "excess"—his extemporizing from and ignoring of notes, his failure to turn lectures into essays, his resistance to capture by would-be recorders of lectures and table talk, all resulting in the loss of a prodigious outpouring—may be engaged in a system designed to create and enlarge a class's "cultural capital," but in his own case "it is well to specify that what was capitalized upon was failure."[6] As Manning and Jon Klancher point out (the latter in an essay called "Transmission Failure"), this "failure" is complex and ambivalent, involving the failure of others to package and transmit Coleridge as well as his own refusal or inability to transform or leverage his talk into recognizable, conventionally circulatable, financially remunerating intellectual "objects."[7] As Manning suggests, while it's productive to see Coleridge's talking in terms of its relation to the poet as producer in a market economy, there is something about the phenomenon of Coleridge's talk that makes it hard to absorb into a decisive account of that relation: It can look like a failed effort to capitalize on intellectual work; like heroic or unintended resistance to the system; or like the ultimate marketing strategy, when Coleridge's "failure" to be or produce recognizable commodities came to define Coleridge's "Genius" for contemporaries and a long line of successors.

In this chapter, I want to shift the terrain a bit. Before we think of Coleridge's talk as a failed gambit or a resistant strategy or a *tour de force* move in some sort of system of exchange, we might ask what qualifies it as a gambit, or strategy, or social transaction at all. Although many acknowledged the highly theatrical nature of the scene of Coleridge talking, his contemporaries also agreed that Coleridge the talker performed the mind radically turned away from its social setting—the mind caught up elsewhere, in some *other* scene. Their accounts make us want to ask what compelled people to listen for hours to talk they almost universally professed not to understand or remember. What is the nature of the relation Coleridge's audience entered into with this figure, who performed a kind of radical insulation from the social setting?

To explore *this* question, we might begin not with failure but delight and wonder. Contemporary accounts of Coleridge in his role as talker, striking both in number and in the degree to which they repeat the same tropes, analogies, and responses, tend to cast him as a marvelous, categorically anomalous figure—the remnant of a lost culture or world, a visitant from another planet. In later life, Hazlitt suggests, having outlived his own past promise and the heady beginnings of British romanticism, Coleridge haunts the streets of London as a ghost or revenant of that self and time: "All he has done of moment, he had done twenty years ago: since then, he may be said to have lived on the sound of his own voice."[8] More dramatically and frequently, contemporaries report that meeting Coleridge transports one to the days of the peripatetic philosophers of ancient Greece, when Isocrates, Milton's "old man eloquent," walked the streets of the city state. When in Coleridge's presence, London becomes Athens, a dinner-party a Symposium.[9] Often, Coleridge appears to have descended from another sphere altogether—as if "dropt from the moon," he makes his way along the Strand of London "*as if* he had been earthy, of the earth."[10] In "My First Acquaintance with the Poets," Hazlitt tells the story of the younger Coleridge at a party in Birmingham "going to sleep after dinner on a sofa, where the company found him to their no small surprise, which was increased to wonder when he started up of a sudden, and rubbing his eyes, looked about him, and launched into a three-hours' description of the third heaven."[11]

But wherever Coleridge comes from and wherever he transports his auditors, one brings little back from one's travels:

> Like his own bright-eyed mariner, he had a spell in his voice that would not let you go. To attempt to describe my own feeling afterward, I had been carried, spiraling, up to heaven by a whirlwind intertwisted with sunbeams, giddy and dazzled, but not displeased, and had then been rained down again with a shower of mundane stocks and stones that battered out of me all recollection of what I had heard, and what I had seen![12]

Although Coleridge himself seemed to store everything that had ever been writing or thought in his capacious memory, the content of his own speech was dramatically and uncannily forgettable, as a host of contemporaries who had hoped to be second Boswells had cause to lament:

> Yet I cannot recall—and I believe I could not recall at the time, so as to preserve as a cherished thing in my remembrance—a single sentence of the many sentences I heard him utter.
>
> . . . and on such occasions I used to leave him as if I were in a waking dream, trying to recall, here and there, a sentence of the many weighty ones I heard him utter, seldom with success.
>
> I think I have never heard Coleridge so very eloquent, and yet it was painful to find myself unable to recall anything of what had so delighted me . . .
>
> I was not unfrequently so engrossed, and absorbed by the almost inspired

look and manner of the speaker, that I was, for a time, incapable of performing the mechanical act of writing.

I left him at night so thoroughly *magnetized*, that I could not for two or three days afterwards reflect enough to put anything on paper.[13]

As Klancher, Manning, and others point out, Coleridge's contemporaries are strikingly unanimous about the inassimilability of his marvelous talk to memory or transcription. It stunned and dis*armed* listeners, including their fine motor skills: Even professional stenographers found themselves unable to take notes on Coleridge's lectures.[14] Crabb Robinson, who recorded everything, ruefully noted that anything he managed to capture of Coleridge's talk was "a *caput mortuum*" to the living performance.[15]

Speculation about why Coleridge's talk eluded capture focused at times on degree: contemporaries compared his prodigious outpouring to a sublime flood or torrent, a "voice of mountain waters" that threatened to overwhelm or drown the recipient, or, perhaps more interestingly, to a kind of mathematical sublime, a mechanical production whose raw materials, being immaterial, were immune to friction or wear, and whose combinations were unpredictable and infinite and in turn fed the motions of the machine. Coleridge, once he got going, "could with difficulty suppress" his talk (the "'art of stopping' must have been to him singularly difficult")[16] and so he went on and on, "never pausing for an instant except to catch his breath (which, in the heat of his teeming mind, he did like a schoolboy repeating by rote his task)"[17]; around his paper of snuff "he revolved, talking and snuffing, snuffing and talking, rewarding every sentence with a pinch"[18], rather like "Babbage's machine," the first modern computer.[19] These differences in degree shaded into a difference in kind, "a talk like no other": The trajectories of Coleridge's arguments were so expansive and the particular illustrations so vivid that one was constantly distracted from the former by the latter; the syntactical turns of the Coleridgean sentence were so surprising and idiosyncratic as to baffle expectation and interrupt concentration (particularly troublesome to the stenographer, who depends on stereotype and predictability); the chaunting delivery, the bright eyes and strikingly transfigured countenance, all seemed spellbinding in a way that sloughed off intellectual grasp, eluded recollection, and foiled capture.

And yet something remained, as the rich archive of contemporary anecdotes attests: not "objects of thought"—nuggets of aphoristic wisdom or truth or some other form of portable property—but the impression of a form of an argument divested of particular content, the cadences of a syntax unencumbered by referential matter—the sense of a prodigal *mode of production* and the bright image of its unearthly, "abstracted" producer. The experience of Coleridge the talker could not be grasped, but instead it returned on one as a haunting, a dream, an echo:

> I regretted I could not exercise the powers of a second Boswell, to record the wisdom and the eloquence that had that evening flowed from the orator's lips. It haunted me as I retired to rest. It drove away slumber; or if I lapsed into sleep, there was Coleridge—his snuffbox, and his 'kerchief before my eyes—[20]

We can think here of Keats, recalling the voice that went on "all the interval."

To experience Coleridge live was thus not to brush up against "life," exactly. Coleridge appears in these remarkably consistent anecdotes as a dematerialized and "abstracted" character (he seemed "to be abstracted from all and everything around and about him").[21] "You could not incarnate him"[22]: One's pleasure was rather "to watch the infirmities of the flesh shrinking out of sight" as he talked on and on, to observe a countenance that "seemed almost spirit made visible without a shadow of the physical upon it"[23]—that, while speaking or in memory, took on the bright, ungrounded character of the aesthetic image, the mental presentation that nonetheless "appears" as a substantial thing before one. What also endures, along with this image of the "abstracted" person, is what Hazlitt calls "the music of thought" ("His voice rolled on the ear like the pealing organ, and its sound alone was the music of thought").[24]

I don't want to suggest that no one ever remembered anything Coleridge said, or that the particular claims of his philosophical and critical thinking had no impact on his listeners; this was obviously not the case.[25] But I'm interested in an insistent strain in the record that suggests that Coleridge's audiences did not measure the value of his talk in terms of what could be transported away from the scene. Rather, in Coleridge's talk they seemed to recognize and value the phenomenon and rhythms of thinking itself. In an obvious but nonetheless curious way, Coleridge staged or incarnated "the life of the mind" for the age. For Hannah Arendt in her book of that title, this life is lived by *anyone* who thinks, while thinking: To think is to remove oneself from ordinary life, and to live, for a time, among mental phenomena not available to the senses and, by extension, to socially available perception. The one who withdraws into a conceptual landscape thus becomes temporarily insulated from common life: "For while, for whatever reason, a man indulges in sheer thinking, and no matter on what subject, he lives completely in the singular, that is, in complete solitude, as though not men but Man inhabited the earth."[26] Anyone who thinks is thus "strange," and philosophers, who choose a life of thinking, live the life of "a stranger." This is Arendt:

> The loss of common sense is neither the vice nor the virtue of Kant's "professional thinkers": it happens to everybody who ever reflects on something; it

only happens more often to professional thinkers. These we call philosophers, and this way of life will always be "the life of a stranger," as Aristotle called it in his *Politics*.[27]

Later, she refers to "Plato's famous saying" that "only the philosopher's body—that is, what makes him appear among appearances—still inhabits the city of men": as though to suggest that "by thinking, men removed themselves from the world of the living."[28]

In a notebook entry of 1808, Coleridge himself connects this mode of estrangement to "Genius":

> And yet I think, I must have some *analogon* of Genius; because, among other things, when I am in company with Mr. Sharp, Sir J. Macintosh, R. and Sidney Smith, Mr Scarlet, & c & c, I feel like a Child—nay, rather like an Inhabitant of another planet—their very faces all act upon me, sometimes as if they were Ghosts, but more often as if I were a Ghost, among them—at all times, as if we were not *consubstantial*.[29]

The feeling, he at first speculates, is like being a child in the company of adults—a difference, perhaps, "of degree," but this modulates into the feeling of being of a different *kind* than ordinary men: being "as if from another planet," "being a Ghost." Rei Terada speculates about this passage that Coleridge's talking is a way of insulating himself from distressing feelings of alienation.[30] I would agree: Here, in an entry that resonates with other moments of self-reflection in the notebooks, including those touched on in the previous chapter, Coleridge casts himself as encapsulated in a kind of thought- and word-balloon, a kind of philosophical bubble-boy. But at the same time this feeling of insularity is turned to account when it suggests he has "some *analogon* of Genius"; in his cordoned-off state, he recognizes himself in the way his contemporaries recognize him, as one who lives among us as a stranger, as the (dis)embodied Genius.

Coleridge's account—of the nonconsubstantiality of himself and ordinary people and the potential reversibility of these effects (I am a ghost, or perhaps, they are ghosts)—is a provocative gloss on the often-noted muteness of his listeners as well as on their inability to transport his language outside of the charmed circle of the talk. Perhaps, we might speculate, his listeners are silent not because they can't get a word in edgewise but because they and Coleridge inhabit separate and parallel universes. We might recall, in this context, Keats's "inquiring with a look" whether he might join Mr. Green's party; or James Fenimore Cooper's account of a pantomimical conversation occurring at a dinner at which Coleridge held forth:

At first I was so much struck with the affluent diction of the poet, as scarcely to think of any thing else; but when I did look about me, I found every eye fastened on him. Scott sat, immovable as a statue, with his little gray eyes looking inward and outward, and evidently considering the whole as an exhibition, rather than as an argument; though he occasionally muttered, "Eloquent!" "Wonderful!" "Very extraordinary!" Mr. Lockhart caught my eye once, and he gave a very hearty laugh, without making the slightest noise, as if he enjoyed my astonishment.[31]

But if Mr. Lockhart's silent laughter suggests the invisible, impermeable barrier that separates the genial Coleridge from the world of ordinary men, the former's eyeing of Mr. Fenimore Cooper reminds us that the talker who cannot be assimilated serves to constellate a social body. The phenomenon of Coleridge the talker thus complicates Arendt's account of the life of the mind, which somewhat surprisingly emphasizes that life's privacy, its insularity, its categorical difference from ordinary, communal life. Her frequent references to the philosophers who live as strangers among us already disturbs that picture, suggesting a social arrangement with a very long history, in which the one who is especially withdrawn into thought appears in a socially resonant way. Given Arendt's quite unremarkable observation that *each* one of us regularly moves between being withdrawn into thought and engaging in the world, what would be the social need or function of this figure? The one who appears as a "stranger among us" can only represent a kind of limit-case: the figure of an exorbitant attachment to thought that resists the pull of collective existence, even the pull of life itself. We tend to believe that conversation depends upon social give and take. But Arendt's accounts of the philosophers gesture toward, and "Coleridge talking" exemplifies, the untoward social attachments a social body might form to the figure who, caught up in some other world, does not have his eyes on the one that includes his audience; the social dynamic that forms around such a one presents the conundrum of a relationship premised upon the absence of an expectation of exchange.

The relations a culture enters into with its foreign bodies vary, of course, and the relations Coleridge's world enters into with Coleridge are particular to this moment. For Thomas de Quincey, the bond between the sage of Highgate and his auditors is the product of a "rare and difficult collusion" resulting in a thoroughly social if "silent" "contract":

All reputation for talking is a visionary thing—and rests upon a sheer impossibility, viz, upon such a histrionic performance in a state of insulation from the rest of the company as could not be effected, even for a single time, without a rare and difficult collusion. . . . It was a silent contract between him and his hearers that nobody should speak but himself.[32]

Hazlitt suggests that what is contracted here is kind of a "division of labour": Coleridge "immediately establishes the principle of the division of labour in this respect, wherever he comes. He takes his cue as speaker, and the rest of the party theirs as listeners—a 'Circean herd'—without any previous arrangement having been gone through."[33] In this particular instance of the "division of labour" that according to Adam Smith characterizes modern labor relations, a person who strikes almost everyone as a throwback to another time and place, in part because he does not "labor," at least in a way that leads to the efficient production of obviously commodifiable goods, talks, while the highly productive members of a new class of professional thinkers that included at various points Mr. Macintosh, Mr. Sharp, Mr. De Quincey, and Mr. Hazlitt, agree—collude—to be silent.

For Hazlitt, one enters into this "arrangement" before a moment of consent presents itself; listeners simply find themselves part of a spellbound "Circean herd." And indeed, reading through this material, one often feels oneself in the presence of what the scientists might call paranormal phenomena. We might think back to Fenimore Cooper's description of the pantomimical dinner party, in which those who seem absolutely cordoned off from Coleridge find themselves at the same time absolutely absorbed, involuntarily mirroring his insulation and captivation: Cooper "struck," every eye "fastened" on the speaker, Scott sitting "immovable as a statue," "looking inward and outward" as though the marvel to which he is a spectator finds its analog within him. Or we could observe the weird way Coleridge's contemporaries, who vary considerably in their degree of infatuation with their subject, still repeat, again and again, the same descriptions, the same figures, the same arrested responses (often evoking Coleridge's own poetry of the supernatural as they do so), almost as if they had all read the same guidebook to the Coleridgean sublime.

If contemporaries draw on the language of magic and sorcery to attempt to capture these effects, in the passage quoted earlier Coleridge deploys a more technically precise Kantian vocabulary to describe his social role—"And yet I think, I must have some *analogon* of Genius." A likeness based on relationship (a:b::c:d), analogy, for Kant, enables objects from one existential order—for example, the ideas of pure reason—to become intelligible in terms derived from another—for example, the world of sensuous appearances. Thus, we might speculate, the one who has some "*analogon* of Genius" potentially mediates between worlds that both Kant and Arendt see as nonconsubstantial—the world of mental concepts, and the world that presents itself to the senses. Yet Coleridgean genius would also seem to destabilize the boundaries the Kantian analogy would effect a crossing between—boundaries between within and without, mental concept and sensuous appearance. The dynamics *this* figure sets in motion resemble less the orderly "transfer" of concepts from one existential order to another than the wilder transferential dynamics that are our modern, psychoanalytic way of explaining the spellbinding, magical dimensions of social relationships. The one who possesses an *analogon* of genius is "like" Genius "itself," the "I AM" that constitutes an "inner" world in an act of doubling over, a reflex at once groundless and self-grounding; the analogon that appears in the world of men, the one who gives himself over to the withdrawn and self-sustaining life of the mind, produces in his audience the captivation and absorption he dramatizes. If each of us at times could be said to be "lost in thought," Coleridge's auditors seemed to have found themselves "lost" in a thinking that appears outside of them in the world of sensuous appearances—a thinking that presents itself as free from the pressure of exchange and without ground or limit.

What signals this arrangement as "modern" is its perceived archaic character, I would argue. Listening to Coleridge talk, his audience seems transported to a lost world—a world perhaps connected to the child's earliest experiences of a time prior to the emergence of "real" objects and systems of exchange, when attachments are to hallucinated constructs and the cadences of a language before it comes to bear reference, to the holding environment in which the infant's reverie is held by the reverie of another.[34] Or, in terms suggested by many of his contemporaries, Coleridge transports them back to an era that precedes the rise of the new class of men whom Kant calls "professional thinkers"—the class to which Coleridge belonged, but as a failure, or at least, as anomaly.[35] In *The Friend*, Coleridge describes his intended public as still collapsed by disappointment in the revolutionary period for which it had held such hope, and thus, as sunk in a stupor of despondence, mistrusting all thought and expecting "help from any quarter but from Seriousness and Reflection," "as if some invisible power would think for us, when we gave up the pretense of thinking for ourselves."[36] In collusion with his contemporaries, I propose, Coleridge takes on the "power" of the thinker who improbably appears "to think for us." In this way he serves as the mildly enchanting "spirit" of a dispirited age, the chosen one who abrogates its terms, injecting into it the possibility of a thinking that escapes the new modes of regulation.

The Spirit of the Age

Hazlitt's "Mr Coleridge," the third essay of *The Spirit of the Age,* begins with a striking account of the present as the dotage of the world:

The present is an age of talkers, not of doers; and the reason is, that the world is growing old. We are so far advanced in the Arts and Sciences, that we live in retrospect, and doat on past achievements. The accumulation of knowledge has been so great, that we are lost in wonder at the height it has reached, instead of attempting to climb or add to it; while the variety of objects distracts and dazzles the looker-on.[37]

The lament is odd given that it follows the portraits of the highly productive Mr. Bentham and Mr. Godwin, each of whom possessed exemplary work habits and perhaps too much optimism about the efficacy of systematic reasoning to address social, moral, and political questions. But here, the spirit of the age manifests itself as a sort of blockage before the sublime of accumulated disciplinary knowledges and their objects, dazzling in their variety. Arrested and disarmed, stuck in and on past accomplishments, including, perhaps, those of the generation primarily represented in Hazlitt's collection, "we" talk rather than *do*.

Hazlitt's account of a talking world evokes a familiar enough complaint about modernity. Yet the opening of "Mr Coleridge" suggests that talking registers more than simply a low-level ennui. Living in retrospect, Hazlitt claims, "we" are "like the spectators of a mighty battle, who still hear its sound afar off, and the clashing of armour and the neighing of the war-horse and the shout of victory is in their ears, like the rushing of innumerable waters!"[38] To be modern is to be subject to a kind of paralyzing tinnitus: traumatic and decisive events in the history of thought, now remote, continue to reverberate in our ears. History, Walter Benjamin claims, belongs to the victors, but Hazlitt's modern Britons—the "we" who are "like" those in whose ear "the shout of victory" echoes—are equivocally and recursively positioned: The image invokes loss more than victory, in part from its suggestion of an unclosable distance between the present time and any living contest of ideas. If Mr. Bentham and Mr. Godwin, each in his way, energetically labored to usher in a new dispensation, Coleridge's setting is the twilight world of the present, a melancholic modernity fixated on and reactive to a political, artistic, and intellectual history whose achievements are all in the past.

In this setting, talking verges on a compulsive and traumatized re-sounding of an overwhelming legacy. Later, Hazlitt will attribute to Coleridge this mariner-like compulsion, "his lips idly moving, but his heart forever still, or, as the shattered chords vibrate of themselves, making melancholy music to the ear of memory!"[39] But at the beginning of the portrait, Coleridge appears less a talker among talkers than the repository and figure of the accumulated stores that paralyze "our" industry. He has read everything; every thought that has ever been thought is folded up in his capacious memory:

Mr. Coleridge has a "mind reflecting ages past": his voice is like the echo of the congregated war of the "dark rearward and abyss" of thought. He who has seen a mouldering tower by the side of a crystal lake, hid by the mist, but glittering in the wave below, may conceive the dim, gleaming, uncertain intelligence of his eye: he who has marked the evening clouds uprolled (a world of vapours) has seen the picture of his mind, unearthly, unsubstantial, with gorgeous tints and ever-varying forms—

"That which was now a horse, even with a thought
The rack dislimns, and makes it indistinct
As water is in water."

. . . Hardly a speculation has been left on record from the earliest time, but it is loosely folded up in Mr. Coleridge's memory, like a rich, but somewhat tattered piece of tapestry: we might add (with more seeming than real extravagance) that scarce a thought can pass through the mind of man, but its sound has at some time or other passed over his head with rustling pinions.[40]

Hazlitt's loosely and richly allusive style, like the mind it describes, glitters with the refracted spoils of intellectual history. Coleridge's mind is like Shakespeare's own "mind reflecting ages past"[41]; his voice is "like the [mutated] echo" of the "war" of Prospero's "dark backward and abysm of time," which Hazlitt's misquotation modulates to bear on *intellectual* history, the history, specifically, of "thought"; the later image of the "evening clouds uprolled," which leads forward to the quotation from *Antony and Cleopatra*, in the context of the near allusion to *The Tempest* also recalls Prospero's final address to the audience in that play, which connects the fading of the illusionistic island refuge to the fading of the play his audience is watching and both to the inevitable fading of "the great globe itself" ("the cloud-capt towers . . . like an insubstantial pageant faded, leave not a rack behind").[42]

The portrait Hazlitt builds here also alludes to two natural phenomena we ourselves might have "seen" or "marked": the reflection of a tower in a lake, the evening clouds uprolled. Most of us have indeed gazed at clouds, but where would we have "seen a mouldering tower by the side of a crystal lake, hid by the mist, but glittering in the wave below"? Perhaps at Ullswater, where we might have been sent by Wordsworth's *Guide to the Lakes*:

Walking by the side of Ullswater upon a calm September morning, I saw, deep within the bosom of the lake, a magnificent Castle, with towers and battlements, nothing could be more distinct than the whole edifice;—after gazing with delight upon it for some time, as upon a work of enchantment, I could not but regret that my previous knowledge of the place enabled me to account for the appearance. It was in fact the reflection of a pleasure-house called Lyulph's

Tower—the towers and battlements magnified and so much changed in shape as not to be immediately recognized. In the meanwhile, the pleasure-house itself was altogether hidden from my view by a body of vapour stretching over it and along the hill-side on which it stands, but not so as to have intercepted its communication with the lake; and hence this novel and most impressive object, which, if I had been a stranger to the spot, would from its being inexplicable have long detained the mind in a state of pleasing astonishment.[43]

This allusion is not footnoted in my edition of Hazlitt and when I came across it Wordsworth's *Guide* was not immediately present to my memory. But I had recently been reading Rei Terada's *Looking Away,* in which she quotes this passage to contrast Wordsworth's careful framing of the scene and its pleasures, linked, she argues, to the commodification of the techniques of spectatorial enjoyment typical of guide book literature, to what she calls Coleridge's "phenomenophilia," his private enjoyment and manipulations of the ephemeral perceptual experiences he calls "spectra."[44] Hazlitt presses Wordsworth's account in the direction of Coleridgean pleasure as Terada defines it: Where Wordsworth initially characterizes this image of the past as a potentially and seductively accessible reserve (an antique castle lodged "deep within the bosom of the lake") and, later, draws on the imagined astonishment of "a stranger to the spot" but only after having demystified the illusion, Hazlitt's re-rendering destabilizes and defamiliarizes the image (we initially think we "see" the tower "by the side of the lake," only to find it "glittering in the wave below"), pointing us to the unsecured and ephemeral "wonder" of this marvelous appearance whose source or ground is "hid."

These accumulated allusions and the contexts Hazlitt gives them also, of course, conjure images from Coleridge's own writings, especially "Kubla Khan" and the *Biographia Literaria.* The effect is to produce a series of loose equivalencies among Coleridge, Shakespeare, Prospero, the poet-figure of flashing eyes and floating hair that emerges at the end of "Kubla Khan," the Imagination's reflexively creative "I AM," Coleridge's mind, the dome that appears "on the waves" or that could be built "in air," Prospero's and Shakespeare's various "insubstantial pageants" (and, for the modern reader, perhaps, the name of Keats that is "writ in water")—equivalencies that suggest at once the atavistic power of Coleridgean Genius and the impermanence of its materials and creations. Coleridge's mind reflects ages past, not as something we might hope to possess (the lure presented by the marvelously intact castle that appears "in the bosom of the lake"—the lure presented by, say, Scott's antiquarian fiction), but as multiple and shifting traces of a vast archive "we" cannot grasp or even access—as the moving, serial combinations of "a variety of objects," denatured, wrenched out of time, their grounding contexts "hid." Thus it seems to limn a rich intellectual tradition at the moment that it is breaking up, fading from us, becoming "strange." And then, it leaves not a rack behind. "With an understanding fertile, subtle, expansive, 'quick, forgetive, apprehensive,' beyond all living precedent, few traces of it will perhaps remain": What flickers into view on the reflective surface of Coleridge's mind is not what will be preserved and folded into "our" history but what will almost certainly become lost to our future.

Like many of Coleridge's contemporaries, Hazlitt casts his subject as an archaic and otherworldly character—the evacuated "spirit" of his own youth and promise, of the youth of romanticism, and of still older dispensations. But if Coleridge himself appears here as a derealized ghost or revenant, he simultaneously functions to mark the evacuated character of the age. Always measuring the present against the heady revolutionary period of the near past in *The Spirit of the Age*, in portrait after portrait Hazlitt points out individual and collective culpability for his generation's swerve from idealism and enthusiasm toward legitimacy. But as they accumulate, the portraits also attend to a different sort of accommodation to power, one that cuts across Hazlitt's subjects, from Mr. Godwin who stays the course to Mr. Southey who does not: Insofar as they are members of a rising class of professional thinkers and writers, Hazlitt's subjects achieve their successes by conforming to modern work standards and conditions—efficiency, productivity, the division and specialization of intellectual labor. The virtues and faults of writers as varied as Mr. Bentham and Mr. Godwin, Mr. Tooke and Mr. Malthus, Mr. Scott and Lord Byron, as Hazlitt sees them, derive from their adherence to the systems in which they have invested in ego and economic terms—systems, he charges, that cannot accommodate history or the vagaries of human behavior, and that are incapable of self-testing or critique.

Coleridge occupies this world. But unlike those who keep their eyes on the prize he is without "discipline" in every sense of the word—tangential, cormorant-like, and unproductive according to the professional or market standards of his day. Unlike many contemporary reporters on Coleridge's talk, Hazlitt does not hesitate to designate this nonproductivity "failure." But his essay's dramatic, mid-course elegiac turn binds the fate of the prematurely exhausted life to that of the exhausted world, a world that fails to sustain the life that could replenish its reserves:

Alas! "Frailty, thy name is Genius!"—What is become of all this mighty heap of hope, of thought, of learning and humanity? It has ended in swallowing doses of oblivion and in writing paragraphs in the *Courier*. Such and so little is the mind of man!

... Proscribed by court-hirelings, too romantic for the herd of vulgar poli-
ticians, our enthusiastic stood at bay, and at last turned on the pivot of a subtle
casuistry to the *unclean side*: but his discursive reason would not let him trammel
himself into a poet-laureate or stamp-distributor; and he stopped, ere he had
quite passed that well-known "bourne from whence no traveler returns"—and
so has sunk into torpid, uneasy repose, tantalized by useless resources, haunted
by vain imaginings, his lips idly moving, but his heart for ever still, or, as the
shattered chords vibrate of themselves, making melancholy music to the ear of
memory! Such is the fate of genius in an age when, in the unequal contest with
sovereign wrong, every man is ground to powder who is not either a born slave,
or who does not willingly and at once offer up the yearnings of humanity and
the dictates of reason as a welcome sacrifice to besotted prejudice and loath-
some power.[45]

"Frailty, thy name is Genius!" Later, and less charitably, Carlyle will accuse
Coleridge of "great and useless Genius," suggesting that "Genius" *could* be
useful.[46] But Hazlitt's formulation is perhaps more suggestive and accurate:
In this age, the age of the invention of romantic "Genius," that type or
name designates a frail archaism characterized by its noninstrumentality, its
uselessness, its out-of-jointness with a social, economic, and political order
that grinds to powder all that fails to accommodate itself to the designs of
capital and nation, to prejudice and power.[47]

Like Arendt, who wrote *The Life of the Mind* after her encounter with
the banality of Eichmann, Hazlitt holds up "the life of the mind" as the
site of a slender, essentially rear-guard resistance that the purposelessness
of thought could offer to an unthinking instrumentalism that functions to
"reduce law to a system, and the mind of man to a machine"—a resistance
to what appears as the givenness of the modern world, and especially its
modes of regulating and containing what it is possible to think. The mind
whose primary attachment is to thinking—"discursive reasoning"—neither
accommodates itself to this world nor is accommodated by or within it, and
so like the baby when it is unsustained by its environment, it perfects the
arts of holding itself, buoyed up by the hallucinated objects of a compelling
mental world and battening "on the sound of [its] own voice." This is, up
to a point, a successful adaptation, on the baby's part and on Coleridge's:
Coleridge actually succeeded in "living on his voice," when person after
person, charmed by this chaunting, abstracted figure, took him up, fed, and
housed him; just as his reputation as a great heap of failed hope—promul-
gated above all by Coleridge himself—promoted the imprint of Samuel
Taylor Coleridge on what were in fact his many ventures into print.[48] And
yet, the baby condemned to batten too long on its hallucinated satisfactions

fails to thrive. It is *this* understanding of Coleridge's "failure" that we are left with here: a radical failure of relation that for Hazlitt redounds to the discredit of the age itself.

Writing on Proust in *Minima Moralia*, Theodor Adorno reflects that "the departmentalization of mind is a means of abolishing mind where it is not exercised *ex officio*, under contract."[49] Or if not abolishing it, Hazlitt might add, as he contrasts Coleridge's situation to that of his contemporaries, of consigning it to the outskirts. At the close of "Mr Coleridge," he charges Wordsworth and Southey with coming "under contract" in Adorno's terms and thereby entering the walls of the city:

> They are safely inclosed there. But Mr. Coleridge did not enter with them; pitching his tent upon the barren waste without, and having no abiding place nor city of refuge![50]

This barren waste is a version of the terrain of the mind itself, where, according to Descartes, "one can live 'as solitary and retired as in the most remote deserts.'" Arendt quotes this passage, and later in *The Life of the Mind* connects this place that is not an "abiding place" to the thinker's I AM, to the *nunc stans*, "this small non-time space in the very heart of time, [which] unlike the world and the culture into which we are born, cannot be inherited and handed down by tradition."[51] (Less sanguine, Coleridge calls this place "limbo.") Arendt would claim that any moment of thinking is wrenched from and lost to collective life and to history; while thinking, the thinking person is both "homeless" and temporally out of joint. Yet for Arendt as well as for Hazlitt, "thinking itself" and the empirical subject who becomes its type or emblem can take historically determinate and resonant forms: like Hazlitt, Arendt writes at a moment when the figure of a thinking without limits can seem to become the bearer of a frail resistance to the social and political forces from which it withdraws.

Arendt suggests that the life of the mind can only come into view as such in the form of an afterimage or afterthought. Drawing together a dazzling array of materials from the Western philosophical tradition in order to read that tradition symptomatically for what it can tell us about thinking itself, her book has affinities with Hazlitt's and his contemporaries' renderings of Coleridge's mind as a rhythm and music divested of particular truth claims, the combinatory elements of which are all that has ever been thought. This mining of the philosophical tradition for new purposes can only happen at the end of a line, Arendt suggests:

> I have spoken about the metaphysical "fallacies," which, as we found, do contain important hints of what this curious out-of-order activity called thinking may

be all about. In other words, I have clearly joined the ranks of those who for
some time now have been attempting to dismantle metaphysics, and philosophy
with all its categories. . . . Such dismantling is possible only on the assumption
that the thread of tradition is broken and that we shall not be able to renew it.[52]

The critical or "dismantling" process in which she engages "only draws
conclusions from a loss that is a fact and as such no longer part of the 'history
of ideas' but of our political history, the history of our world."[53] Philosophy
as a current in a presumptively autonomous "history of ideas" comes to an
end for historical reasons, which in this case include the emergence of the
academic disciplines and the modern university, as well as the ascendency of
modes of political and social critique, including critiques coming from within
the philosophical tradition that gathered impetus from Kantian thought. This
end cannot be precisely marked, and indeed, the older tradition continues
posthumously, as it were, into the new dispensation. The moment Arendt describes, in which the thread of a tradition is broken, stretches at least from the
romantic period into Arendt's and our own time, during a period in which
"philosophy" also became and remains an established academic discipline.

The figure of Coleridge occupies this juncture at which the old, posthumously surviving philosophical tradition coexists with its breakup. The cost
of philosophy's posthumous survival is its transmutation into a professional
"discipline," with the circumscribed range and reach that this entails—part
of a more general disciplining and constriction of "mind" itself under modernity, Adorno suggests; one symptom of the tradition's breakup is the
way its conceptual language becomes available for conscription to new uses,
including the emerging psychological and psychoanalytical discourses that
Coleridge had a part in fashioning and that I discuss in the previous chapter. The figure of Coleridge thus brings into relief the equivocality of the
moment Arendt describes. The bearer of heady new philosophical ideas that
would prove to vitalize English philosophical thought and connect it to a
disciplinary mainstream, he simultaneously came into view as "the one who
thinks" for a melancholy age that had already accommodated itself to the end
of the line. The pathos and wonder, the forms of attachment, identification,
envy, frustration, and boredom that attach to the figure of Coleridge the
talker—all suggest the degree to which he performs a life of the mind that
Arendt suggests is always and intrinsically "out-of-order," but that under
modern conditions can only be imagined as the exclusive activity of the one
who exists beyond the pale while yet walking among us.

Coda

Hannah Arendt's *The Life of the Mind* winds down with an elegiac turn. Once you have dismantled the old philosophical systems, Arendt observes,

> What you then are left with is still the past, but a *fragmented* past, which has lost its certainty of evaluation. About this, for brevity's sake, I shall quote a few lines which say it better and more densely than I could:

> Full fathom five thy father lies,
>   Of his bones are coral made
> Those are pearls that were his eyes.
>   Nothing of him that doth fade
> But doth suffer a sea-change
>   Into something rich and strange.
>   *The Tempest*, Act I, Scene 2

> It is with such fragments from the past, after their sea-change, that I have dealt here. That they could be used at all we owe to the timeless track that thinking beats into the world of space and time. If some of my listeners or readers should be tempted to try their luck at the technique of dismantling, let them be careful not to destroy the "rich and strange," the "coral" and the "pearls," which can probably be saved only as fragments.[1]

Like William Hazlitt, who invokes Prospero's "dark backward and abysm of time" to describe the talk of "Mr Coleridge," Arendt turns to *The Tempest* to evoke the record of the life of the mind, the timeless tracks of which flicker into our view as the glittering detritus of a lost world.[2] Released from their moorings, these fragments appear at once alien, precious, and frail—and, she adds, worthy of our care, even though our relation to these withdrawn things can only be something of a nonrelation. The landscape Arendt evokes has affinities with Coleridge's talk as Hazlitt describes it in *The Spirit of the Age* that extend beyond the shared Shakespeare allusion: Both are *poetic,* in that the counters of older modes of thought, loosed from their original contexts, have become the rhetorical elements of new combinations—ever-shifting, "rich and strange" in the way of the aesthetic, and, salient for this study, in the way of the poetry of second-generation romanticism when it revives and deploys the materials of "a *fragmented* past." The images of the lives of Keats, Shelley, and Coleridge, I've been arguing here, take on the charge of this long melancholic moment: They appear as figures for the long practices that have come to feel out of joint with the times, for a sense of calling that seems to fail or to exceed the demands of new disciplinary regimes; and they gesture to what is felt to be irrecoverably lost at a moment when new social arrangements, including newly negotiated "contracts" between a culture and its thinkers and artists, are in the making.

At the close of his portrait of "Mr Coleridge," Hazlitt charges Wordsworth and Southey with coming "under contract" in Adorno's terms and thus landing "safely enclosed" within the walls of the city. Sinecured as stamp-collector and poet-laureate, their lives suggest the collusion of aspects of a late romantic aesthetics with the designs of nation, empire, and capital, designs that entail a restructuring and disciplining of work, including intellectual work itself.[3] The lives of the dead poets that I have been examining in these pages fall in with this broader program. More than the image of Wordsworth, perhaps, their stories have functioned historically to cultivate passionate readerly attachments to British canonical literature and the values embedded in a high literary tradition. But by virtue of an ostentatious turning away, the turn by which something becomes "image"—the turn, Benjamin reminds us, that is at once that of the singular aesthetic object and of the commodity—they also bring into view the costs of such conscription. In the period that stretches from Wordsworth's time to our present, poetry's rich and strange "life," deriving from the movement of the virtual trope or figure, continues as it always has done. What changes, always, are the conditions of existence for its makers and readers: the increasing reach of a commodity capitalism that works by a process of abstraction of singular thing into image; the consequently threatened sacrifice or loss of what was "human in the past" to this regime; the human condemned to a failure to thrive. It is this conscription of the human to the life of the image that the poetry of second-generation romanticism dramatizes and to which its biographical figures attest.

The poet of Coleridge's "Kubla Khan" builds a dome "in air" and, at the end of the poem, a conjured "all" recognize him as inhabiting the *nunc stans,* the charged, cordoned-off no place within which art and thought perform their magic. At the end of her book, Arendt urges us to preserve magical spaces like this, by checking our impulse to critique or "dismantle" them too completely. We should perhaps steer away from this sort of nostalgia. Hazlitt's portrait of Coleridge suggests that under modern social, political, and economic arrangements the *nunc stans* can take the form of a barren waste, the outskirts to which society consigns those who work without, or beyond, discipline or hope; while the history I have been tracking here suggests that the rich and strange figures of poetry and thought, circulating within a disenchanted world and infusing it with a sort of magic, can potentially function to support the unsupportable. At this time of constantly intensified assault on public and higher education, and especially on the arts and humanities, professional romanticists are rightfully wary of celebrating or granting undue social power to the charged insularity that characterizes the arrested figures of Keats, Shelley, and Coleridge, or, for that matter, to the professional work that, engaging romantic writing, at once constitutes our threatened "discipline" and moves us beyond reason. And yet—again, on that negative "other hand" conjured by Coleridge's late notebook entry—pressing on these particular images of the lives of poets opens us to dimensions of romantic writing that continue to speak to the long moment that includes our present and our future. This writing registers the costs of the contracts modernity strikes with the arts, allowing these losses to be felt on our pulses as our own condition; it flags turnings away that are also poetically generative despite, or because of, the sentence of death under which poetry labors; and it bears forward—as immured, as-yet-undetonated possibilities—movements of thought that gain their impetus and power from an abstruse pressing away from function, aim, and end.

Acknowledgments

Earlier versions of portions of Chapter 2 were published in *European Romantic Review* and *Romantic Praxis*, and an earlier version of Chapter 4 was published in *Romantic Praxis*. Williams College contributed to the production costs of Fordham Press and has also provided generous sabbatical support over the years.

This project has evolved over a long period of time, and along the way I have received support, feedback, and encouragement from many colleagues in the field. I would especially like to acknowledge the interlocutors who appeared just as I began to try to wrestle a handful of fugitive pieces into the shape of a book. These include the participants in the 2012 Summer Friends of Coleridge Conference: I especially thank Tim Fulford, who invited me to present the work on Coleridge that became the book's final chapter. My gratitude also goes to participants and audiences at North American Society for the Study of Romanticism panels on "Romantic Brevity," and especially to David L. Clark and Jacques Khalip, who proposed the topic and invited me to present new work on Keats. As I was completing a draft of the entire manuscript I had the chance to present a large portion of it over two days at the Cogut Institute for the Humanities at Brown University: I thank Marc Redfield and Jacques Khalip for inviting me, the Cogut Institute staff for organizing the visit, and the wonderfully generous and helpful Brown faculty and students who attended the various events, read much of the manuscript, and offered valuable encouragement and advice at a critical moment.

Closer to home, Williams colleagues and students have contributed to this work in particular and general ways. They include Stephen Fix, Suzanne Graver, Walter Johnston, Katie Kent, Anjuli Raza Kolb, John Limon, Patricia Malanga, Peter Murphy, Bernie Rhie, and Shawn Rosenheim, along with the many Williams students with whom I have thought and talked about romanticism and poetry. Cassandra Cleghorn, Jessica Fisher, David L. Smith, and Dorothy Wang were part of a Williams Oakley Center workshop on poetics that sparked new ways of thinking about romantic lyric. Emily Vasiliauskas proved a wonderfully helpful writing partner late in the project. Julie Joosten, former student, now poet and fellow romanticist, provided insightful, detailed, and hugely useful responses to a particularly recalcitrant section of the manuscript. I am also indebted to the members of a small Williams writing group—Theo Davis, Gage McWeeny, Christopher Pye, Anita Sokolsky, and Stephen Tifft—who provided valuable feedback just as I was trying to conceive of this as a book project. Chris Pye, Steve Tifft, and Anita Sokolsky, especially, go way back: I can't begin to say how formative our long history together has been for me and how much I owe to their work and to their generous responses to mine. I send especially warm thanks to Chris, with whom I learned how to write, and to Anita for her forbearance with and transformative attention to this particular project—for the many incisive responses she has provided to the many drafts she has read.

It has been a pleasure to work with everyone involved in Fordham University Press's Lit Z Series: with Sara Guyer and Brian McGrath, the series editors; with Thomas Lay, who has overseen the whole process; with Eric Newman, the managing editor; and with Edward Batchelder, a most scrupulous and judicious copy editor. Brian McGrath and the two anonymous readers of the manuscript all provided sound, smart suggestions for revisions. Elizabeth King provided the stunning cover image.

Finally I want to thank the members of the extended Swann and Paisley families: my brothers, Rick, Don, and Scott, and their families; and Rose, Greg, Lola, Viva, Chloe, and Rufus. Various as they are, they all share a bent for intense, energetic absorption—in creative and intellectual projects, in friendships and relationships—that has been truly sustaining, enlivening, and inspiring to me over many years. In this spirit I want especially to acknowledge Doug Paisley and Anna Swann-Pye, who never stop surprising and delighting me, who keep opening my ways of thinking and being. Their intellectual sparkle, their creative energy, and their love have enriched this project and life itself, and I dedicate this book to them.

Notes

Introduction

1. Particularly interesting examples of the long cultural fascination with Keats's and Shelley's deaths extending into our own moment include many contemporary poems on this subject: See, for example, Ben Belitt's "This Scribe, My Hand," in *This Scribe, My Hand: The Complete Poems of Ben Belitt* (Baton Rouge: Louisiana State UP, 1998), 65, cited by Jacques Khalip in *Anonymous Life: Romanticism and Dispossession* (Stanford: Stanford UP, 2009), 25; and Alan Halsey, *The Text of Shelley's Death* (Sheffield, U.K.: West House Books, 2001), both late entries in a long lineage of poems on the deaths of Keats and Shelley; see also Stanley Plumly, *Posthumous Keats* (New York: W.W. Norton, 2008). For accounts of the role biography has played in Keats's reception, see for instance Susan Wolfson's "Keats Enters History: Autopsy, *Adonais*, and the Fame of Keats," in *Keats and History*, ed. Nicholas Roe (Cambridge: Cambridge UP, 1995); Wolfson suggests that the "cultural processing of Keats" is "one of the main routes by which the 'romance' of 'romanticism' emerged in the nineteenth century," 19. See also Adela Pinch, "A Shape All Light," in *Taking Liberties with the Author: Selected Essays from the English Institute,* ed. Meredith McGill (Ann Arbor, Mich.: English Institute in collaboration with the American Council of Learned Societies, 2013), http: hdl.handle .net/2027heb.90058.0001.001, on the particular forms of the endurance of Shelley-love through the Victorian period; see also Ann Wierda Rowland, "John Keats, English Poet (Made in America)," *Keats-Shelley Journal* 65 (2016): 112–35, for an account of Keats-love during the same period.

2. Marc Redfield, *The Politics of Aesthetics: Nationalism, Gender, Romanticism* (Stanford: Stanford UP, 2003), 32.

3. Samantha Matthews, *Poetical Remains: Poet's Graves, Bodies, and Books in the Nineteenth Century* (Oxford: Oxford UP, 2004).

4. Andrew Bennett, *Romantic Poets and the Culture of Posterity* (Cambridge: Cambridge UP, 1999), 2. The first three chapters of Bennett's book elaborate this argument (9–91).

5. Deidre Shauna Lynch, *Loving Literature: A Cultural History* (Chicago: U of Chicago P, 2015). See especially Chapter 1, "Making it Personal" (21–64), and 220, 257.

6. For accounts of Mary Shelley's editorial work that touch on some of these controversies, see for example Michael Gamer, "Shelley Incinerated," *Wordsworth Circle* 39, no. 1–2 (2008), 23; see also Eric O. Clarke, "Shelley's Heart: Sexual Politics and Cultural Value," *Yale Journal of Criticism* 8 (1995); and Richard Monckton Milnes, *The Life and Letters of John Keats* (London: Moxon, 1867).

7. Robert Metcalf Smith's *The Shelley Legend* (New York: Charles Scribner's Sons, 1945), 1–36, is an especially virulent attack on Mary Shelley's sanitizing of Percy Shel-

ley; I discuss these quarrels within the Shelley circle in Chapter 3 of this volume. For a richly textured account of the Coleridge circle's initial responses to plagiarism charges and Sara Coleridge's subsequent handling of the matter, see Alan D. Vardy, *Constructing Coleridge: The Posthumous Life of the Author* (Basingstoke, U.K.: Palgrave Macmillan, 2010).

8. Thomas Pfau, *Romantic Moods: Paranoia, Trauma, and Melancholy, 1790–1840* (Baltimore: Johns Hopkins UP, 2005), 336.

9. These perceptions of the complicity of the author's biography in aesthetic ideology have traversed a range of critical accounts of romanticism. Recall, for example, Paul de Man's famous pronouncement on the way biography is wielded to transform unstable texts into commemorative objects in "Shelley Disfigured": "For what we have done [with the dead bodies of romanticism] is simply to bury them. . . . They have been transformed into historical and aesthetic objects," in *The Rhetoric of Romanticism* (New York: Columbia UP, 1983), 120. At about the same time, in "Keats and the Historical Method," Jerome McGann argues for the tendency of biographical reading to deflect from the social contexts and ideological imbrications of literature; see *The Beauty of Inflections* (Oxford: Clarendon Press, 1988), 48–49.

10. Redfield, *The Politics of Aesthetics*. See especially the book's introduction, "The Politics of Aesthetics," 1–42.

11. Bennett and Lynch are alive to these tensions and contradictions, although their projects, focused on a broad picture, do not center on them. But see for instance Bennett's observation that the Genius whose work lives on into posterity is a *writing* subject means that this subject survives as inscription; thus romantic writing "tends to inscribe the dissolution of identity into its ideal of the writer," in *Romantic Poets and the Culture of Posterity*, 2. For a sensitive account of the limitations of Bennett's argument—that it relies on a trap-like sense of causality that "misses" what is always potentially missed by the future—see Emily Rohrbach, *Modernity's Mist: British Romanticism and the Poetics of Anticipation* (New York: Fordham UP, 2016), 16–17.

12. Khalip, *Anonymous Life*; Pfau, *Romantic Moods*; Sara Guyer, *Romanticism after Auschwitz* (Stanford: Stanford UP, 2007); Rohrbach, *Modernity's Mist*.

13. William Wordsworth, 1800 "Preface" to *Lyrical Ballads*, in *Lyrical Ballads and Other Poems 1797–1800,* ed. James Butler and Karen Green (Ithaca, N.Y.: Cornell UP, 1992), 746–47; and Walter Benjamin, "On Some Motifs in Baudelaire," in *The Writer of Modern Life,* ed. Michael Jennings (Cambridge, Mass.: Belknap, Harvard UP, 2006), for example 170–72.

14. Hyder Edward Rollins, ed., *The Keats Circle* (Cambridge, Mass.: Harvard UP, 1948) I:88. John Keats, *The Letters of John Keats*, ed. Hyder Edward Rollins (Cambridge, Mass.: Harvard UP, 1958), I:387.

15. From anecdotes collected in Richard Willard Armour and Raymond Floyd Howes, eds., *Coleridge the Talker* (Ithaca: Cornell UP: 1940), 222, 230.

16. William Hazlitt, "Mr Coleridge," in *The Spirit of the Age* (London: Collins, 1969), 62.

17. Armour and Howes, *Coleridge the Talker,* 260, 223, 230, 274, 362, 141. Andrew Bennett's *Romantic Poets and the Culture of Posterity* includes a chapter on Coleridge's talk (116–38); see also Chapter 5 of this volume.

18. *Samuel Taylor Coleridge, The Notebooks of Samuel Taylor Coleridge*, ed. Kathleen Coburn (Princeton: Princeton UP, 1973), III:3324.

19. Lynch sees this "abstracted" and "ghostly" or "revenant" character of even living authors as they appear in accounts from this period as pointing to the way authorship more generally has been connected to the illustrious dead authors of the British canon. Her reading is persuasive. My own interest is in the eerie reversibility of these moments: If they serve to bind a public to a national literature, as Lynch argues, they also suggest ways that our attachments subject us to the mechanistic working of literary figure, bringing home the "revenant" quality of our present. Lynch, *Loving Literature*, 235–75.

20. Thomas Hogg, *Shelley at Oxford* (London: Methuen, 1904), 31–33, 25–27, 41. The rhythms that interest me, here and elsewhere in this study, are explored by Denise Gigante, who connects them to the period's interest in vitalist theories of organic life. See her *Life* (New Haven: Yale UP, 2009). I would argue that these rhythms are, precisely, unnatural: They belong to the order of the denatured, virtual figure. The figure's unsettling capacity to toggle between rigidity and animation is central to Theresa Kelley's account of allegory in *Reinventing Allegory* (Cambridge: Cambridge UP, 1997); see especially "Romantic Ambivalences 1" and "2," 93–175.

21. *Manfred* II:i, 38. In Byron, *The Complete Poetical Works,* ed. Jerome J. McGann (Oxford: Oxford UP, 1986), IV:68.

22. Lynch, *Loving Literature*, 235–75.

23. My understanding of allegory is indebted, in ways that are difficult to footnote, to the work of Walter Benjamin, especially *The Origin of German Tragic Drama*, ed. George Steiner, trans. John Osborne (London: Verso, 1998) and the essays on Baudelaire recently collected in *The Writer of Modern Life*; to the work of Paul de Man, especially but not exclusively to the essays collected in the volume *Allegories of Reading* (New Haven: Yale UP, 1979); and to numerous critical texts that absorb, extend, and reflect upon that work, especially, in this chapter, Pfau's *Romantic Moods* and Rei Terada's *Feeling in Theory: Emotion after the "Death of the Subject"* (Cambridge, Mass.: Harvard UP, 2001). My own study is mainly concerned with the dimensions of belatedness and cultural exhaustion (and the attendant affects of melancholy and pathos) explored by these writers. Theresa Kelley's impressively rich, historically ranging, and always provocative account of allegory, while less exclusively focused on these particular dimensions of allegorical figures, traces ambivalences within allegory itself—the way allegorical figures veer between ghostly attenuation and compulsive liveliness, and the fascination these figures subsequently compel, often under the sign of danger—that are very pertinent to the modes of "life" possessed by the biographical figures I examine here. Kelley, *Reinventing Allegory*.

24. Again, see Kelley's *Reinventing Allegory* for a related take on these rhythms: A limit-case of petrified abstraction, allegory also performs "the necessary surplus or excess of figure" (132–34).

25. William Hazlitt, *Selected Writings,* ed. Duncan Wu (London: Pickering and Chatto, 1998), 2:134; cited by Pfau in *Romantic Moods*, 338.

26. Benjamin, *The Writer of Modern Life*, 142.

27. Benjamin, *The Writer of Modern Life*, 140.

28. Benjamin, *The Writer of Modern Life*, 178.

29. Rei Terada, "After the Critique of Lyric," *PMLA* 123, no. 1 (2008): 198.

30. Lynch's Burkean account of this filiative strategy chimes with James Chandler's work on Wordsworth as the poet of a Burkean "second nature"; see Lynch, *Loving Literature*, 21–61; and Chandler, *Wordsworth's Second Nature* (Chicago: U of Chicago P, 1984). My argument here is that the work of the second generation of romantic writers, including Coleridge in his later writing, tends to challenge narratives of interiorization and acculturation.

31. Most pertinently, in "Autobiography as De-Facement," in de Man, *The Rhetoric of Romanticism*, 67–83.

32. Paul Monette, *Last Watch of the Night* (San Diego: Harvest Books, 1994), 95. Monette's essay ("3275," 89–115) strikes me as such a project, open to sentimentality in a way that suggests an appreciation and a future for romanticism's nonmonumentalizing modes of preservation and remembrance.

33. At the conclusion of the first volume of his biography of Coleridge, which ends with Coleridge setting off for Malta, Richard Holmes speculates about what Coleridge's reputation would have been had he died at this point. See Holmes, *Coleridge: Early Visions* (New York: Pantheon, 1989).

34. John Keats, *The Poems of John Keats*, ed. Miriam Allott (London: Longman, 1970), 525.

35. I write about this poem in a somewhat different context in "The Strange Time of Reading," *European Romantic Review* 9, no. 2 (1998): 275–82.

36. *John Keats: Complete Poems*, ed. Jack Stillinger (Cambridge, Mass.: Belknap, Harvard UP, 1982), 164. Subsequent references to Keats's poetry come from this volume.

37. Again, see de Man, "Autobiography as De-Facement," for an extended reading of this sort of "shock" as it moves through Wordsworth's writing (67–83, especially 73–74). For an analysis that applies de Man's thinking to scenes of death and suspension in Keats's work, see Brendon Corcoran, "Keats's Death: Towards a Posthumous Poetics," in *Studies in Romanticism* 48 (2009), 325.

38. This sort of moment is connected to the reading experience Forest Pyle describes in *Art's Undoing: In the Wake of a Radical Aestheticism* (New York: Fordham UP, 2014): "At certain moments in certain texts we find ourselves *too close* to the text, rendered incapable of reading and stuck in a kind of auratic fascination that we dispel only by turning away, what Barthes called becoming 'unglued' " (21). Samantha Matthews makes the relevant point that during this period, the poetical "remains" also connoted "a disconcerting corporeal disintegration"; see *Poetical Remains*, 7.

39. By now, many introductions of many books on romantic writing offer good critiques of the new historicism. My interest here is in effects that consistently evade a positivist account of context as something that can be authoritatively brought to bear on poetic materials: Rather, poetic materials trigger experiences in which a sense of provenance befalls the reader, in a manner that suggests the resilience of either domain to explication by the other. Again, this sort of experience resembles those that are the subject of Pyle's *Art's Undoing*; see, for instance, his accounts of aesthetic experience as "involuntary," as "something that approaches the status of an event," as a moment of "arrest" (10).

40. Samuel Taylor Coleridge, *The Notebooks of Samuel Taylor Coleridge*, ed. Kathleen Co-

burn (Princeton: Princeton UP, 1973), III:4073. Chapter 4 includes a more extensive and somewhat differently inflected reading of this notebook entry.

41. As Morton D. Paley points out in his reading of this poem in *Coleridge's Later Poetry* (Oxford: Clarendon Press, 1996), there is a history of identifying this figure with Coleridge (51).

42. The Brocken specter is an Alp-effect by which a backlit figure casts a shadow on the mist. The last lines of "Constancy to an Ideal Object" cast an "enamoured rustic," in pursuit of the "image with a glory round its head," as not knowing that he "makes the shadow he pursues." As Jacques Khalip argues in *Anonymous Life*, this is a figure for subjectivity as simulacrum (21). In *Aids to Reflection* Coleridge connects this optical effect to the special case of the image of genius, in a way that suggests that at the center of the shadow that a culture (mis)recognizes as a "real" thing, the genius might recognize a black hole. *Samuel Taylor Coleridge, Aids to Reflection,* ed. John Beer (Princeton: Princeton UP, 1993), 227.

43. Although, see Sara Guyer's reading of the figurations of "flesh and blood" that underwrite and unsettle these claims, in *Romanticism after Auschwitz*, 46–70.

44. De Man, "Autobiography as Defacement," 78.

45. Jennifer Bajorek, *Counterfeit Capital* (Stanford: Stanford UP, 2009), 22.

46. Adela Pinch, *Strange Fits of Passion: Epistemologies of Emotion, Hume to Austen* (Stanford: Stanford UP: 1996), 8, 69. See also Anita Sokolsky's "The Resistance to Sentimentality: Yeats, de Man, and Aesthetic Education," in which she cites Cleanth Brooks's expression of disdain of the "sentimental poem" as one "which fails to secure at all—or achieves only a specious reconciliation of attitudes"; see *Yale Journal of Criticism* 1 (1987), 68, 83. This form of "specious reconciliation," I propose, is related to allegory.

47. See especially Marjorie Levinson's path-breaking *Keats's Life of Allegory* (London: Basil Blackwell, 1988), as well as Pfau's *Romantic Moods*, which in its analysis of Keats responds in part to Levinson's work (309–78).

48. Another gloss on this passage from *Isabella* might be Terada's comment on de Man's reading of emotion in Rousseau's *Julie* in *Feeling in Theory*: Emotions can travel about "unhinged from the expressive hypothesis" (50). In *Reinventing Allegory*, Theresa Kelley describes the capacity of allegorical figures to inspire passion as participating in a crisis of representation that characterizes romantic aesthetics; see especially 132–34. See also David Ferris, "Fragments of an Interrupted Life: Keats, Blanchot, and the Gift of Death," for a reading of "This Living Hand" that connects this sort of (invited, impossible) exchange to the question of the afterlife of romanticism, in *The Meaning of "Life" in Romantic Poetry and Poetics,* ed. Ross Wilson (New York: Routledge, 2009), 103–24.

49. Keats's assessment is reported by Richard Woodhouse in a letter to John Taylor; see *The Letters of John Keats*, II:162.

50. Levinson, *Keats's Life of Allegory*, 24–25. For versions of the second possibility, in addition to Pfau's work, see Jack Stillinger's influential argument about Keats's "anti-romances" in "The Hoodwinking of Madeline: Skepticism in *The Eve of St. Agnes*," reprinted in *Keats's Poetry and Prose,* ed. Jeffrey N. Cox (New York: W.W. Norton and Co., 2009), 604–14.

51. Sokolsky, "The Resistance to Sentimentality," 83.

52. Redfield, *The Politics of Aesthetics,* 26. See also Eve Kosofsky Sedgwick's related reflections in "Paranoid Reading and Reparative Reading, or, You're So Paranoid, You Probably Think This Essay Is about You," in *Touching Feeling* (Durham, N.C.: Duke UP, 2003), 123–52.

53. The transcript of the discussion following de Man's Cornell Messenger Lecture on Walter Benjamin's "The Task of the Translator" includes some of de Man's most direct statements about "intention" as separable from subjectivity; see "Conclusions: Walter Benjamin's 'The Task of the Translator,'" in *The Resistance to Theory* (Minneapolis: U Minnesota P, 1986), 94.

54. Pfau, *Romantic Moods,* 309–39.

55. Hazlitt, *The Spirit of the Age,* 67.

56. Terada, *Feeling in Theory,* 5.

57. Terada, *Feeling in Theory,* 51, 69, 52.

58. Benjamin, *The Origin of the German Tragic Drama,* 139.

59. My thinking about "worklessness" and a romantic recalcitrance about being put to work, articulated most fully in this study in Chapter 4, which explores Coleridge's "work without hope," is indebted both to Guinn Batten's *The Orphaned Imagination: Melancholy and Commodity Culture in English Romanticism* (Durham, N.C.: Duke UP, 1998), and to Tilottama Rajan's "Keats, Poetry, and the 'Absence of the Work,'" *Modern Philology* 95, no. 3 (1998), 334–51.

60. Guyer, *Romanticism after Auschwitz* (Stanford: Stanford UP, 2007), 20. See also Rohrbach's *Modernity's Mist* for a discussion of modes of thinking about history and the future in terms of what is "missed," and thus, that cannot or may not be absorbed into any totalizing story.

61. Tricia Lootens, *Lost Saints: Silence, Gender, and Victorian Literary Canonization* (Charlottesville: UP of Virginia, 1996).

62. On the "feminizing" of Keats, see especially Susan Wolfson's "Feminizing Keats," in *Critical Essays on John Keats,* ed. Hermione de Almeida (Boston: G.K. Hall, 1990), 317–56, and "Keats Enters History." Fine recent essays on the deaths of female poets include Samantha Matthews's chapter on Tighe in *Poetical Remains,* 77–112; Tricia Lootens, "Reviving the Legend, Rethinking the Writer: Letitia Landon and the Poetess Tradition," in *Romanticism and Women Poets: Opening the Doors of Reception,* ed. Harriet Kramer Linken and Stephen C. Behrendt (Lexington: UP of Kentucky: 1999); and Ghislaine McDayter, "Celebrity, Gender, and the Death of the Poet: The Mystery of Letitia Elizabeth Landon," in *A Companion to Romantic Poetry,* ed. Charles Mahoney (Chichester, U.K.: Wiley-Blackwell, 2001), 337–53. Lootens's *Lost Saints* (Charlottesville: UP of Virginia, 1996) is a comprehensive study of the way the path to "canonization" for female poets ultimately disqualifies them for inclusion in what came to count as the "canon."

63. As I write this, the Trump administration is threatening the absolute defunding of the arts—news that arrives daily in my inbox and on social media pages together with multiple "poems of the day," announcements of readings and workshops, appeals from and advertisements for small presses, and information about how to mobilize in support of the arts and the human.

1. Tracing Keats

1. Andrew Bennett, *Keats, Narrative, and Audience: The Posthumous Life of Writing* (Cambridge: Cambridge UP, 1994).

2. Stanley Plumly, *Posthumous Keats* (New York: W.W. Norton, 2008). See especially Chapter 1, "On he flared," 23–55.

3. One can now order one's own copy of Haydon's life mask from the National Portrait Gallery: www.NPG.org.uk. Recent instances of the cropping up of Keats's masks include Michelle Stacy's account of the Keats-Shelley Museum in Rome in *The Paris Review* (Feb 23, 2016 [http://www.theparisreview.org/blog/2016/02/23/writ-in-water/]); *The New York Times*'s reporting on the estate of Maurice Sendak, which includes photographs of Sendak's death mask of Keats (http://www.nytimes.com/2014/12/02/books/maurice-sendaks-estate-debating-where-the-things-go.html); and the photographer John Dugdale's self-portrait with the death mask owned by Sendak, an image of which appears on the cover of Kaja Silverman's *The Miracle of Analogy* (Stanford: Stanford UP, 2015).

4. I am thinking of a strain of Keats criticism to which I will be returning in this chapter and which shares an interest in dimensions of Keats's work that cannot be accommodated by, and tend to challenge, expressive paradigms of the lyric: These include its flagging of literary conventions and the signs and techniques of "literariness," the "impersonality" or "anonymity" of its personae, and its refusals of narratives of individual transformation or historical progress. This strain descends from Marjorie Levinson's path-breaking *Keats's Life of Allegory: The Origins of a Style* (Oxford: Basil Blackwell, 1988); the constellation of critics who have become touchstones for my own thinking includes Levinson, Jacques Khalip (*Anonymous Life: Romanticism and Dispossession* [Stanford: Stanford UP, 2009]); Thomas Pfau (*Romantic Moods: Paranoia, Trauma, and Melancholy, 1790–1840* [Baltimore: John Hopkins UP, 2005]), and Rei Terada (*Feeling in Theory: Emotion after the "Death of the Subject"* [Cambridge, Mass.: Harvard UP, 2001]).

5. The image "peeled off" from its context is the frequent object of Walter Benjamin's thinking about baroque allegory in *The Origin of German Tragic Drama*. But similar formulations occur in his later writing on Baudelaire, especially, which connect Baudelaire's allegorical practices with the poetry's engagement with modern commodity culture. See for example these lines in "Central Park": "That which the allegorical intention has fixed upon is sundered from the customary contexts of life: it is at once shattered and preserved" (*The Writer of Modern Life: Essays on Charles Baudelaire*, ed. Michael W. Jennings [Cambridge, Mass.: Belknap, Harvard UP, 2006], 143). Marc Redfield's summary account of "the aesthetic" as a discourse of "framing" that at once severs the realm of the aesthetic from historical and political context and necessarily violates that frame is germane here; see *The Politics of Aesthetics: Nationalism, Gender, Romanticism* (Stanford: Stanford UP, 2003), 17–18.

6. Khalip, *Anonymous Life*. See also Levinson's *Keats's Life of Allegory*, on the challenge Keats's verse was seen to pose to expressive paradigms of the lyric (1–44); and Pfau's *Romantic Moods*, on "Keats's contestation of Wordsworthian lyric form" (313).

7. Pfau, *Romantic Moods*, 336. In *Art's Undoing: In the Wake of a Radical Aestheticism*

(New York: Fordham UP, 2014), Forest Pyle, commenting on Roland Barthes's "The Death of the Author," offers a neat formulation of this "irony": "The irony is, of course, that perhaps no author's death in the Anglo-American tradition has done more to secure what Barthes calls the 'empire' of the author than that of John Keats" (84).

8. Walter Benjamin, *The Origin of the German Tragic Drama,* ed. George Steiner, trans. John Osborne (London: Verso, 1998), 139.

9. The Keatsian images I have in mind can be described as "apathetic" and are subject to Terada's observations in *Feeling in Theory* about the "revenant" character of emotions, which can find pathos in vacated forms (82–89). For a discussion of the potentially problematic nature of the distinction between "the sentimental" and "the pathetic," see the introduction to this book.

10. Redfield ventriloquizes without endorsing this truism in *The Politics of Aesthetics*: "It is, after all, a movement destined to die young or end badly, bequeathing only its promise to us as our own utopian possibility" (32).

11. Hyder Edward Rollins, ed., *The Keats Circle* (Cambridge, Mass.: Harvard UP, 1948), II:73–74. (Hereafter cited in the text as *KC*; here and elsewhere, I omit Rollins's editorial tracking of edits and of inconsequential MS lacunae.) Plumly's *Posthumous Keats* is an extended meditation on this period of Keats's "posthumous life."

12. *KC* II:104.

13. John Keats, *The Letters of John Keats: 1814–1821,* ed. Hyder Edward Rollins (Cambridge, Mass..: Harvard UP, 1958) II:378. (Hereafter cited as *LJK*.)

14. This epitaph is not only on Joseph Severn's tombstone, but on John Hamilton Reynolds's as well.

15. Commenting on this passage in *Anonymous Life* Khalip suggestively describes Keats's "I" here "as the effect of a substitution" (2), and later investigates the passage as an expression of anxiety and skepticism about the dynamics of sympathetic identification (44–47). These observations are of a piece with my argument here, that the materials of the posthumous life themselves partake of modes of resistance to expressive paradigms and conventions.

16. I discuss some of this material in an earlier essay on Keats's death, "The Strange Time of Reading" (*European Romantic Review* 9, no. 2 [1998]), 275–82.

17. The citation from Benjamin appears in "Central Park" (*The Writer of Modern Life,* 143). See Pfau's extended account of Keats's melancholic, allegorical early verse in *Romantic Moods,* 309–78, which is inspired by Benjamin's account of allegory. See also Khalip's description of romantic subjectivity as caught up with strategies of "strategic reticence" in *Anonymous Life,* 3.

18. In this context, Andrew Bennett's description of Keats's verse as evincing a preference for the sensuous to the thetic properties of language are relevant; see *Keats, Narrative, and Audience,* 1. See my "The Strange Time of Reading" for an earlier reflection on these materials. See also Brendan Corcoran, "Keats's Death: Towards a Posthumous Poetics," *Studies in Romanticism* 48, no. 2 (Summer 2009), 321–48, for a related account of the awareness of the "post-human" at the core of these late writings of Keats. My sense of the way all these materials resist the working through of loss are in general much indebted to Guinn Batten's *The Orphaned Imagination* (Durham, N.C.: Duke UP, 1998); see especially 1–20.

19. And indeed, romanticism as an aesthetic movement can be said to emerge as a response to these new conditions of modernity: In the context of British literature, think for instance of William Blake's wide-ranging critique of the encroaching regulatory systems that are commodity capitalism's conditions of possibility. In *Romantic Moods*, Pfau explicitly gathers Keats, Hazlitt, and Heine into poetic responses to modernity that Benjamin identifies with Baudelaire (313); he also argues that Hazlitt and Keats "prefigure" the work of the Frankfurt School (358).

20. Benjamin, *The Writer of Modern Life*, 170–210; see especially 170–81.

21. Benjamin, *The Writer of Modern Life*, 171–72.

22. Writing on Benjamin's argument, Samuel Weber points to these and other paradoxes of the "shock effect": "Perhaps this is what is most shocking about 'shock': the inseparability of danger and of the effort to defend against it" (*Mass Mediauras: Form, Technics, Media*, ed. Alan Cholodenko [Stanford: Stanford UP, 1996], 98). See also Jennifer Bajorek's discussion of Benjamin's work on Baudelaire in *Counterfeit Capital: Poetic Labor and Revolutionary Irony* (Stanford: Stanford UP, 2009), especially her account of the "traumatophilia" of Benjamin's Baudelaire, 96–106.

23. Benjamin, *The Writer of Modern Life*, 175.

24. Bajorek, *Counterfeit Capital*, 110–14.

25. Quotations from Keats's poetry are taken from *Keats's Poetry and Prose*, ed. Jeffrey N. Cox (New York: W.W. Norton & Co., 2009), and will be subsequently cited in the text.

26. This is Pfau's argument in *Romantic Moods*. In *Anonymous Life*, Khalip makes a related argument about what he suggestively calls Keats's "poetics of nothingness" (58), a poetry of emptied out "I"s and objects. See also Theresa Kelley's description of the "frozen" figures of allegory that yet excite pathos and desire, in *Reinventing Allegory* (Cambridge: Cambridge UP, 1997), 165.

27. This is an often-made point. See for example Jack Stillinger's "The 'story' of Keats" in *The Cambridge Companion to Keats*, ed. Susan J. Wolfson (Cambridge: Cambridge UP, 2001), 246–60; and Andrew Bennett's *Romantic Poets and the Culture of Posterity* (Cambridge: Cambridge UP, 1999), which focuses on the importance of Milnes's edition, accompanied by the biography, to Keats's "after-fame" (141–44).

28. In *Keats: The Critical Heritage*, ed. G. M. Mathews (London: Routledge and Kegan Paul, 1971). Leigh Hunt's *Memoir of John Keats* was first published in *The Poetical Works of Coleridge, Shelley, and Keats* (Paris: A. and W. Galignani, 1829), 545–47. I am grateful to Matthew Sangster for pointing me to this edition, as evidence that I am not the first to have collected these poets in one volume!

29. The phrase "labour of love" comes up frequently in the correspondence between Milnes, Coventry Patmore, and members of the Keats circle (see for example *KC* II:172, 201, 235), and Milnes uses the phrase in his dedication of the edition to Francis Jeffrey (*Life, Letters, and Literary Remains of John Keats*, ed. Richard Monckton Milnes [London: Edward Moxon, 1848], vi). Milnes draws heavily on the letters of the posthumous life in his biography, and indeed, at the end of the text his voice almost drops out as he defers to Severn's epistolary accounts of Keats's last days.

30. Hannah Arendt, in her introduction to Walter Benjamin, *Illuminations: Essays and Reflections* (New York: Schocken Books, rept. 2007), 2.

31. Levinson, *Keats's Life of Allegory*. See especially 1–44.

32. This is related to the series Pfau identifies as Keats's "dismayingly interchange-able protagonists" (*Romantic Moods,* 364). I personally am more charmed by these fig-ures, although I agree with Pfau that they exist in the way of the commodity; see my "*Endymion*'s Beautiful Dreamers," in *The Cambridge Companion to Keats,* 20–36. Jerome Christensen identifies a similar series of equivocal youths in Byron's biography and poetry in *Lord Byron's Strength* (Baltimore: Johns Hopkins UP, 1993); see especially Chapter 3.

33. Pertinent here and to the rest of this section is Khalip's comment on Keats's pas-tiche style: "Keats's poetics thus exemplify an adept technique of instant reproducibility; since poetry is seemingly devoid of a governing author, it might have been written by anyone at any time—a fear the lurks behind John Lockhart's famous attack on Keats in *Blackwood's*"; see also his account of Keats's "empty fame or negative celebrity" (*Anony-mous Life,* 59, 47).

34. I discuss the reviews and the formation of the Keats circle in defensive response to them in "*Endymion*'s Beautiful Dreamers," 32–35. Woodhouse is especially interesting for his expression of support of Keats in terms of an ethic of succoring art to which the example of Chatterton is central ("Whatever People regret that they could not do for Shakespeare or Chatterton, because he did not live in their time, that I would embody into a rational principle and (with due regard for certain expediencies) do for Keats" [*KC* I:83]). This ethic has a kind of back-to-the-future fantasy about it ("Keats is the new Chatterton; perhaps I could retroactively change the narrative"); the fantasy is of course one Keats had a role in generating by his dedication of the volume to the mem-ory of Chatterton. In *Romantic Poets and the Culture of Posterity*, Bennett discusses the ubiquity and availability of the Chatterton narrative by this time; see 21–22, 143–44. Woodhouse is an early moment in a long history of efforts to "rescue" Keats—from the reviews, from neglect, from "sentimental" readings, from aspersions on his "manliness," on his poetic seriousness, etc. In his work on the elegy, R. Clifton Spargo provides an insightful gloss on these efforts: "Mourning frequently deploys a psychological trick of time, treating its retrospective concern for the other as if it were anticipatory or poten-tially preventive of loss" (*The Ethics of Mourning: Grief and Responsibility in Elegiac Litera-ture* [Baltimore: Johns Hopkins UP, 2004], 4).

35. "Charisma" derives from the Greek *kharis,* "favor" or "grace." See also Bennett, *Romantic Poets and the Culture of Posterity,* 58–59, for a discussion of Coleridge's expla-nation of the etymology of "fame," which he derives from the Latin *fari,* a root it shares with "fate," described by the OED as "a sentence or doom of the gods."

36. That Keats is so often described in the retrospective accounts of his contempo-raries collected by Milnes as withdrawn into himself and/or wishfully rapt by another landscape suggests this peeling free of the emblematic figure from its context, the sacri-fice of particular life to the life of the "type." In this context, Benjamin's remarks on the German *Trauerspiel* are germane: "All of the things which are used to signify derive, from the very fact of their pointing to something else, a power which makes them appear no longer commensurable with profane things." Quoted in Pfau, *Romantic Moods,* 327.

37. Baldwin's *London Magazine* (April 1821), 3.426–27; reprinted in *Keats: The Critical Heritage*. Samantha Matthews makes this point about the proleptic feel of Bryan Waller Procter's ("Barry Cornwall"'s) obituary in *Poetical Remains,* 113.

38. *KC* II:273. In his correspondence with Milnes, Bailey also describes Keats as "a young Apollo," like "a fine Greek statue" (*KC* II:269).

39. Jack Stillinger, "The 'Story' of Keats," *The Cambridge Companion to Keats*, 246–60.

40. In his 1966 introduction to the Signet edition of Keats's poetry, Paul de Man writes about the "defensiveness" of biographies and assessments of Keats (which I presume include the then-recent work of Walter Jackson Bate, always alluded to as "magisterial," and of Robert Gittings). See de Man's "Introduction to the Poetry of John Keats," reprinted in *Critical Writings, 1953–1978*, ed. Lindsay Waters (Minneapolis: Minnesota UP, 1989), 180.

41. Pfau, *Romantic Moods*, 335. The passage could also, of course, be read as an instance of what Levinson calls the early poetry's "badness"; see *Keats's Life of Allegory*, 1–44. I discuss this scene in "*Endymion*'s Beautiful Dreamers," 22–25, from which this draws.

42. See note 33 of this chapter.

43. The character of the absorption staged in this scene can be related, I think, to Benjamin's suggestive and fascinating reflections about the tendency of the petit bourgeoisie at a certain cusp moment (when it is not yet fully aware of its decline, which will bring new opportunities for limited "enjoyment" at the expense of "power"), to empathize and identify with the commodity—to bring to the commodity "a sensitivity that perceived charm even in damaged or decaying goods." *The Writer of Modern Life*, 88–89.

44. Bennett's *Keats, Narrative, and Audience* describes the "uncertain but irreducible and scandalous instabilities" that I am trying to adumbrate here (1). The possibilities of reading roughly correspond to those proffered by Christopher Ricks (*Keats and Embarrassment* [Oxford: Oxford UP, 1984]), Levinson, and Pfau: While all grant to Keats's early poetry a certain nonconformity with and exposure of poetic convention and decorum, they diverge in terms of the degree of self-consciousness about and mastery of these effects they grant the poetry, and about the extent of its challenge to poetic and cultural norms. Again, Khalip's remarks about the effects of a pastiche poetry "seemingly devoid of a governing author" are astute and helpful here; see *Anonymous Life*, 59–60.

45. Pfau, *Romantic Moods*, 357. Marc Redfield's argument that critical disagreements about whether romantic poetic effects are complicit with or critical of a dominant ideology are pertinent to these debates about Keats, especially, perhaps, to the disagreement between Levinson and Pfau: "The mutual implication of aesthetics and theory accounts for the endless back and forth of criticism, whereby literary or other aesthetic works are by turns judged ideologically complicit and subversive" (*The Politics of Aesthetics*, 26).

46. See Chapter 2 of this volume.

47. In *Feeling in Theory*, Terada, reading Jameson reading Warhol's "Diamond Dust Shoes," comments on the effects of pathos generated by the reproduced: Jameson, she observes, "associates pathos with mediation in images—with the realization that images are being produced in series. The image seems off-present, either too early or too late, a pre- or after-image. Parallel to this experience in the image-world is pathos in the emotion-world" (13). The effect I am interested in—the "pathos" that attaches to "Keats"—partakes in the relation of this figure to seriality, I would argue.

48. For an argument about the charges of "sentimentality" that stick to the reception of Keats, see the introduction to this volume.

49. Terada, *Feeling in Theory,* 69.

50. See Forest Pyle's fine account of the ambivalences of the introductory strophe in *The Ideology of Imagination: Subject and Society in the Discourse of Romanticism* (Stanford: Stanford UP, 1995), 136–39, where he argues that the passage poses the ideological predicament and challenge taken on by the poem.

51. As Moneta suggests, the "allegorical" structure of the poem is acknowledged by the belatedness of the poet's arrival, first in the garden where he eats of a feast of leftovers, and then here; it is also suggested by the detritus (linens, tongs, censors, etc.) heaped in the space. See Benjamin: "That which the allegorical intention has fixed upon is sundered from the customary contexts of life: it is at once shattered and preserved" (*The Writer of Modern Life,* 143). Later Benjamin links this wrenching of things from their contexts in allegory to the placement of commodities (148).

52. Thus the poet's mode of survival may be like that of Benjamin's Baudelaire, who "apes" the poet and in this way sustains the virtual endurance of that figure, for an audience no longer in need of the real thing (*The Writer of Modern Life,* 140). See also Jonathan Mulrooney, "How Keats Falls" (*Studies in Romanticism* 50, no. 2 [Summer 2011], 251–73), for an argument about Keats's shaping of a new poetry out of a recognition of poetry's lack of place in the new order.

53. In this context, Pfau's account of Keats's poetry as sounding an overdetermined, phantasmagorical, and claustrophobia Regency landscape (*Romantic Moods,* 309–78) is pertinent, as is Pyle's account of the poem as staging a confrontation with the materiality (and ideological givenness) of language (*The Ideology of Imagination,* 136–39). Terada's provocative, demoralizing, but increasingly felt on the pulses reading of the *Hyperion* poems connects their ossified world to the long postwar theater (post-Waterloo to our present) in which "trapped thought" faces "the wholeness of the false." See "Looking at the Stars Forever," *Studies in Romanticism* 50, no. 2 (Summer 2011), 275–309.

54. Pyle, *Art's Undoing,* 95. See also David Ferris's "Fragments of an Interrupted Life: Keats, Blanchot, and the Gift of Death" for an account of "This Living Hand" and *Hyperion* as texts that insist on the preservation of history as a "problem"—the only mode of the past that can have purchase on the future (*The Meaning of "Life" in Romantic Poetry and Poetics,* ed. Ross Wilson [New York: Routledge, 2009], 103–24).

55. Bringing Benjamin's thinking about "shock," so deeply bound up with the sense of the shutter speed of the camera, into conjunction with this moment of excruciatingly slowed time might seem forced. The poet's eye, however, is cast here as a neutral aperture: If the instant of the involuntary human "blink" analogizes the shock defense, this scene suggests the poet's eye, through strenuous discipline, aspiring to the condition of the camera as a neutral registering mechanism, the timing of which can be set and altered—it can be held open for long exposure. Terada suggests that the "eye" in this and other passages of the *Hyperion* poems anticipate a cinema still on Benjamin's horizon, Italian postwar cinema as described by Gilles Deleuze, in which "time suffuses the shot" ("Looking at the Stars Forever," 275–309). In *Art's Undoing,* Pyle argues that the first *Hyperion* breaks off when it arrives at a radical sense of the inassimilability of history to its articulation, and that the second poem dramatizes and takes on this crisis of knowledge (95). Critics who along with Pyle have produced compelling accounts of the *Hyperion* poems' exploration of nonrecuperable, nonredemptive, and nonprogressive

history and temporality include Mulrooney, Terada, Khalip, Ferris, and Tilottama Rajan ("Keats, Poetry, and 'The Absence of the Work,' " *Modern Philology* 95, no. 3 [Feb. 1998], 334–51). Emily Rohrbach's *Modernity's Mist: British Romanticism and the Poetics of Anticipation* (New York: Fordham UP, 2016) offers an account of the context in which Keats's thinking about history and temporality unfolds.

56. See Pyle's *The Ideology of Imagination*, 136–39, for an account of the poem's dramatization here of the incompatibility of the human (and especially, the ethical and redemptive potential of poetry) and the inhuman "blank splendor" of poetic language; in *Art's Undoing* he returns to this scene and the challenge it dramatizes, seeing in it the predicament that only a "radical aestheticism" can meet. Khalip also addresses the scene as dramatizing an ethical relationship and challenge, the poetry's effort to envision "non-proprietary relationships with art and persons" (*Anonymous Life*, 64). Like them, I see the scene dramatizing a coming into poetic calling that burdens the human poet with the relationship to the inhuman; my emphasis here is on how the "call"—the moment of being held by this nonhuman look—interpellates the poet so that he too becomes a hollowed figure in this world; this is implied by Khalip's accounts of the "anonymous life" of the poet.

57. In various ways, then, the poet here describes an entrance into "the space of literature," a step that demands the depersonalization of the writer as he becomes of the order of literature. The phrase is from Blanchot: "What speaks in [the writer] is the fact that, in one way or another he is no longer himself; he isn't anyone anymore" (cited in Khalip, *Anonymous Life*, 22–23). Blanchot describes what I have called elsewhere a "neutral" or structural fatality, connected to the so-called "the death of the author" as an effect of writing. Yet as many others have pointed out, this structural demand takes on a particular gravity during the long "moment" Keats inhabits: The "love of literature" is dramatized here as a fatal attraction, a "pull" into a claustrophobic, oppressively given world which admits no hope. For a slightly differently inflected account of the way Keats's poetry opens to death, see Corcoran, "Keats's Death."

58. Benjamin, *The Writer of Modern Life*, 202, 204.

59. For a reading of this passage that similarly applies its insights to images of impossible exchange and "grasp" in Keats, see David Ferris, "Fragments of an Interrupted Life."

60. Benjamin, *The Writer of Modern Life*, 289n77. See also Mutlu Konuk Blasing's related claim that language "carries" "the historical truth of a linguistic community—those who share a particular experience of the trauma that produces 'humans' " (*Lyric Poetry: The Pain and the Pleasure of Words* [Princeton: Princeton UP, 2007], 10).

61. These associations with the figure and name of "Moneta" are noted and traced in K. K. Ruthven, "Keats and *Dea Moneta*" (*Studies in Romanticism* 15, no. 3 [July 1976], 445–59). See also Theresa Kelley, *Reinventing Allegory* (Cambridge: Cambridge UP, 1997), on the allegorical sign presenting as a "riddle" (20).

62. Levinson, *Keats's Life of Allegory*, 1–44. Saturn's temple becomes a sort of safe deposit box for these cultural markers and riches: "Robes, golden tongs, censer, and chafing-dish, / Girdles, and chains, and holy jewelries" "all in a mingled heap" (78–80).

63. Benjamin, *The Writer of Modern Life;* see, for instance, 148, 165, 183–86.

64. Levinson, *Keats's Life of Allegory*, 4.

65. Benjamin, *The Writer of Modern Life*, 289n77.

66. See Pfau's critique of this sort of developmental narrative in *Romantic Moods*, 334–37.

67. Bajorek, *Counterfeit Capital*, 22.

68. Benjamin, *The Writer of Modern Life*. On "long practice," see, for example, 202; on the figure of the poet as simulacrum, see, for example, 140.

69. Samuel Weber, *Mass Mediauras: Form, Technics, Media*, ed. Alan Cholodenko (Stanford: Stanford UP, 1996), 104–5.

70. See Khalip's comment that in Keats, fame is "envisioned as inseparable from the lifelessness of commodity culture," *Anonymous Life*, 48.

71. Benjamin, *The Writer of Modern Life*, 202.

72. See Mulrooney's "How Keats Falls" for an argument about *Hyperion* as an investigation of the constrained conditions of poetry, out of which a new poetry emerges. Pfau and Terada make bleaker versions of the same claims: that Keats's poetry comes out of an address of the claustrophobic, given, "false whole" of post-Waterloo Europe; see Terada, "Looking at the Stars Forever," and Pfau, *Romantic Moods*, 338. In his "Traumatic Poetry: Charles Baudelaire and the Shock of Laughter" (*Trauma: Explorations in Memory*, ed. Cathy Caruth [Baltimore: Johns Hopkins UP, 1995], 236–55), Kevin Newmark provides an account of what this "new" poetry might register that is in line with the account I have been giving of Keats's *Fall of Hyperion*: "Memory also would be the place where the wholly unexpected and accidental can now happen to the subject, making it into something different or other than it previously was, as was the case when 'modernity' occurred historically to interrupt once and for all the unified structure of what we continue to call 'traditional' experience. Memory . . . names the place where the subject of knowledge and experience is always susceptible to being overcome and transformed by the disruptive force of shock" (238).

73. In "Fragments of an Interrupted Life," Ferris reads Keats's "living hand" as a figure for a living on that breaches the opposition of life and death. For a more extensive analysis of Keats's "hands" and the relation of their appearance to gestures of sacrifice and modes of ethical obligation, see Pyle, *Art's Undoing*, 81–92.

2. The Art of Losing: Shelley's *Adonais*

1. Bion, *Lament for Adonis,* and Moschus, *Lament for Bion,* in *Theocritus, Moschus, Bion,* ed. Neil Hopkinson (Cambridge, Mass.: Loeb Classical Library, 2015). R. Clifton Spargo discusses the elegiac delusion and the call to "haste" as imbricated in the elegy's ethical relation to the dead in *The Ethics of Mourning* (Baltimore: Johns Hopkins UP, 2004), 4, 7.

2. Percy Bysshe Shelley, *Shelley's Poetry and Prose*, ed. Donald H. Reiman and Neil Fraistat (New York: W.W. Norton, 2002).

3. For a more extensive discussion of Shelley's stilled forms, see Chapter 3 of this volume; on this passage from *Endymion*, see Chapter 1. Andrew Bennett provides a fuller account and analysis of these proleptic effects in *Romantic Poets and the Culture of Posterity* (Cambridge: Cambridge UP, 1999); see especially the introduction and "Keats's Prescience."

4. The rich texture of Shelley's allusions to Keats's verse is traced by Donald Reiman in "Keats and Shelley: Personal and Literary Relations," in *Shelley and His Circle:*

1773–1822, ed. Donald Reiman (Cambridge, Mass.: Harvard UP, 1986) V:426. Stuart Curran's "Adonais in Context" makes a persuasive and moving case for *Adonais*'s deep, appreciative engagement with Keats's work (*Shelley Revalued: Essays from the Gregynog Conference*, ed. Kelvin Everest [Towtowa, N.J.: Barnes & Noble Books, 1983], 165). Kelvin Everest also engages the rich texture of these allusions in "Shelley's Adonais and John Keats." *Essays in Criticism*, 57, no. 3 (2007), 237–64.

   5. *Shelley's Poetry and Prose*, 413n2.

   6. See the introduction to *Theocritus, Maschus, Bion*, vii–xv.

   7. Thus biographical fascination, although it may engage with and shore the monumentalizing projects of aesthetics, has the structure of trope as Paul de Man describes it, for example, in "Autobiography as De-Facement" (in *The Rhetoric of Romanticism* [New York: Columbia UP, 1984], 67–81). See also Neil Hertz, "Lurid Figures," in *Reading de Man Reading*, ed. W. Godzich and L. Waters (Minneapolis: U of Minnesota P:1988), and "More Lurid Figures," in *diacritics* 20, no. 3 (1990), 2–27, for his tracing of a "pathos of uncertain agency," connected with uncertain effects of biographical reference, through de Man's work in a way that is suggestive for thinking about these effects.

   8. For a summary of this history and these views, see Susan J. Wolfson, "Keats Enters History: Autopsy, *Adonais*, and the Fame of Keats," in *Keats and History*, ed. Nicholas Roe (Cambridge: Cambridge UP, 1995), 17–45.

   9. *Defense of Poetry*, in *Shelley's Poetry and Prose*, 483.

   10. Critics offering a range of perspectives on Shelley's efforts to engage, chastise, and reconfigure a contemporary culture of letters include Kenneth Neill Cameron, in *Shelley: The Golden Years* (Cambridge, Mass: Harvard UP, 1974), 422–44; James Heffernan, "*Adonais:* Shelley's Consumption of Keats," *Studies in Romanticism* 23 (1984), 295–315; William A Ulmer, "*Adonais* and the Death of Poetry," *Studies in Romanticism* 32 (1993): 425–51; Wolfson, "Keats Enters History"; and Everest, "Shelley's Adonais and John Keats."

   11. As many critics have pointed out, Shelley's choice of the pastoral form allows him to engage a tradition closely linked to the mourning of a youthful subject and a fellow-poet, a tradition that includes Theocritus, Virgil, Moschus, Spenser, and Milton. These elegies often charge the world with contributing to the death: this is most explicit in Moschus's elegy for Bion, a direct influence on *Adonais*, which charges that Bion was made to drink poison. As Stuart Curran points out in "*Adonais* in Context," the form is "deeply social in import" (168). My sense of the way *Adonais* reorders the social world around the fraternal dynamics of pastoral elegy and of the Hunt circle is indebted to Jeffrey Cox's *Poetry and Politics in the Cockney School* (Cambridge: Cambridge UP, 1998); see especially Cox's pages on *Adonais*, 209–18. In *The Ethics of Mourning* (Baltimore: Johns Hopkins UP, 2004), R. Clifton Spargo describes conventions of elegiac tradition in which the elegist does combat with the enemies of the dead, which he attributes to a fantasy that one could retroactively "rescue" the dead from their deaths: waging "war against the injustice of the death of the other, it demands from its society a reconfiguration of the very idea of ethics itself" (6). His remarks are suggestive in the context of the rescue fantasies that have marked the history of Keats's reception.

   12. Anthony D. Knerr provides an overview of the poem's critical reception in the commentary to *Shelley's Adonais: A Critical Edition* (New York: Columbia UP, 1984), 119–35. Stuart Curran, who summarizes the contentions (along a Wasserman/Cameron

divide) shaping more recent critical assessments of the poem, comments: "Of Shelley's major poems *Adonais* has been perhaps the most consistently respected and inconsistently read" ("*Adonais* in Context," 165).

13. For another overview of what is at stake in critical disagreements about the poem, see William Ulmer, "*Adonais* and the Death of Poetry" (*Studies in Romanticism* 32 [1993], 427–28); see also Karen Weisman's comment, in "Shelley's Lyricism," that "*Adonais* must represent the extreme end of consensus-breaking" (*The Cambridge Companion to Shelley,* ed. Timothy Morton [Cambridge: Cambridge UP: 2006], 56). For an extreme instance of the view that Shelley capitalizes on Keats's death, see Heffernan's "*Adonais:* Shelley's Consumption of Keats," which calls Shelley's story of the death of Keats by review a "fabrication" and an "insult" (301). See also Wolfson, "Keats Enters History."

14. In Chapter 1, in the section titled "Reviving the Empty World," I discuss these responses more fully; see especially note 34.

15. Wolfson, "Keats Enters History," 19.

16. Peter Sacks, *The English Elegy* (Baltimore: Johns Hopkins UP, 1985), 90 ff., 118–37. In this context, see also Ulmer's observation that Shelley's project of reviving Keats was a textual one involving the revival of "a dying tradition" ("*Adonais* and the Death of Poetry," 434).

17. See Percy Bysshe Shelley, *The Letters of Percy Bysshe Shelley,* ed. Frederick L. Jones (Oxford: Clarendon P, 1964), II 221 (on re-reading *Endymion*), 284, 289–90 (on *Hyperion*). See Everest's speculations about Shelley's careful re-reading of Keats after hearing of his death in "Shelley's Adonais and John Keats," 253.

18. Marjory Levinson relies heavily on the responses of Byron and the hostile *Endymion* reviews in the case she builds for the innovative and scandalous "badness" of Keats's early verse in *Keats's Life of Allegory: The Origins of a Style* (Oxford: Basil Blackwell, 1988); see especially the introduction, 1–44. In his analysis of Keats's early verse in *Romantic Moods: Paranoia, Trauma, and Melancholy, 1790–1840* (Baltimore: Johns Hopkins UP, 2005), Thomas Pfau builds on Levinson's account of the allegorical character of Keats's verse, but takes issue with a tendency, shared by Levinson, to distinguish between "early" and "late" verse; see especially 333–37. I will return to with this contention between Levinson and Pfau, which has partly to do with the degree of knowingness one grants to Keats. See also Jerrold Hogle, *Shelley's Process* (Oxford: Oxford UP, 1988), for a discussion of Shelley's allegory as a mode of deferral from one figure to another (318).

19. Pfau, *Romantic Moods* (Baltimore: Johns Hopkins UP, 2005), 348.

20. In this context, see also Karen Weisman, who argues that Shelley appropriates pastoral conventions in a way that reveals them as "signs of insufficiency." "The Lyricist," in *The Cambridge Companion to Shelley*, ed. Timothy Morton (Cambridge: Cambridge University Press, 2006), 57.

21. See Wasserman's pivotal reading of the poem in *Shelley: A Critical Reading* (Baltimore: Johns Hopkins UP, 1971) for the skeptical view, 462–502.

22. See especially Levinson's *Keats's Life of* and Pfau's *Romantic Moods.*

23. For Heffernan, Shelley has brought these strains of criticism on himself ("*Adonais:* Shelley's Consumption of Keats"). Paul de Man offers a decisive formulation

of an opposed view in "Shelley Disfigured" (*The Rhetoric of Romanticism* [New York: Columbia UP, 1984]): we "bury" Shelley and the other dead bodies of romanticism into "their own texts made into epitaphs and monumental graves" (121). In this context, see also Pfau's charge that romantic studies remain bound in sentimental responses to Keats's death, in *Romantic Moods*, 336.

24. Walter Benjamin, *The Origin of German Tragic Drama*, ed. George Steiner, trans. John Osborne (London: Verso: 1998), 139.

25. These claims thread through Benjamin's work on Baudelaire, but see for example section [32a] of "Central Park," collected in *The Writer of Modern Life* (Cambridge, Mass.: Belknap, Harvard UP, 2006), 159.

26. Hogle's reading of *Adonais* in *Shelley's Process* also describes Shelley as working with exhausted signs; see for example 301; for an argument that lands in a place closer to my own, see Ulmer, "*Adonais* and the Death of Poetry," 425–51.

27. In their work on romantic emotion, both Adela Pinch and Julie Ellison illuminate the kinds of effects and responses I describe here. See Adela Pinch, *Strange Fits of Passion: Epistemologies of Emotion, Hume to Austen* (Stanford: Stanford UP, 1996), and Julie Ellison, *Cato's Tears and the Making of Anglo-American Emotion* (Chicago: Chicago UP, 1999).

28. Samuel Johnson, *Life of Milton*, ed. Stephen Fix, in *The Lives of the Poets* (New Haven: Yale UP, 2010), 176. Jerrold Hogle provides a complex and illuminating account of Johnson's criticism and Shelley's thinking about these dimensions of *Lycidas*; see *Shelley's Process*, 298–99.

29. Sacks (*The English Elegy*), Curran ("*Adonais* in Context"), and Ulmer ("*Adonais* and the Death of Poetry"), especially, emphasize Shelley's identification with Keats; in this group also belongs Michele Turner Sharp, whose "Mirroring the Future: *Adonais*, Elegy, and the Life in Letters" argues for this identification on the basis of a shared life in letters (*Criticism* 42, no. 3 [2000], 299–316). Heffernan ("*Adonais*: Shelley's Consumption of Keats") and to some extent Wolfson ("Keats Enters History") argue that Shelley sacrifices Keats to his own ambitions.

30. See Julia Kristeva's account of the language of melancholy in *Black Sun*, trans. Leon Roudiez (New York: Columbia UP, 1989), 33–68. The facticity and conventionality of this "frail form" is widely acknowledged, as for example by Angela Leighton in "Deconstruction Criticism and Shelley's *Adonais*" (in *Shelley Revalued*, ed. Kelvin Everest [New York: Barnes and Noble Books, 1983]); Curran in "*Adonais* in Context"; Ulmer in "*Adonais* and the Death of Poetry"; and Sharp in "Mirroring the Future." Leighton suggests that recognizing this conventionality is a rebuttal to charges of sentimentality; I would argue that these charges are intimately linked to the perception of conventionality.

31. At the beginning of his "Poetry as Reanimation in Shelley," Ross Wilson quotes a passage from a letter Shelley wrote to Peacock that is germane here, and to this whole study:

The curse of this life is that whatever is once known can never be unknown. You inhabit a spot which before you inhabit it is as indifferent to you as any other spot upon the earth, & when persuaded by some necessity you think to leave it, you leave it not,—it clings to you & with memories of things which in your experience of them gave no such promise, revenges your desertion. Time flows on, places are changed, friends who were with us are no longer with us, but what has been, seems yet to be, but barren & stript of life.

The passage is from *The Letters of Percy Bysshe Shelley*, ed. Frederick L. Jones (Oxford: Clarendon Press, 1964), II:6; Wilson's essay is in *The Meaning of "Life" in Romantic Poetry and Poetics*, ed. Ross Wilson (New York: Routledge, 2009), 125–45.

32. See Michele Turner Sharp's "Mirroring the Future" for an argument about the poem that acknowledges and reads these effects as the risks of existence in print culture.

33. For Shelley's self-consciousness about pronouns as suggesting the way identity is produced out of substitutive relations, see "On Life": "The words *I,* and *you* and *they* are grammatical devices invented solely for arrangement and totally devoid of the intense and exclusive sense usually attached to them" (*Shelley's Poetry and Prose,* 508), and Khalip's comment on them in *Anonymous Life,* 100. I would argue that the "Preface" to *Adonais,* often read as evidence that Shelley actually *believes* his story about Keats, produces similar effects through the odd profusion of citations and voices that compose these claims.

34. Marc Redfield's introduction to *The Politics of Aesthetics* (Stanford: Stanford UP, 2003) describes postures like these as belonging to rhythms by which "literary or other aesthetic works are by turns judged ideologically complicit and subversive" (26). See the introduction of this book for an account of the way this rhythm structures charges of and defenses against sentimentality or self-indulgence in responses to romantic biographical figures.

35. Wolfson suggests all these possibilities in "Keats Enters History": in *Adonais,* Keats "dies out of popular scorn to be reconstituted for elite consumption" (33); Shelley, unwittingly, "[stages] his own martyrdom" (35), although the plan is to establish his own majority and masculinity vis a vis Keats (25).

36. For accounts of these early critical responses, see Anthony D. Knerr's summary in *Adonais: A Critical Edition,* 119–35, and Wolfson.

37. In a discussion following his Cornell Messenger Lecture of 1983 on Walter Benjamin's "Task of the Translator," Paul de Man offers an account of "non-subjective" intention, the "intention" of "language" as it is "oriented to meaning" (*The Resistance to Theory,* foreword by Wlad Godzich [Minneapolis: U Minnesota P, 1986], 94).

38. See de Man on the volatile "passions" of reading in "Semiology of Rhetoric": These passions are not "an emotive reaction to what language does, but . . . an emotive reaction to the impossibility of knowing what it might be up to" (*Allegories of Reading* [New Haven: Yale UP, 1979], 19). Rei Terada's *Feeling in Theory* (Stanford: Stanford UP, 2001) offers a comprehensive reading of de Man's theory of emotion, to which I am indebted; see especially 48–89.

39. For just some examples, see Wasserman (*Shelley: A Critical Reading* [Baltimore: Johns Hopkins UP, 1971], 496–99); Sacks (*The English Elegy,* 149–51); Hogle (*Shelley's Process,* 310–12); Spargo (*The Ethics of Mourning,* 149).

40. Tilottama Rajan, "Keats, Poetry, and the Absence of the Work" (*Modern Philology* 95, no. 3 [1998]), 334–51.

41. See Sacks, *The English Elegy*, 180, for a suggestion that Urania listens to poetry from which Shelley wants to distance himself.

42. Sacks, *The English Elegy*, 148–49.

43. This account of maternal (in)attention is indebted to the work of D. W. Winnicott; see for example "The Capacity to be Alone," in *The Maturational Processes and the Facilitating Environment* (Madison, Conn.: International Universities Press, 1965), 29–36. See also my discussion of maternal reverie in Chapter 4.

44. Here we might think of Forest Pyle's account of Shelley's thinking about and performance of the "spell" and "spellings" of poetry by which poetry participates in and undoes the spells of ideology (*Art's Undoing: In the Wake of a Radical Aestheticism* [New York: Fordham UP, 2014], 29–65). My argument here is that the poem is not "throwing a stone" at Urania, in the words of the "Preface," so much as acknowledging dimensions of literature in which poems and readers necessarily participate.

45. For an account of the way Keats's own poetry plays with this sense of death at the core of verse, see Brendan Corcoran, "Keats's Death: Towards a Posthumous Poetics," *Studies in Romanticism* 48, no. 2 (Summer 2009), 321–48. In this context, see also Jonathan Culler's "Lyric, History and Genre," which argues that apostrophe, a central trope of lyric, "works to constitute a poetic speaker taking up an active relation to a world or element of the world constructed as addressee, an addressee which is often asked to respond in some way, as if the burden of this apostrophic event were to make something happen" (*The Lyric Theory Reader*, ed. Virginia Jackson and Yopie Prins [Baltimore: Johns Hopkins UP: 2014], 68). Shelley's imagined scene of reading, more than exposing the delusive structure of apostrophe, casts it as a ruse and distraction.

46. Freud, *The Interpretation of Dreams*, trans. James Strachey (New York: Avon Books, 1965), 547–48.

47. Freud, *The Interpretation of Dreams*, 548–49.

48. Jacques Lacan, "Seminar IX" in *The Seminar of Lacan: Four Fundamental Concepts of Psychoanalysis*, ed. Jacques-Alain Miller, trans. Alan Sheridan (New York: W.W. Norton and Co: 1998), 57 ff.

49. Cathy Caruth, *Unclaimed Experience* (Baltimore: Johns Hopkins UP, 1996), 103–4.

50. In *The Ethics of Mourning* (Baltimore: Johns Hopkins UP, 2004), R. Clifton Spargo provides another perspective on Caruth's insights here, in a discussion of "belatedness" as one of the challenges to the process of mourning (129).

51. Caruth, *Unclaimed Experience*, 103.

52. For other reflections about the experience of the temporality of missed experience, see Sara Guyer's *Romanticism after Auschwitz* (Stanford: Stanford UP, 2007): The book as a whole is an extended account of such "missings," but see especially Chapter 1 (25–45); and see Emily Rohrbach's *Modernity's Mist: British Romanticism and the Poetics of Anticipation* (New York: Fordham UP, 2016), 5.

53. See *The Letters of Percy Bysshe Shelley* II:107, 108, 122, for Percy Shelley's account; see Anne K. Mellor, *Mary Shelley: Her Life, Her Fiction, Her Monsters* (New York: Routledge, 1988) for an account of the same period. See also Julie A. Carlson's work on Mary Shelley's responses to and perspectives on this period in *England's First Family of Writers: Mary Wollstonecraft, William Godwin, Mary Shelley* (Baltimore: Johns Hopkins UP, 2007), 162–211.

54. My sense of the dead mother, here and elsewhere in this book, is highly indebted to Andre Green's essay of that name, included in *On Private Madness* (Madison, Conn.: International Universities Press, 1972), 142–73.

55. *The Letters of Percy Bysshe Shelley*, II:104.

56. This reading is thus offered as an alternative to charges on the part of critics of the poem that Shelley infantalizes Keats in a way that demeans; see, for example, Heffernan, "*Adonais:* Shelley's Consumption of Keats," and Wolfson, "Keats Enters History," 26, 28. Julie Carlson's work provides an insightful and persuasive account of the ways in which Mary Shelley's writing during this period in fact strives to find ways to move beyond the stuckness of mourning and the "designated mourner" role; see especially Chapter 5, "Living Off and On: The Literary Work of Mourning," in *England's First Family of Writers*, 162–211.

57. See Sacks for a claim that the elegy, from its beginnings, can be seen as part of a "contest for inheritance" (*The English Elegy*, 36–37). I would argue that Shelley's elegy reflects on the problematic of "inheriting" anything; that it rather posits modes of the unrecuperated survival of the dead into posthumous time. For a related perspective, see Carlson's ventriloquizing of Mary Shelley's riposte to William Godwin, contained in the writing she produced during this time: "Why focus on illustrious men? Talk about the calamity of a child's death, which under any definition is loss of the virtually all-potential" (*England's First Family of Writers*, 170).

58. I thank William Keach for pointing out to me the suggestiveness of Shelley's allusion here to the cenotaphic pyramid of Caius Cestius, a "flame turned to marble," in this context—a monument (to Cestius, to empire) the supposed content of which has vanished and cannot be passed down.

3. Shelley's Pod People

1. Percy Bysshe Shelley, *The Complete Poems of Percy Bysshe Shelley, with notes by Mary Shelley* (New York: The Modern Library, 1994), 150. Quotations from *The Witch of Atlas* and Mary Shelley's introduction are also from this edition.

2. Edward Trelawny, *Records of Shelley, Byron, and the Author* (New York: Benjamin Blom, 1878).

3. Cited by David Crane, *Lord Byron's Jackal: A Life of Edward John Trelawny* (New York: Four Walls Eight Windows, 1999), 339.

4. Trelawny, *Records of Shelley, Byron, and the Author*, 211.

5. Trelawny, *Records of Shelley, Byron, and the Author*, 212–13. Samantha Matthews's reconstruction of these events at once draws from Trelawny's and scrutinizes his role; see her *Poetical Remains: Poets' Graves, Bodies, and Books in the Nineteenth Century* (Oxford: Oxford UP, 2004), 134–39.

6. For accounts of the heart controversy, see Robert Metcalf Smith, *The Shelley Legend* (New York: Charles Scribner's Sons, 1945), 1–2; Leigh Hunt, *The Autobiography of Leigh Hunt*, ed. Roger Ingpen (London: Archibald Constable and Co, 1903), II:100–102. Hunt's obituary is reprinted in Newman Ivey White, *The Unextinguished Hearth: Shelley and His Contemporary Critics* (Durham, N.C.: Duke UP, 1938), 321. For an astute account of the way the heart becomes emblematic of and imbricated in contestations about

Shelley's cultural value, see Eric O. Clarke, "Shelley's Heart: Sexual Politics and Cultural Value" in *Yale Journal of Criticism* 8 (1995), especially 188–89; and see Matthews, *Poetical Remains*, 139–43.

7. One could say that Trelawny's function was to bear Shelley's remains into the Victorian period of Shelley-love explored by Adela Pinch in "A Shape All Light" in *Taking Liberties with the Author: Selected Essays from the English Institute,* ed. Meredith McGill (Ann Arbor: English Institute in collaboration with the American Council of Learned Societies, 2013. http://hdl.handle.net/2027//heb.90058.0001.001).

8. Paul de Man, "Shelley Disfigured," in *The Rhetoric of Romanticism* (New York: Columbia UP: N.Y., 1984), 122.

9. De Man, "Shelley Disfigured," 121.

10. Thomas Jefferson Hogg, *Shelley at Oxford* (London: Methuen, 1904), 6–13.

11. Hogg, *Shelley at Oxford*, 40–41.

12. William Hazlitt, *The Collected Works of William Hazlitt,* ed. A. R. Waller and Arnold Glover (London: J. M. Dent and Co, 1904), X:257.

13. Trelawny, *Records of Shelley, Byron, and the Author*, 22.

14. Cited in Kenneth Neill Cameron, *Shelley: The Golden Years* (Cambridge, Mass.: Harvard UP, 1974), 60.

15. Trelawny, *Records of Shelley, Byron, and the Author*, 22.

16. Trelawny, *Records of Shelley, Byron, and the Author*, 103.

17. Trelawny, *Records of Shelley, Byron, and the Author*, 91.

18. Paul de Man, "Shelley Disfigured," 109.

19. Adela Pinch provides an account of an important moment in this history, the period immediately following the demises of the members of the circle, when this "shape" of the author comes fully loose from what had anchored it in life; see "A Shape All Light."

20. Hunt, *The Autobiography of Leigh Hunt,* II:105.

21. Trelawny, *Records of Shelley, Byron, and the Author*, 189–90.

22. For another argument about the way the poet's bodily remains enter into analogy with poetic "remains" during this period, see Matthews, *Poetical Remains.* Matthews also speculates about the potential significance of Shelley being arrested in the form of a reader of Keats; see 132–34.

23. Stuart M. Sperry, *Shelley's Major Verse* (Cambridge, Mass.: Harvard UP, 1988), 154.

24. Theodor Adorno, *Aesthetic Theory,* ed. and trans. Robert Hullot-Kentor (Minneapolis: U Minnesota P, 1997), 12.

25. In *Shelley's Process* (Oxford: Oxford UP, 1988), Jerrold Hogle argues that the poem's sport—its playfully capricious relation to plot and readerly expectations—*is* its mode of social engagement: The poem works to break the hold of mythic narrative, including those deployed to shore up a repressive modern order (211–22). I find his argument persuasive, but would add that lining and countering this play is the poem's proliferation of figures of the "not-in-play": images that on the one hand gesture toward an art radically incommensurable with social experience, but on the other, verge upon the sort of fixity, glamour, and ideological potency Hogle claims the poem as a whole critiques.

26. Shelley, *The Complete Poems*, 462–63.

27. For an account of this period, see Richard Holmes, *Shelley: The Pursuit* (London: Quartet Books, 1976), Chapters 24–25. See also Julie A. Carlson's chapter on Mary Shelley's efforts to work through the trauma and grief of this period, often through writing that engages the work of Percy Shelley and that of her parents. *England's First Family of Writers: Mary Wollstonecraft, William Godwin, Mary Shelley* (Baltimore: Johns Hopkins UP, 2007), 162–211.

28. Ovid, *Metamorphosis,* trans. Rolfe Humphries (Bloomington: Indiana UP, 1955), 244–300.

29. Ovid, *Metamorphosis*, 287–390.

30. My reading here disagrees with Denise Gigante's in *Life: Organic Form and Romanticism* (New Haven: Yale UP, 2009), where she proposes that the poem is about the "vitalism" of the witch (155–207); it is in sympathy with what Theresa Kelley describes as a romantic interest in "shapes" becoming "marble," in persons becoming statuary; see her *Reinventing Allegory* (Cambridge: Cambridge UP, 1997), especially 171–72, but also throughout her discussion of romantic "abstraction."

31. My discussion here is indebted to Maurice Blanchot's "Two Versions of the Imaginary," in *The Gaze of Orpheus*, ed. P. Adams Sitney, trans. Lydia Davis (Barrytown, N.Y.: Station Hill, 1981).

32. See Holmes, *Shelley: The Pursuit*, 605.

33. Sigmund Freud, "The Relation of the Poet to Daydreaming," in *Delusion and Dream,* ed. Philip Rieff (Boston: Beacon Press, 1956).

34. D. W. Winnicott, "The Sense of Guilt," in *The Maturational Processes and the Facilitating Environment* (Madison, Conn.: International Universities Press, 1996), 26.

35. Guinn Batten makes a related argument about romanticism more generally in *The Orphaned Imagination: Melancholy and Commodity Culture in English Romanticism* (Durham, N.C.: Duke UP, 1998).

36. This is the argument of Maria Torok's "The Illness of Mourning and the Fantasy of the Exquisite Corpse." My discussion here and throughout the latter part of this essay is deeply indebted to *The Shell and the Kernel*, ed. Nicholas Rand (Chicago: U of Chicago P, 1994), the collection of essays by Nicholas Abraham and Torok in which Torok's essay appears.

37. See Holmes, *Shelley: The Pursuit*, 518, 596.

38. See, for example, Percy Shelley's two short poems to Mary Shelley from this time, each entitled "To Mary Shelley" (Shelley, *The Complete Poems*, 621). See also Carlson's *England's First Family of Writers* for an account that suggests Mary Shelley's responses to these deaths were less frozen than Percy Shelley and many biographers suggest (162–211).

39. See the more extensive exploration of this scene in Chapter 2 of this volume.

40. For an especially virulent expression of this preference, see Smith, *The Shelley Legend*, 1–36. Bette London's "Mary Shelley, *Frankenstein*, and the Spectacle of Masculinity" begins with a brief, suggestive account of the gender dynamics implicit in various representations of the poet's death (*PMLA* 108, no. 2 [March 1993], 253–65); and see Matthews's *Poetical Remains* for a sympathetic and nuanced account of Mary Shelley's reactions to Percy Shelley's death both at the time and in her later work as an editor of Percy's remains (127–53).

4. Late Coleridge

1. William Hazlitt, *The Spirit of the Age,* ed. E. D. Mackerness (London: Collins Publishers, 1969), 56.

2. Walter Benjamin, *The Writer of Modern Life,* ed. Michael Jennings (Cambridge, Mass.: Belknap, Harvard UP, 2006), 142.

3. In Richard W Armour and Raymond F. Howes, eds., *Coleridge the Talker* (Ithaca: Cornell UP, 1940), 199.

4. Samuel Taylor Coleridge, *The Notebooks of Samuel Taylor Coleridge,* ed. Kathleen Coburn (Princeton: Princeton UP, 1973), III:4073. Future references to this volume will be abbreviated as *CN* and included in the text. In most instances, as here, I leave out Coburn's tracking of Coleridge's edits.

5. Samuel Taylor Coleridge, "Preface" to "Kubla Khan," in *The Complete Poetical Works of Samuel Taylor Coleridge,* ed. Ernest Hartley Coleridge (Oxford: Oxford UP, 2000), 295. Future references to this edition will be abbreviated as *PW* and included in the text.

6. Samuel Taylor Coleridge, *Collected Letters of Samuel Taylor Coleridge,* ed. Earl Leslie Griggs (Oxford: Clarendon Press, 1971), V:758.

7. William Wordsworth, *Lyrical Ballads and Other Poems 1797–1800,* ed. James Butler and Karen Green (Ithaca: Cornell UP, 1992).

8. The "old man eloquent," a description of Isocrates, is habitually used by contemporaries to describe Coleridge. See for example Henry Hood's account included in *Coleridge the Talker,* 264; and see Chapter 5 of this volume. Morton D. Paley points out in his reading of "Limbo" in *Coleridge's Later Poetry* (Oxford: Clarendon Press, 1996) that there is a history of identifying the blind man with Coleridge (51).

9. For an account of Coleridge's "abstruse research" and his sense of its connection to personal travail, see Neil Vickers, "Coleridge's 'Abstruse Researches,'" in *Samuel Taylor Coleridge and the Sciences of Life,* ed. Nicholas Roe (Oxford: Oxford UP, 2001), 155–56.

10. Paley tracks this flea and its progenitors in *Coleridge's Later Poetry,* 45–49.

11. The most famous of these moments are recorded in "Dejection: An Ode" and "To William Wordsworth" (*PW* 362, 403).

12. For a fascinating and related meditation on Coleridge's abjects, see Tilottama Rajan, "Coleridge, Wordsworth and the Textual Abject," *The Wordsworth Circle* 24, no. 2 (1993), 61–69.

13. My sense of this positioning is indebted to the work of André Green. See especially "The Borderline Concept" in *On Private Madness* (Madison, Conn.: International Universities Press, 1972), 60–83.

14. In this context, Green's account of how a manifestation of "the negative" in an analysand projects into a "blind spot" in the analyst, indirectly serving the purpose "of blinding and suspending interpretive work," is suggestive: The reader of the poem engages in a mode of reading that feels like groping. André Green, *The Work of the Negative,* trans. Andrew Weller (London: Free Association Books, 1999), 10.

15. In *Anonymous Life: Romanticism and Dispossession* (Stanford: Stanford UP, 2009), Jacques Khalip describes the equivocal subjectivity at once shored up and made fragile by these efforts of self-positioning (19–20).

16. This is the poem published as "Ne Plus Ultra" (*PW* 431).

17. My thinking in this chapter, especially about the illimitability of Coleridge's work, is indebted to the broader arguments of both Guinn Batten's *The Orphaned Imagination: Melancholy and Commodity Culture in English Romanticism* (Durham, N.C.: Duke UP, 1998), and Tilottama Rajan's "Keats, Poetry, and the 'Absence of the Work,'" *Modern Philology* 95, no. 3 (1998), 334–51. See also David Collings for an analysis of Coleridge's pursuit of "the negative" in a different late poem, "Human Life," that chimes with my analysis here, although Collings interest is primarily in Coleridge's exploration of the force of the negative within philosophical and theological discourses: "Positive Negation: On Coleridge's 'Human Life,'" in *Romanticism and the Rights of the Negative*, ed. Tilottama Rajan (Romantic Praxis Series [June 2017], web resource: https://www.rc.umd.edu/praxis/negative/praxis.2017.negative.collings.html).

18. Richard Holmes's *Coleridge: Darker Reflections* (New York: Pantheon Books, 1998) includes a full account of this crisis (210–20). In *Coleridge's Later Poetry*, Paley brings this biographical context to bear on a reading of this poem (41ff.).

19. See especially William Hazlitt's essay "Mr. Coleridge," in *The Spirit of the Age,* ed. E. D. Mackerness (London: Collins Publishers, 1969), 54–67. For a sensitive, nuanced account of the vicissitudes of "hope" in Coleridge's late poems, see Tilottama Rajan's chapter on Coleridge's late lyrics in *Dark Interpreter* (Ithaca: Cornell UP, 1980), especially 242–43, as well as her "Coleridge, Wordsworth and the Textual Abject." See also Paley's *Coleridge's Later Poetry* for a reading of the poem that draws on this biographical context (41–57).

20. There is of course a distinction to be made between what "late" Coleridge actually produced, objectively speaking, including major works like *Biographia Literaria, The Statesman's Manual, Aids to Reflection, On the Constitution of Church and State,* and others, and his and others' sense of him as not fulfilling his promise and his promises. In the terms of D. W. Winnicott, what Coleridge "has not got" (for example, the great work on the logos) serves to shadow or negate any of his particular achievements. See D. W. Winnicott, *Playing and Reality* (New York: Routledge, 1991), 24.

21. Richard Holmes, *Coleridge: Early Visions* (New York: Pantheon Books, 1989), 362–64.

22. For an account of the various published versions and editorial history of the poems that he calls the "Limbo Constellation," see Paley's *Coleridge's Later Poetry*, 42.

23. These dimensions of "the negative" are the subject of Green's *The Work of the Negative.*

24. In her chapter on Coleridge in *Looking Away* (Cambridge, Mass.: Harvard UP, 2009), Terada traces the distinctions Coleridge makes between (pleasurable) "spectra"— optical illusions, idiosyncratically available perceptions—and "spectres" (the hallucinatory phenomena of dreams, obsessive states) (35–72). This poem, I argue, traces and speculates about the process by which one converts to the other.

25. Terada describes Coleridgean reverie as a negotiation with the given, which this poem performs, and at one point connects reverie to infantile experience; see *Looking Away*, 44–45.

26. This account is especially indebted to the work of D. W. Winnicott; see especially his essays "The Capacity to be Alone" and "The Theory of Parent-Child Relationship"

in *The Maturational Processes and the Facilitating Environment* (Madison, Conn.: International Universities Press, 1965), 29–55.

27. Green, "The Dead Mother," in *On Private Madness*, 142–73.

28. These possibilities are explored by André Green in *The Work of the Negative*; see especially his account of "negative hallucination" as the obverse of hallucinatory satisfaction (55). The attachment to what one "has not got" refers to a phrase from D. W. Winnicott to which Green often returns (*Playing and Reality*, 24).

29. Dante, *The Inferno*, trans. Mark Musa (London: Penguin Books, 1971), 98 (Canto iv, 42).

30. Green, *On Private Madness*, 275.

31. In this context, see Coleridge's citation of Hartley Coleridge, on the fancies of the brain: "It is not nothing," and Terada's discussion of this passage in *Looking Away*, 62–63.

32. Terada, *Looking Away*, 51–53.

33. See Green, *The Work of the Negative*, 76.

34. In this context, see Rajan's observation in *Dark Interpreter* that Coleridge's late verse is especially engaged with a strain of Renaissance verse that focuses on the absence of the beloved (212); in *Coleridge's Later Poetry*, Paley unfolds the poem's engagement with its Renaissance contexts (38–40).

35. This understanding of modern allegory is indebted to the work of Walter Benjamin, especially *The Origin of German Tragic Drama* (London: Verso, 1998); see the introduction to this volume for a fuller account of the allegorical dimensions of romantic poetics that interest me here. Rajan astutely observes that Coleridge's late verse regularly engages with the mode of allegory, despite his famously stated preference in *The Statesman's Manual* for symbol over allegory. She argues that he intentionally adopts a minor or failed mode in these late explorations of the potentially irremediable gap between appearance and substance (Rajan, *Dark Interpreter*, 236–38). For an account of "the negative" as it inhabits romantic "anonymity" and preoccupies critical theory, see Khalip, *Anonymous Life*: Anonymity signals "a negative excess or melancholic obstinacy from within the paradigms of knowledge" (175).

36. See, for instance, Green's "The Dead Mother" in *On Private Madness*, 150–55. Adam Phillips's work consistently reflects on what propels intellection; see, for example, *Terrors and Experts* (Cambridge, Mass.: Harvard UP, 1995).

37. Green, *The Work of the Negative*, 276; see also his chapter, "Hegel and Freud," in the same volume (26–49). In this context, see also Terada's analysis in *Looking Away* of Kant's "noumenon" as the posited blank that allows us to grant minimal acceptance to appearance (88–96). See also Collings, "Positive Negation: On Coleridge's 'Human Life,'" for a suggestive account of the way Coleridge's interest in "negation" uncovers a lining or "counterside" *within* philosophical and theological discourses.

38. See the introduction to Green's *The Work of the Negative*, 1–13.

39. In *Looking Away*, Terada observes that Coleridge's "psychic life reads like an involuntary flight from critical philosophy" (6): and he flies, she argues, to the spectra, which afford minor and transient opportunities for negotiation with the givens of appearance. I would argue that this flight in turn propels him toward anatomizings of the mechanism of flight itself, among other things. His examination remains engaged with

a reaction to "appearance," and thus he tends to see it as another torque—toward the mode of negativity—of his abstruse research into sense perception and sensation.

40. *PW* 455. This is an overly schematized account of this poem, to which I will return. For a reading that beautifully traces the ambivalences and equivocations of this first strophe, see Rajan, *Dark Interpreter*, 257.

41. Winnicott, *Playing and Reality*, 24.

42. "Frost at Midnight," *PW* 240. The phrase "pastimes and killtimes," accompanied by a descriptive list, occurs in Coleridge's *Biographia Literaria,* ed. James Engell and W. Jackson Bate (Princeton: Princeton UP, 1983), 48 n. See Rajan's *Dark Interpreter* for an account of a poetic "restlessness" in Coleridge's late work that suggests the continual positing and deferring of hope (242–43).

43. Writing on Immanuel Kant, both Terada and David L. Clark focus on Kantian philosophy's creation and protection of spaces that can exist "privately," away from the pressures and regulations of the social, in ways that seem pertinent to the dimensions of Coleridge's thinking that I am tracing here. Terada, *Looking Away*, 73–76; David L. Clark, "Kant's Aliens: The 'Anthropology' and Its Others," *CR: The New Centennial Review* 1, no. 2 (Fall 2001), 201–89; see especially 238, 251.

44. In *The Work of the Negative,* Green appreciates the French language as particularly well-suited to exploring the work of the negative, which presents a challenge to articulation (19). Without recourse to French, Coleridge's vocabulary for describing this work is at times strikingly nonvernacular: It can feel like an Englishization of European philosophical terms. In this context, see also Rajan on Coleridge's turn to "allegorical" writing during this period (*Dark Interpreter*, 236–38).

45. John Beer collects many of these references to "outness" in a note to his edition of Coleridge's *Aids to Reflection* (Princeton: Princeton UP, 1993), 391n26.

46. In "Coleridge's 'Abstruse Researches,'" (*Samuel Taylor Coleridge and the Sciences of Life,* ed. Nicholas Roe [Oxford: Oxford UP, 2001]), Neil Vickers explores Coleridge's identification of his "abstruse research" with the period of his partnership with Thomas Wedgwood; the essay investigates inquiries into sense and touch in ways pertinent to my thinking. See also Jerome Christensen's *Coleridge's Blessed Machine of Language* (Ithaca: Cornell UP, 1981) for a description and interpretation of Coleridge's experiments with Wedgwood that informs my analysis here; see especially 85–90.

47. On the blindness at the heart of vision in Coleridge, see Rajan, *Dark Interpreter,* 257.

48. Green, *The Work of the Negative,* 211.

49. Green, *The Work of the Negative,* 5.

50. In "Kant's Aliens," Clark's account of the conditions that allowed Kant to function—the closet as a space for the privacy of thinking how the solitary work of philosophy can fit into a universe of production and consumption (238); the flagging of illness and hypochondria, which allowed the "surfacing of heterogeneous knowledge in the context of elevation of disciplinary work"—seem extremely suggestive as a gloss on "late Coleridge," although on the surface the avowed relations to work ethic and philosophical "discipline" seem so divergent. Clark describes Kant's work as asserting "the right to keep to oneself, to the privacy of one's ideas" (251): one could perhaps think of Coleridge's *Notebooks* as a sotto voce performance of a "keeping to oneself."

51. Describing this lyric, Tilottama Rajan notices that "the poem gives itself and doesn't give itself to its own illusions" (*Dark Interpreter,* 20).

52. Rajan, *Dark Interpreter,* 20. See also Khalip's reading of the Brocken specter as a figure for subjectivity as simulacrum in *Anonymous Life,* 21.

5. Coleridge the Talker

1. John Keats, *The Letters of John Keats,* ed. Hyder Edward Rollins (Cambridge, Mass.: Harvard UP, 1958), II:88–89.

2. Samuel Taylor Coleridge, *Table Talk,* ed. Carl Woodring (Princeton: Princeton UP, 1990) I:325.

3. Richard W. Armour and Raymond F. Howes, eds., *Coleridge the Talker* (Ithaca: Cornell UP, 1940), 141–42.

4. Armour and Howes, *Coleridge the Talker; S. T. Coleridge: Interviews and Recollections,* ed. Seamus Perry (Basingstoke, U.K.: Palgrave, 2000); Coleridge, *Table Talk.*

5. Peter J. Manning, "Manufacturing the Romantic Image: Hazlitt and Coleridge Lecturing," in *Romantic Metropolis: The Urban Scene of British Culture, 1780–1840,* ed. James Chandler and Kevin Gilmartin (Cambridge: Cambridge University Press, 2005), 227–45.

6. Manning, "Manufacturing the Romantic Image," 237–38.

7. Jon Klancher, "Transmission Failure," in *Theoretical Issues in Literary Study,* ed. David Perkins (Cambridge, Mass.: Harvard University Press, 1991), 173–95.

8. William Hazlitt, *The Spirit of the Age* (London: Collins, 1969), 56.

9. All quoted in *Coleridge the Talker.* John Heraud compares him to one of the "philosophers of old" (260); George Gilfillan (223), Samuel Carter Hall (230), William Jerdan (274), and Richard Aris Willmot (362) all name him "the old man eloquent"; Charles Cowden Clarke compares him to the "old peripatetic philosophers" (133).

10. *Coleridge the Talker,* 222 (George Gilfillan); 230 (Samuel Carter Hall).

11. *Coleridge the Talker,* 248.

12. *Coleridge the Talker,* 141–42.

13. *Coleridge the Talker,* 230, 231, 334, 141.

14. *Coleridge the Talker,* 145 (Henry Nelson Coleridge).

15. *Coleridge the Talker,* 241–42.

16. *Coleridge the Talker,* 318 (Bryan Waller Proctor); 305 (Thomas A. Methuen).

17. *Coleridge the Talker,* 133 (Charles Cowden Clarke).

18. *Coleridge the Talker,* 223 (George Gilfillan).

19. *Coleridge the Talker,* 298 (Harriet Martineau). Carl Woodring, who draws on many of these contemporary accounts in his introduction to *Table Talk,* hones in on accounts of Coleridge's talk as a "river" (xli–lxii); see also Andrew Bennett's chapter on Coleridge in *Romantic Poets and the Culture of Posterity* (Cambridge: Cambridge UP, 1999), which describes the "compulsiveness" of Coleridge's talking based on these contemporary accounts (120).

20. *Coleridge the Talker,* 201 (Thomas Frognall Dibdin).

21. *Coleridge the Talker,* 201 (Thomas Frognall Dibdin).

22. *Coleridge the Talker,* 149 (Henry Nelson Coleridge).

23. *Coleridge the Talker*, 109 (Washington Allston).

24. William Hazlitt, *Lectures on the English Poets,* in *The Collected Works of William Hazlitt,* ed. A. R. Waller and Arnold Glover (London: J. Dent, 1902), V:167. See also Bennett's *Romantic Poets and the Culture of Posterity* for an account of contemporary descriptions of the "flow" of Coleridge's talk (118–19).

25. For example, David Vallins's essay on Coleridge's conversation both explores the engagement of the fragments collected in *Table Talk* with the philosophical questions that preoccupied him throughout his life, and suggests the ways in which the fragmentary character of "talk" performs the restless and open movements of thought that Coleridge connects to genius. "Coleridge as Talker," *The Oxford Handbook of Samuel Taylor Coleridge,* ed. Frederick Burwick (Oxford: Oxford UP, 2009), 307–22.

26. Hannah Arendt, *The Life of the Mind* (San Diego: Harcourt Brace, 1978), I:47.

27. Arendt, *The Life of the Mind*, I:53.

28. Arendt, *The Life of the Mind*, I:79.

29. Samuel Taylor Coleridge, *The Notebooks of Samuel Taylor Coleridge,* ed. Kathleen Coburn (Princeton: Princeton UP, 1973), III:3324. Future references to this volume will be abbreviated as *CN* and included in the text. In most instances, as here, I leave out Coburn's tracking of Coleridge's edits.

30. Rei Terada, *Looking Away* (Cambridge, Mass.: Harvard UP, 2009), 41.

31. *Coleridge the Talker,* 182.

32. *Coleridge the Talker,* 198.

33. *Coleridge the Talker,* 255.

34. See D. W. Winnicott, "The Capacity to be Alone" and "The Theory of Parent-Child Relationship" in *The Maturational Processes and the Facilitating Environment* (Madison, Conn.: International Universities Press, 1965), 29–55.

35. Cited in Arendt, *The Life of the Mind* I:53.

36. Samuel Taylor Coleridge, *The Friend,* ed. Barbara E. Rooke (Princeton: Princeton UP, 1993), I:123.

37. Hazlitt, *The Spirit of the Age,* 54.

38. Hazlitt, *The Spirit of the Age,* 54.

39. Hazlitt, *The Spirit of the Age,* 62.

40. Hazlitt, *The Spirit of the Age,* 54–55.

41. From "On Worthy Master Shakespeare and His Poems," reprinted in *Notes and emandations to the text of Shakespeare's plays, from early manuscript corrections in a copy of the folio, 1632,* ed. J. P. Collier (London: Collier, 1852), cclxxi.

42. *The Tempest* I:ii, 50; *Antony and Cleopatra* IV:14, 9–11; *The Tempest* IV:i, 152–56. *The Arden Shakespeare Complete Works,* ed. Richard Proudfoot, Ann Thompson, and David Scott Kastan (London: Arden, 1996).

43. William Wordsworth, *Guide to the Lakes,* ed. Ernest de Sélincourt (Oxford: Oxford UP, 1977), 108.

44. Terada, *Looking Away*, 64.

45. Hazlitt, *The Spirit of the Age,* 62.

46. *Coleridge the Talker,* 112.

47. In the spirit of Hazlitt, Carl Woodring, in his introduction to *Table Talk*, describes

Coleridge as a "model" for an age given over to "utilitarian self-interest, *laissez-faire*, and the blindness of common sense" (xxxix).

48. Bennett argues that by virtue of his talk, Coleridge at once defies and becomes integrated into romanticism's "culture of posterity" (*Romantic Poets and the Culture of Posterity*, 116–38).

49. Theodor Adorno, *Minima Moralia* (London: Verso, 2005), 21.

50. Hazlitt, *The Spirit of the Age*, 67. See also Carlyle, cited in *Coleridge the Talker*: "He had not the courage . . . to pass resolvedly across void deserts to the firm land of Faith beyond—he preferred to create logical fatamorganas on that nether side" (120).

51. Arendt, *The Life of the Mind*, I:47, 210.

52. Arendt, *The Life of the Mind*, I:211–12.

53. Arendt, *The Life of the Mind*, I:212.

Coda

1. Hannah Arendt, *The Life of the Mind* (San Diego: Harcourt Brace, 1978), I:212.

2. William Hazlitt, *The Spirit of the Age* (London: Collins, 1969), 54.

3. Theodor Adorno, *Minima Moralia* (London: Verso, 2005), 21; Hazlitt, *The Spirit of the Age*, 54.

Index

About the Author

Karen Swann is Morris Professor of Rhetoric Emerita in the Williams College English Department. She currently teaches at Bard Microcollege Holyoke.

Sara Guyer and Brian McGrath, series editors

CPSIA information can be obtained
at www.ICGtesting.com
Printed in the USA
LVHW040600010319
609175LV00001B/3/P